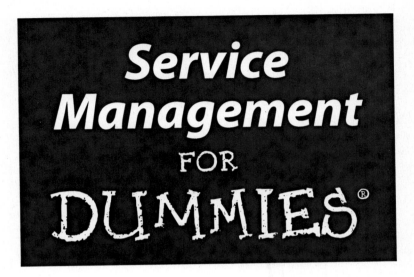

Service Management

FOR

DUMMIES®

**by Judith Hurwitz, Robin Bloor,
Marcia Kaufman, and Fern Halper**

WILEY

Wiley Publishing, Inc.

Service Management For Dummies®

Published by
Wiley Publishing, Inc.
111 River Street
Hoboken, NJ 07030-5774

www.wiley.com

WILEY

About the Authors

Judith Hurwitz is a technology strategist and thought leader, as well as president of Hurwitz & Associates, a business technology strategy firm that helps companies gain business benefits from their technology investments. In 1992 she founded the Hurwitz Group, a technology research group. She has worked in various corporations, including John Hancock, Apollo Computer, and Patricia Seybold Group, and she has written numerous white papers and publishes a regular blog. Judith holds BS and MS degrees from Boston University. She is a coauthor of *Service Oriented Architecture For Dummies,* 2nd Edition, and *IBM Information on Demand For Dummies,* Custom Edition (both from Wiley Publishing, Inc.). Judith provides strategic guidance to both vendors and customers of distributed technologies and is a frequent keynote speaker at industry events. She was named a distinguished alumnus of Boston University's College of Arts & Sciences in 2005. She is also a recipient of the 2005 Massachusetts Technology Leadership Council Award.

Robin Bloor, a partner in Hurwitz & Associates, has been an IT consultant and technology analyst for almost 20 years. He lived and worked in the United Kingdom until 2002, founding the IT analysis company Bloor Research, which published comparative technology reports that covered everything from computer hardware architecture to e-commerce. Robin is the author of the 2000 UK business best seller *The Electronic B@zaar: From the Silk Road to the E-Road* (Nicholas Brealey Publishing), which analyzes and explains the field of e-commerce. He is a coauthor of *Service Oriented Architecture For Dummies,* 2nd Edition (Wiley). In 2002, Robin moved to the United States; he now resides in Austin, Texas. He merged his U.S. analyst company with Hurwitz & Associates in 2005, and in 2006, he began to take an interest in the expanding area of service oriented architecture (SOA). Robin has become an influential and respected commentator on many corporate IT issues and is in great demand as a presenter at conferences, user groups, and seminars.

Marcia Kaufman, a founding partner in Hurwitz & Associates, has 20 years of experience in business strategy, industry research, SOA, software quality, information services, and analytics. In addition to publishing a regular technology blog, Marcia has written extensively on SOA, information management, and the business value of information technology. Marcia has worked on financial services industry modeling and forecasting in various research environments, including Data Resources, Inc. She holds a BA in mathematics and economics from Connecticut College and an MBA from Boston University. Marcia is a coauthor of *Service Oriented Architecture For Dummies,* 2nd Edition, and *IBM Information on Demand For Dummies,* Custom Edition (both from Wiley).

Fern Halper, PhD, a partner in Hurwitz & Associates, has more than 20 years of experience in data analysis, business analysis, and strategy development. Fern has published numerous articles on data analysis and content management. She has done extensive research, writing, and speaking on the topic of text analytics. Fern publishes a regular technology blog. She has held key positions at AT&T Bell Laboratories and Lucent Technologies, where she was responsible for developing innovative data analysis systems as well as strategy and product-line plans. She has taught courses in information technology at several universities. Fern received her BA from Colgate University and her PhD from Texas A&M University. Fern is a coauthor of *Service Oriented Architecture For Dummies,* 2nd Edition, and *IBM Information on Demand For Dummies,* Custom Edition (both from Wiley).

Dedication

As a group, the authors dedicate this book to our colleague Carol Caliendo, whose spirit and attention to detail helped make this book happen.

Judith dedicates this book to her family, Warren, Sara, and David; to her mother, Elaine; and in memory of her father, David.

Robin dedicates this book to Judy, for her encouragement, support, and advice; and to his children, Maya, Jude, Hannah, Jacob, and Seth.

Marcia dedicates this book to Matt, Sara, and Emily, and to her network of family and friends whose laughter, love, and support helped her through her treatment for breast cancer in 2008.

Fern dedicates this book to her husband, Clay, and to her daughters, Katie and Lindsay. She also dedicates this book in memory of her parents, Stanley and Phyllis.

Authors' Acknowledgments

We heartily thank our friends at Wiley, most especially Katie Feltman and our development editor, Kathy Simpson.

We learned a tremendous amount from all our interactions with IT executives who willingly and graciously shared their experiences and knowledge about those experiences with service management. We would like to acknowledge the following individuals: Elizabeth Kubycheck, George Maroulakos, and Keenan Phelan of CIBER; Guillermo Diaz, Jr. and Sean Worthington of Cisco; Philippe Caron of Commission scolaire de la Région-de-Sherbrooke; Harry K. Butler III of Elbit Systems of North America; Eric Norman and Bill Peer of InterContinental Hotels Group; Nick Robak of Independence Blue Cross; Isaac Ramsingh and Patrice Briley of The Medical Center of Central Georgia; Steve Flammini and Mary Finlay of Partners HealthCare; Michael Zucker of Sisters of Mercy Health System; Dan DuBeau and Meryl Ginsberg of Varian Medical Systems; and Robert Fort of Virgin Entertainment Group.

Thank you to our friends representing many of the vendors, systems integrators, and industry associations in the service management community: Al Zollar, Doug Brown, Kristin Hansen, Bill Powell, Caroline Robertson, Pierre Coyne, Rich Esposito, Pat Reynolds, Kathleen Holm, Alan Ganek,

Laura Sanders, Terese Knicky, and Patty Rowell of IBM; Erin Smith of Axeda; Elaine Korn and Bill Emmett of BMC; Janice Thomas, Nicole Buffalino, and Julie L. Henderson of CA; Craig B. Librett and Jane Emerson of EMC; Clay Bogusky of Iron Mountain; Heath Durrans and Thomas J. Cozzolino of LiquidHub; Joy H. Garner of Numara Software, Inc.; Kristen Wilson of Blanc & Otus; Michael McDonough of Corporate Ink; Liz Boal of Greenough Communications; and Kathy Tebben of LSH Communications.

Publisher's Acknowledgments

We're proud of this book; please send us your comments through our online registration form located at http://dummies.custhelp.com. For other comments, please contact our Customer Care Department within the U.S. at 877-762-2974, outside the U.S. at 317-572-3993, or fax 317-572-4002.

Some of the people who helped bring this book to market include the following:

Acquisitions and Editorial

Project Editor: Kathy Simpson

Acquisitions Editor: Katie Feltman

Copy Editors: Tonya Cupp and Kathy Simpson

Technical Editor: Brenda M. Michelson

Editorial Manager: Jodi Jensen

Editorial Assistant: Amanda Foxworth

Sr. Editorial Assistant: Cherie Case

Cartoons: Rich Tennant
(www.the5thwave.com)

Composition Services

Project Coordinators: Lynsey Stanford and Patrick Redmond

Layout and Graphics: Carl Byers, Melissa Jester

Proofreaders: Caitie Copple, Leeann Harney

Indexer: Sharon Shock

Publishing and Editorial for Technology Dummies

Richard Swadley, Vice President and Executive Group Publisher

Andy Cummings, Vice President and Publisher

Mary Bednarek, Executive Acquisitions Director

Mary C. Corder, Editorial Director

Publishing for Consumer Dummies

Diane Graves Steele, Vice President and Publisher

Composition Services

Debbie Stailey, Director of Composition Services

Contents at a Glance

Table of Contents

Introduction

Welcome to *Service Management For Dummies*. We think a service-driven economy makes this topic increasingly important. Clearly, the way people manage business and IT services is changing dramatically. Companies get into trouble when they don't look at their physical *and* business assets as a unified measure of their ability to manage customers' expectations and experiences.

We think you should focus on the intersection of business strategy, IT strategy, planning, and operations. Companies that plan to create an integrated service management platform are in a great position to evolve as opportunities and threats emerge.

Service management isn't a quick fix: It's stages of maturity that make your company better able to compete in a changing world. We hope that this book inspires you to take a different look at this very complicated and important area.

About This Book

Service management is a big topic covering lots of important issues that you must understand, whether you're managing a data center, virtualizing your computing environment, looking for best practices, or getting a handle on all the technologies you need. We tie our service management discussions directly to the issue that companies care about most: meeting the key performance indicators for their businesses. We think that understanding service management from a business perspective better prepares you to help your company succeed.

We recommend starting with Part I, because it puts into context the new way of thinking about managing the services that define your company. When you're ready, dive into the technical details in Parts III and IV. In Part V, you're rewarded with case studies that give you a taste of what real companies are doing to make their service management strategies work.

Foolish Assumptions

We think this book will be useful to many people, but we have to admit that we chose a segment of the world to focus on when writing *Service Management For Dummies*. Here's who we think you are:

- ✔ **You're thinking about technology from a business perspective.** You care more about IT-enabled business services than about technical systems. Perhaps we're preaching to the choir. We think you understand that you're doomed to failure if your organization continues treating IT like an isolated fiefdom.

- ✔ **You're a businessperson who wants results from the IT you've invested in over the past decade.** You want a business-driven service management strategy.

- ✔ **You're an educated IT person who's having trouble focusing on service management (versus server or systems management).** You want to see how you can better leverage your existing capabilities and resources to satisfy customer expectations and improve value.

Whoever you are, we welcome you on this journey!

How This Book Is Organized

We organized this book into six parts for easy consumption. Feel free to skip about.

Part 1: Introducing Service Management

In this section, we provide an overview of how to think about service management. We summarize the business drivers and the technical focus, and provide a perspective on the all-important customer.

Part 11: Getting the Foundation in Place

Before you can get into the details of service management, you need some context for best practices and standards. Starting with a strategy is important, and strategy is an important focus of Part II.

Part III: Service Management Technical Foundation

Service management has a lot of important technical underpinnings. In this part, we put the foundation in context with governance principles.

Part IV: Nitty-Gritty Service Management

The data center and its many supporting services and infrastructure are the heart of this part. If you want to know how the data center is changing — with virtualization and cloud computing becoming important, for example — this is the part for you. We cover important enablers of service management, including security, business service management, and desktop management.

Part V: Real Life with Service Management

There's nothing like hearing from real people who've made a difference for their real organizations with service management. In this part, some of those people share their best practices.

Part VI: The Part of Tens

If you're new to the *For Dummies* treasure trove, you may be unfamiliar with the Part of Tens. Here, Wiley editors torture *For Dummies* authors into creating useful, accessible lists of ten (more or less) elucidating elements. We started these chapters kicking and screaming but ultimately were very glad that they're here. We think you'll be glad too.

Icons Used in This Book

 We use this icon to indicate a particularly useful point that saves you time.

 Pay attention to this icon. The bother you save may be your own.

 This icon means that we're trying to make sure we're getting our point across to you.

 You can ignore this icon if you insist, but you techies probably will love these details.

Where to Go from Here

In this book, we give you an overview of service management and introduce all of its significant components. Each of the issues we discuss in this book could be the subject of a full-length book, however.

Service management is a big theme for us at Hurwitz & Associates. We invite you to visit our Web site at www.hurwitz.com and sign up for our newsletter.

Part I
Introducing
Service
Management

The 5th Wave

By Rich Tennant

"Our customer survey indicates 30% of our customers think our service is inconsistent, 40% would like a change in procedures, and 50% think it would be real cute if we all wore matching colored vests."

In this part . . .

*E*xactly what is service management, beyond what the two words themselves imply? In this part, we provide a graphical and reasonably simple way of looking at service management that explains it from both a business perspective and a technical perspective.

Chapter 1

Understanding Service Management

A service can be something as simple as preparing and delivering a meal to a table in a restaurant or as complex as managing the components of a data center or the operations of a factory. We're entering an era in which everything is a service.

A *service* is a way of delivering value to a customer by facilitating the expected outcome. That definition sounds simple enough, but it can be rather complicated when you look deeper. Suppose that you're hungry, and you want to get something to eat at a restaurant. You have some decisions to make. How quickly do you want or need a meal? How much time do you have? How much money do you want to spend? Are there types of food that you prefer? We make these types of decisions every minute of the day. So if you're hungry, have 20 minutes and a limited amount of money, and want something familiar to eat, you might go to a fast-food restaurant, and your expectations probably will be met. In fact, you probably didn't notice or even pay attention to any of the inner workings of the fast-food service provider. If the customer can find, order, receive, and be satisfied with the service — without incident — good service management is in place.

But what if something weird happened? You walk into that fast-food restaurant, expecting to get the sandwich you always order quickly, but instead, a hostess greets you and informs you that the wait for a table will be 20 minutes. Lovely music is playing, and every table has a white tablecloth.

Naturally, you're confused. You start thinking about the inner workings of service management in that restaurant. What has gone wrong? Is someone not doing his job? Is some information about customer expectations missing? Is someone changing the expected outcomes without informing customers? You might even start trying to solve the problem by asking probing questions. In your confusion, you walk out of the restaurant and find somewhere else to get a sandwich.

Why are we telling you this crazy story? When you're thinking about *service management* (monitoring and optimizing a service to ensure that it meets the critical outcomes the customer values and stakeholders want to provide), many dimensions and aspects may not be apparent at the outset.

In this chapter, we give you a glimpse into the new world of service management. Clearly, effective service management requires an alignment of the overall business goals and objectives. This type of alignment isn't a one-time task: An iterative cycle is involved, not only on a strategy level, but also within each stage of service management. Creating a valuable customer experience requires a lot of behind-the-scenes work that the customer never sees unless something goes wrong. As we show in the examples in this chapter, you can't ignore one element of the overall service management process without affecting the way that the entire system works.

Knowing That Everything Is a Service

In an increasingly interconnected business world, everything is becoming a service. In fact, the very definition of *service* has changed. In the old days, when we talked about a service, we meant labor provided by the traditional services economy: restaurants, hotels, health care, banks, retail stores, and education. The services sector of the economy is filled with jobs for people who provide services, such as a teacher who educates your children, a nurse who cares for you in the hospital, or a doorman who opens the door for you at a hotel. Jobs in the shrinking industrial sector of the economy include operating machinery or computers as part of the process of producing a product, such as securing an engine in a new automobile or welding components to make a bridge. Many people in the industrial sector continue to provide physical labor as part of the production process, but this process is increasingly augmented and transformed by technology. Now, as a result of the influx of technology, the manufacturing process has been transformed, and we need to talk about the manufactured products as services.

How is this possible? Well, think about manufactured products. At one time, manufacturing a product was straightforward. A manufacturer would decide the most efficient way to create a product and continue to improve on that process until each new product was created in the least amount of time with the best results. In fact, this was precisely what Henry Ford did when he revolutionized the car industry in the early part of the 20th century. As long as the market and the technology remained the same, tweaking processes to gain efficiencies was remarkably reliable.

But technology has changed dramatically over the past decade, and it has fundamentally changed the way we can build products. Technology can become the essence of both cost reduction and strategic differentiation between winners and losers. As building new, innovative products and bringing them to market in novel ways has become easier, the nature of creating products and managing services is changing.

Looking at How the Digital World Has Turned Everything Upside Down

Most manufacturers have replaced the traditional assembly line with a computer-driven process that focuses as much on capabilities and innovation as on efficiency. But this transformation has gone far beyond the manufacturing plant, extending to the way that products function after they leave the manufacturer. Today, products themselves have evolved to the point at which they are actually based on digital services.

Many types of manufactured products have been transformed into digitally based services. Some examples are medical devices, bridges, air-traffic-control systems, digital cameras, and even toasters. In the old days, all these products were mechanical. A typical toaster, for example, had a mechanical timing mechanism that popped up your toast based on how you tuned the dial. If you wanted very dark toast, you set the dial to dark, which set the toaster's timer for 75.4 seconds or so. You, the consumer, decided how much time was needed to make your toast. From a service management perspective, the service provider (toaster) and the customer (you) collaborated to provide the value that you wanted. The service provider made an asset that you owned (bread) into something that was more valuable to you (toast). Today, a toaster may have sensors that detect that you're toasting a large bagel, for example; therefore, it adjusts the toasting time to that type of bread. The new toaster requires additional understanding on the part of the customer to get the full value from the service relationship.

Take this idea to the next level. X-ray machines have evolved from devices that put images on film into digital imaging machines that transform images into huge volumes of digital data — and that example is just the tip of the iceberg. Products today are designed with complex sensors, scanners, and wireless systems based on radio-frequency identification (RFID); therefore, a vast array of manufactured goods is actually a complex array of digital services that need to be managed, monitored, optimized, and transformed based on the market, as well as on regulatory and business demands. We are indeed entering a new world in which everything has become a service. For many organizations, the implications of managing in a service-based world are dramatic.

Implementing Service Management

What does "everything is a service" mean for how you implement service management? In brief, you need to do a lot more management of the services representing your business if they're going to work efficiently.

We start with an example from the real world that everyone is familiar with: the automated teller machine (ATM). If you need to deposit money or get cash quickly, you use an ATM. To the casual observer, this idea may seem simple. (In fact, in the early days of the evolution of the ATM, its innovation was to help solve the process bottleneck caused by too many customers standing in line for too few tellers.) Behind the scenes, however, an ATM involves a complex business process.

The world of service management has two sides: the customer experience and the behind-the-scenes services that support the customer. True success in service management means that customers' expectations are met or exceeded in a predictable way. The behind-the-scenes activity is a complex business process, however. Whereas the service requires active collaboration between you (the customer) and the ATM (the service provider), the customer isn't required to understand the complexities of service management that occur behind the scenes. The customer must perform activities according to agreed-to rules and terms, and the provider must perform activities according to the same set of rules and terms, but the customer isn't required to understand the complexities of the entire service management system that makes everything work.

Start with the customer view of the service. You walk up to the machine, insert your bank card, input your personal identification number (PIN), and tell the system what type of transaction you want to make (such as "I need $20 from my checking account"). An automated system reads your account information and matches it against your PIN; then it checks to make sure that you have enough cash in your account. Within a few seconds (assuming that your PIN is right and you do have the money), cash appears in the tray. You get a printed receipt verifying that your balance has been debited $20. Then you go about your business, never really thinking about what happened behind the scenes.

In a competitive business world, banks recognize that it isn't enough to use the familiar ATM only as a cash-transaction machine. The ATM is part of a (fictional) financial corporation that we call ABC Financial, which offers products and services such as insurance, loans, and certificates of deposit (CDs). ABC Financial decides that it could increase revenue if it leverages its relationship with the ATM customer.

From a customer experience perspective, the marketing department adds some new screens to the ATM, displaying messages such as this: "We offer wonderful new CDs at incredible interest rates. Do you want to learn more?"

If the customer indicates that she is interested in the CD, ABC Financial has a series of screens set up that immediately display information or provide options to receive a brochure or set up an appointment with a sales rep.

Such components, both technical and business, transform the ATM from a simple box that allows customers to avoid the teller line to a sophisticated service engine.

Managing Services Effectively

Managing services is not a one-time process. It involves making sure that all the moving parts work together as a system. You need to establish checks and balances for customer goals, financial goals, and marketing goals. Therefore, service management must be understood based on many dimensions, ranging from customer experience metrics and business performance indicators to how individual components operate and interrelate. In Chapter 2, we show you the building blocks that you need to begin your journey toward service management.

Behind-the-scenes management activities

Behind the brightly colored ATM screen, a lot is going on. Here's a sample of the type of service management that happens in the background:

- ✔ Data center management ensures that the banking transactions are handled in a secure, predictable, and reliable manner.

- ✔ The financial institution manages the ATM machines. In addition, the institution may support ATMs owned by other financial institutions. The contact between banks and banking systems has to be managed on both business and operational levels.

- ✔ A service desk is designed to help customers and the branch location deal with problems with the ATM.

- ✔ A business process is designed based on the way the company interacts with customers on marketing, regulatory, and oversight issues.

- ✔ Management ensures that the performance indicators that support business objectives are met by new and existing product offerings.

- ✔ A system collects data generated by the various systems to make sure that the systems are operating in the correct manner, such as ensuring that each ATM has enough cash.

- ✔ A process is in place to handle incidents when they occur.

The company also has to answer a variety of questions such as these:

- ✔ What happens when an ATM fails? Who gets notified, and what happens next?

- ✔ How do we track where problems are happening?

- ✔ Do we know whether the network behind the ATM is the problem?

- ✔ Where do we keep track of the configuration of the parts that make up the ATM and the relationships among the parts, and how do we make changes in one part without interrupting the service?

- ✔ What level of service is required? Is the level of service something that we can dictate, or is it dictated by customer expectations?

- ✔ Can customer expectations be influenced? With a better understanding of customer expectations, could we build the service in such a way that customers prefer our service to other options, and what are those other options?

Because many systems have to interact to ensure that ABC's ATM business is performing well, ABC needs a way to optimize the performance of the business. Some regulations may apply in a particular state or region but not in another, for example. ABC needs to ask itself the following questions:

- ✔ Are we in compliance with both state and national rules?

- ✔ Can we prove that we're in compliance?

In addition, the competitive market is changing. ABC needs to consider its approach to influencing customer behavior — how this year's approach differs from last year's, for example, and what factors influence customers' buying and use behaviors.

Provider/customer collaboration

Service is a complex and dynamic collaboration between provider and customer. Therefore, companies continually need to optimize the interactions of all the components that make up the service to ensure that changing business objectives are met, and they need to improve both the customer interaction and relationship over time.

Clearly, many issues affect the way that the seemingly simple ATM affects a business on a regular basis. If all systems of checks and balances are in place, and all components are managed in an efficient and effective manner, life is good. As in every process and every business, however, small issues can have a major impact — which is where service management comes in.

Suppose that ABC Financial is pleased with its ATM network; the network is well managed and secure, so everyone is happy. One day, an ATM services manager comes up with an idea to improve efficiency and save money: A third party could take over ATM repairs, which could save ABC as much as $100 million by replacing its in-house repair staff. ABC Financial learns a hard lesson, however. It doesn't spend the time managing the effectiveness of the service provided by the third party; therefore, repair times are double what they had been. The repair processes may be efficient, but customers are unhappy, and they begin to call the support line in great numbers — and ABC Financial is forced to hire more call-center staff to address service issues.

A critical distinction exists between a management process and the service itself. In the ABC example, the company could establish a task force to try to find out why the level of customer satisfaction has dropped so rapidly, but as managers research the problem, customers begin to move to competing banks.

In the next couple of chapters, we walk through a holistic view of service management and show how all the parts relate to one another. This journey is a fun one, so we hope that you'll jump onboard.

Chapter 2

Getting Inside Service Management

*I*n this chapter, we introduce a very simple model of a service, looking at it from the inside. By providing some examples and figures, we help you understand how just about everything around you can be viewed as a service or a component of a service. To create a strategy for service management, you need to start by understanding some basic principles of service delivery and management. This chapter provides this basic level of information about managing services. To keep things simple, we ignore the fact that every service has a consumer and consider just what makes up a service from the inside.

Keep in mind one simple but important principle: The customer doesn't really want to know what makes the service tick. He wants a service that provides a valuable result or outcome.

Building a Foundation for Service Management

In Chapter 1, we stake a huge claim and say that everything is a service. Although we're a little cavalier in defining the term that way, we don't have much choice, because what we're really doing is focusing on every activity to which you can apply service management, such as delivering food in a restaurant, responding to customer service queries, or producing manufactured goods.

Think of every activity within a commercial organization as being a service or a component of a service.

We define *service* this way:

> A service is a purposeful activity carried out for the benefit of a known target.

In this chapter, we're interested primarily in the first half of that definition: *A service is a purposeful activity*. We focus on what a service looks like from the inside, as shown in the diagram in Figure 2-1.

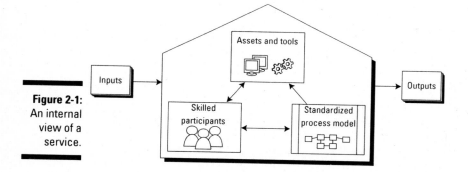

Figure 2-1:
An internal view of a service.

As Figure 2-1 indicates, a service has inputs and outputs. The *input* is a request for the service — something that triggers the activity. The *output* of a service is an outcome. The outputs of a service provider can include both products and service outcomes, which can be anything from a product (an Apple iPod) to an outcome (a mowed lawn) to a product *and* service outcome (a meal and restaurant service). The internal activity of the service transforms the inputs into the outcomes. It typically involves people, whom we refer to in Figure 2-1 as *skilled participants*. It involves the *assets and tools* (which can be as simple as a pen and paper or as complex as a manufacturing plant) that are used to execute the service. The service also involves a *standardized process model* — a method for delivering the service. This process may be so simple that the skilled participants can pick it up in a few hours, or it may be complex, consisting of sets of rules that shape systems and determine how a whole department within an organization carries out its work.

The services that we're most interested in are the activities carried out by large organizations.

Services are often made up of a group of component services, some of which may also have component services.

You can think of an accounting department, for example, as providing a service to other departments, to the executive board, and also to the share-holders. You can consider what an accounting department does as a single service, and from the auditing perspective, you probably should. But you can also consider an accounting department to be a collection of services because it contains multiple distinct activities: accounts receivable, general ledger, and so on. You can view each activity as being a component service.

Inputs and outputs

The delivery of a service usually involves a request that initiates the delivery of the service and the processing of a set of inputs that delivers the desired outputs. Figure 2-2, which looks extremely simple but masks a fair amount of complexity, illustrates this process.

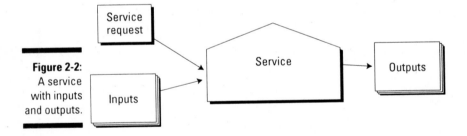

Figure 2-2:
A service with inputs and outputs.

Services of all kinds can be very *immersive* (meaning that you become part of the process) or not particularly immersive (meaning that the process hap-pens without your interaction). Visiting an automated teller machine (ATM) to get money, for example, isn't particularly immersive because the customer activity is very simple. The customer requests the service by inserting her card into the ATM. The only other inputs that the customer provides are a personal identification number (PIN), entered for the sake of security, and information about the amount of money required. The ATM checks to see whether the customer is entitled to withdraw money and delivers the money with a receipt.

The whole transaction probably takes less than a minute, and the customer isn't exposed to any of the complexities that make such a service possible. The service is simple, and it works as long as the customer performs the customer activities and the provider performs the provider activities under an agreed-to set of rules.

Now contrast this example with being taken to a hospital with appendicitis, having an appendectomy, and then recovering in a hospital room. Clearly, this service is highly immersive, and the customer is thoroughly exposed to a great deal of the activity that delivers the service. In this example, the customer for the service is also one of the inputs to the service. The same is true of other services, such as providing training to a group of people to increase their skills in some way.

Services, as we define them, always transform something, and they complete by delivering an output, whether that output is cash from your bank account or relief from appendicitis.

Assets and tools

You may wonder why we choose to use the symbol of a building to contain the elements of a service in Figure 2-1 and Figure 2-2, earlier in this chapter. Our intention is to provide an impression of a space in which a service is carried out. Every service is carried out somewhere, perhaps in a collection of places, and it may even be distributed around the world via a process involving many call centers and computers.

You use essentially three types of assets and tools to deliver a service:

- ✔ Work environments (buildings)
- ✔ Mechanical tools (vehicles)
- ✔ Digital tools (computers and communications devices)

What assets and tools have in common is that they all cost money and need to be maintained — and possibly replaced — over time. Digital tools are devoted primarily to collecting and managing information, whereas mechanical tools are related primarily to manipulating or moving things, and the environment is the space within which the activity takes place.

If you think of a very complex service, such as providing a passenger flight from one place to another, you see that the assets and tools are highly diverse, involving airports (including hangars and runways) as well as call centers and offices in many places. The associated machinery is complicated, too, given the engineering and logistical support that an airplane needs. The computer and communications systems also are complex.

Neither could we claim that our example of an ATM service is simple in this respect. The service is simple enough at the interface — the card goes in and the money comes out — but as we show in Chapter 1, an array of complex information technology (IT) systems is involved in making the service happen.

A standardized process model

Every process, from tying your shoelaces to sending astronauts to the moon, involves an activity-based workflow. Processes are sometimes newly invented. Gold-medal Olympian Dick Fosbury, for example, invented the Fosbury Flop, an original technique for executing the high jump that changed the way that the event is executed today. Most of the time, though, the elements that compose processes evolve, improving to some degree over time.

Even the simplest of services has to be managed as a process. The process flow may be stated explicitly and documented somewhere, or it may not be. It may influence the way that assets and tools are deployed, or it may not. It may demand that staff members be trained to understand how it works, or the process may be obvious. All these factors can vary.

Figure 2-3 depicts the process model as a flow diagram, representing the proper activity for taking the inputs of a service and transforming them into desired outcomes.

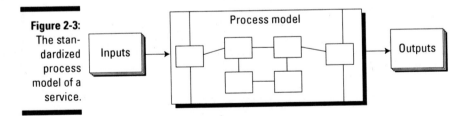

Figure 2-3: The standardized process model of a service.

We can describe the ATM cash withdrawal service in a standardized process model by showing the input (the ATM user inserts the card and enters the requested information), the process (the ATM verifies the PIN against encoded information on the card and checks the amount of money requested against data in the user's bank account), and the output (the ATM dispatches money).

If we include all the surrounding management activities that support the service, however, the process model is more complicated. In this case, the model has to include the activities of various support systems throughout the bank's network, such as check depositing and check clearing, as well as the scheduling of security personnel to deliver money to the ATM at various times as the machine begins to run short.

The more complicated model shows that some of the activities are actually defined as computer programs that automate part of the service (such as the process that debits the money from the ATM user's account). The whole process is built and automated to work with very little intervention from human beings, and the part of the process model that describes what human beings have to do is very simple.

After you clearly define a service, you have to work through how you'll manage that service. The process model describes how the service is delivered. Service management describes how you'll manage the service, addressing such questions as these:

- How will you keep track of the configuration of the service?
- How will you manage changes to the service?
- How will you manage incidents that may occur?
- How will you monitor the service?
- How will you manage requests related to the service?

For all repeated services, a process is employed to carry out the service, and a set of service management processes is used to manage the service.

Skilled participants

The most flexible part of most services is the staff. To carry out their work, the members of the staff must have the following traits:

- Good judgment
- Intelligence
- Proper skills
- Knowledge of their roles
- Flexibility

The activity of automating service of any kind involves automating the predictable and repeating elements of it, leaving the exceptional cases to the people who are involved.

In most services of any size, the staff members who deliver the service have specific roles that involve them in specific activities. In many instances, they need to be trained in specific skills, and they were hired because they have the requisite intelligence and judgment.

In many circumstances, although a standardized process is in place, it's almost wholly enshrined in the knowledge of the person who's carrying out the task. In fact, many services have two information systems: the computer system and the skilled staff members who deliver the service.

Seeing the Importance of Oversight

We think of the oversight system (or service management system) as recording all the information about the service or any aspect of the service that can be useful in any way. Thus, the oversight system may refer to the standardized process model to gather measurements about the speed of any given activity or the speed of flow from one activity to another. It may take readings from sensors embedded in machinery or from programs that monitor the activity of computer systems, and it may take information directly from the skilled participants who carry out the service.

This book is about service management, but our model of a service currently includes nothing that relates to managing the service. We address that problem in Figure 2-4 by adding the element of oversight.

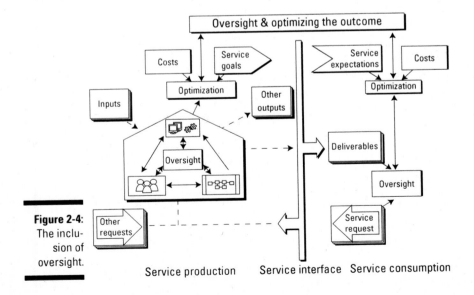

Figure 2-4: The inclusion of oversight.

As far as oversight is concerned, you shouldn't think simply in terms of computer systems gathering and analyzing information. You also need to include physical systems, such as the fire-alarm system that's deployed throughout the working space, the central heating system, or even a nuclear power plant.

The point is that for most services, many individual oversight systems operate within the overall service management system, contributing to the proper performance of the service, but you should have most interest in the oversight systems that provide feedback to those who carry out the service. Oversight systems that provide feedback on how efficiently the service is running are especially useful to the people or computers that carry out the service. Their primary role is to ensure that the service is delivered at a level that is acceptable to the service user.

Balancing the Physical World and IT Systems

Take a moment to review Figure 2-1, earlier in this chapter. In this section, we discuss that figure from the service management point of view.

The first thing to note is that service management doesn't concern itself only with what we think of traditionally as computer and communications systems. Information technology is now embedded inside most assets that in the past may not have been thought of as IT assets. In fact, an increasingly blurry line divides *enterprise physical assets* (such as buildings, furniture, landline phones, and security systems) and *IT assets* (servers, laptops, and mobile devices) as all assets become increasingly smart, interconnected, and instrumented by design.

Physical and IT systems

Although many of us think about managing computers and communications systems, this example is only the tip of the iceberg. Service management really looks to manage physical environments (plants, facilities, trucks, and so on) as well as IT systems, and it defines processes, functions, and roles for people. In our ATM example, we aren't talking just about IT technology. The ATM service also relies on trucks, the people who replenish the cash, and the paper on which receipts are printed.

When you examine the mission-critical activities of your organization, you usually discover that computer systems play a central role. As far as this discovery is concerned, we have good news and bad news:

- ✔ The good news is that IT service management involves similar activities, no matter what the various technology and systems are doing.

- ✔ The bad news is that service management is, in many ways, a complex and highly skilled activity.

Luckily, businesses have been using IT (including computers, applications, networks, storage devices, and security firewalls) for decades, and in doing so, they've accumulated a mass of experience and a wealth of assets. The experience that businesses have accumulated spans all these areas; more important, more physical assets are transforming into IT assets with the inclusion of smart chips and sensors that allow them to be managed as IT assets. An explosion of computerization or smartening of dumb assets is occurring, allowing service management to control the broad set of assets more easily and adding complexity to what were once simple applications, systems, and networks.

Service best practices

The service management experience is embodied to a great extent in the hundreds of thousands of computer professionals who run the systems. The assets include a wide range of software that's purpose-built to assist in service management. Much of this software has evolved over many years. In addition, we have standardized process models and best practices for service management, such as the Information Technology Infrastructure Library (ITIL), the enhanced Telecom Operations Map (eTOM), and Control Objectives for Information and Related Technology (COBIT). (For more information, see Chapter 4.) Any organization that needs to consider implementing or changing the way that it manages the services it delivers can leverage these resources to augment its service management planning.

Service delivery and oversight

In this chapter, we consider only the internal operation of a service. A service has inputs and outcomes, involves the use of tools and assets in a specific environment, and is carried out by skilled participants who implement a standardized process model, and the whole environment is subject to the oversight of the service management system.

What we haven't done is discuss the nature of that oversight and what it involves in detail, but you've probably deduced that it involves service management. The notions of both service and service management are critical. The staff members who deliver a service take pride in their activities and also seek to improve their efficiency so as to make the service better over time. In addition to the delivery of the service, many activities are required to manage the service. You need to consider the following questions:

- ✔ How will you plan and manage changes to the service?

- ✔ How will you monitor service levels and service costs?

- ✔ How will you manage incidents that may occur?

- ✔ How will you manage the availability and continuity of the service in the event of a major unplanned disruption?

- ✔ How will you manage the security of information within the service?

- ✔ How will you direct, evaluate, and monitor compliance with required regulations or polices?

- ✔ How will you manage exceptions?

Service management needs to be effective to answer these questions, but in the end, the execution of the service itself must be done in such a way that the customer finds the outcomes to be valuable, convenient, and correctly priced.

Chapter 3

The Customer Is King

*W*e look at a service from the inside in Chapter 2, so it seems logical that in this chapter, we take a look at a service from the outside. In Chapter 2, we focus on the first part of the definition of a service *(a service is a purposeful activity)*; in this chapter, we focus on the second part *(carried out for the benefit of a known target)*.

We could say *for the benefit of the customer,* but we don't. In most circumstances, satisfying the customer isn't the only driver that shapes a service. If the service is delivered by a public company, for example, you also need to satisfy the shareholders. You can quite easily make the customers happy and still go out of business, and the shareholders are unlikely to approve such a business strategy. So in addition to executing the activities of a well-defined service in a high-quality manner, service management needs to include both a customer satisfaction process and a stakeholder-requirements management process to ensure that the needs of all stakeholders are known and managed.

So when we say *for the benefit of a known target,* we may be talking about a need to satisfy multiple targets, each of which has a specific expectation of the service. The shareholders care about profitability, whereas the customers care about the quality of service.

Understanding Customers' Expectations

The most important thing to understand about customer expectations is that they're defined by context. If you want to deliver an appropriate service, you need to satisfy the expectations of the customer. Like most people, you've probably been to expensive restaurants and also to fast-food joints, for example. Although you were the same person in both types of restaurants, you definitely weren't the same customer. At an expensive restaurant, you expected excellent service, an intriguing menu, a wine list, a pleasant environment, and so on. At a fast-food joint, you expected swift service and predictable food.

As customers, people are defined by their expectations. Thus, if you want to deliver an appropriate service, you need to satisfy the customers' expectations.

Consider an automated teller machine (ATM) transaction. ATM customers' expectations are very easy to define. Customers expect the ATM to work properly, dispense money in a reasonable amount of time, and keep their financial data secure. Customers don't really care *how* an ATM accomplishes these tasks as long as it works the way they expect it to. As far as they're concerned, the ATM can involve a vast integrated computer and communications system, or someone could be hiding inside the machine with a wad of bills, pushing them out of the slot when requested. Both systems are the same as far as the customer is concerned; how the service is achieved is irrelevant.

Another important aspect is selection. Customers either select a service or have no choice. A person entering the United States through an airport, for example, is stopped by the U.S. Customs Service. The customer in this instance can't say, "I don't think I like this customs service; I'll use Canada's instead." The fact that the U.S. Customs Service has a monopoly at all U.S. borders, however, doesn't prevent it from wanting to provide unobtrusive service to innocent travelers while preventing banned substances and smugglers from entering the country.

The expectations of the customer are defined primarily by context.

Looking at a Service from the Outside

The customer of a service sees only the external view of the service interface, as shown in Figure 3-1.

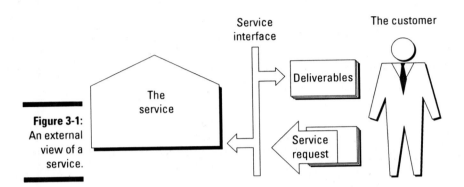

Figure 3-1:
An external
view of a
service.

Although the service may have many inputs and outputs, the customer is directly aware of only the outcomes provided directly by the service and the inputs (such as a security code) she provided, along with the service request (such as the amount of money she wants to withdraw).

Suppose that you take your shoes to a cobbler and tell him what's wrong with them. Later, you collect the shoes, and you judge the level of service primarily by whether the cobbler mended the shoes effectively.

In this situation, the cobbler managing the service probably focuses on the quality of workmanship and the time taken to complete the work. Unless he measures factors such as customer satisfaction, transaction trends, pricing trends, and margin trends, however, he'll have no idea whether he's delivering the appropriate service level based on both customer and stakeholder requirements.

In evaluating service quality, measurements of customers' and stakeholders' satisfaction are the most important.

If the cobbler pays special attention only to the quality of the work, he may be investing in the wrong thing. Perhaps he has a good location filled with wealthy customers and no nearby competitors, so he may be able to spend more time on repairs and charge more without driving away customers. If his method of providing service is sustainable, he needs to gather information from his customers. If he's going to be successful, he needs to discover the key factors that will satisfy his customers. On the other hand, if the cobbler measures only the customer experience and fails to track progress on stakeholder requirements, he may go out of business. He may spend so much time or charge so much for each shoe repair that his customers would have been better off buying new shoes.

Understanding Service Management

Service management is

> The management of a service to ensure that it meets the critical outcomes the customer values and the stakeholders want to provide.

Before we go any further, we need to distinguish between the execution of a service and service management. The *execution of a service* is the process of performing the task, whereas *service management* is the process of making sure that the task is performed according to expectations.

An ATM is a good example of a service because the service outcomes desired by the customer and stakeholders are simple and not subject to debate. The customer wants quick, accurate, secure, affordable, and always-available service transactions, and the stakeholders want seamless delivery of the service at an affordable price with the right level of oversight.

Those features are all that the customer — we'll call her Jane — expects, but her expectations actually are high. Jane expects the ATM to be available 24/7, to be free of errors, and to be fast. If she turns up at an ATM at 4 a.m. and the ATM isn't working, she's much more likely to get annoyed and curse the bank than to think, "After all, it's 4 a.m. Perhaps I was optimistic in expecting to get money at this time of day."

As far as ATM service is concerned, the critical customer service needs are well understood. Ever since ATMs were introduced, customers have had high service expectations, and because banks can save money and even generate revenue by deploying ATMs, financial institutions are willing to make the investment to deliver the quality of service that customers demand.

In fact, the ATM service was highly automated from the get-go, and even at the outset, the level of automation was such that the service was delivered primarily by purpose-built computers and communications technology.

The assets and tools that are involved in providing the ATM service include the ATM devices, the secure communications links from the ATM to the bank's data centers, the applications that manage customer checking accounts, the systems that manage cash distribution, the bank's customer support center, and the processes for recording lost or stolen cards. (For more information on how assets and tools fit into the service management model, refer to Chapter 2.)

The service management systems monitor the ATM's service systems to prevent those systems from failing and affecting customers' service expectations.

A system isn't necessarily made up only of technology. A typical system, in fact, is made up of people, processes, technologies, and information. In addition to the service management system, service providers need good governance to minimize performance declines during periods of change and innovation.

Service management systems are the systems that support the systems that deliver the service.

Dealing with the Commercial Reality

To keep customers satisfied, you need to identify key service performance indicators as well as key goal indicators — and monitor them closely so that you meet both customers' and stakeholders' expectations, as illustrated in Figure 3-2.

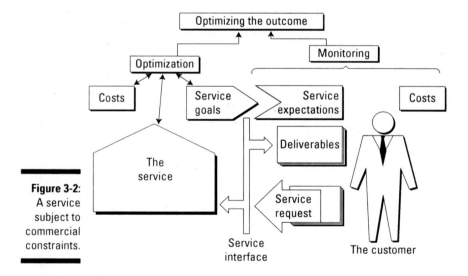

Figure 3-2: A service subject to commercial constraints.

The important point is that in most situations, clear commercial constraints apply. The service provider has costs, and as the service level delivered increases, so do the costs of delivering the service. The role of the key service performance indicators is to set the acceptable service level so that the level of customer satisfaction is high. Then you can optimize the delivery of the service so that you deliver the highest service level at the lowest cost.

You mustn't lose sight of the customer, however. The customer also has costs (the price he pays for the service) and service expectations. Because we live in a competitive world, the customer's service expectation probably won't always be the same. Most likely, the customer will expect to get more for his money as time passes.

To optimize your outcome over time, you need to monitor customers' expectations on an ongoing basis; simply assuming that current service goals will remain static isn't good enough. The situation is dynamic, and when customers' expectations change, the service provider needs to recognize and respond to the changes.

To achieve this goal, measure both performance and desired outcomes. You can measure customers' expectations by conducting customer feedback surveys and by monitoring customer responses to changes in price or other factors that affect the delivery of services. Companies use a variety of traditional surveys and Web-based monitoring tools to measure sales and customer relationship effectiveness and to keep track of performance at many levels. You must measure service activities for aspects such as cost, duration, human effort, and quality. You also need to measure progress toward the outcomes that both the customer and the stakeholders had in mind when the service was established.

Gaining Control of Services and Service Components

If you want to optimize a service, you have to optimize the whole service rather than each individual service component. In the ATM example, there's little point in ensuring that the ATM is always well stocked with money if the system that provides information about the customers' bank balances fails. You have to optimize the ensemble of services holistically.

The activities that deliver a service usually can be broken into multiple other activities. You can consider each of these component services to be a service in its own right, in which case it also has a customer. The customer for each *component service* isn't the ultimate customer of the whole service, however, but simply the receiver of its outputs.

This relationship gets very complicated. If you consider an ATM service, you can envisage a whole set of coordinated component services, such as the marketing of certificates of deposit (CDs) and the provision of insurance forms. Suppose that the marketing department of ABC Financial has added some new screens to the ATM and that each screen is backed by a new component service. The two component services — marketing CDs and providing insurance forms — are actual services that a human teller might provide, and the ATM has been programmed to provide a form of these services as well. The consumer receives the outputs and benefits by getting answers to questions immediately rather than waiting to speak with a teller.

The same is true for service providers and consumers. Customers have customers who have customers. Suppliers have suppliers who have suppliers. The extent of the service management system almost reverberates into eternity. Individual people both give and receive service all day long, and it's human nature to worry about the part of the service management system that you control. In today's complex world, however, you also need to care about the connections among services and the dependencies among services. In other words, if your supplier takes a risk, it's your risk too.

Consider the activity or service of delivering cash to the ATM. The ATM has a defined service to dispense cash. A *key performance indicator* (KPI) for this service component includes delivery of the right amount of cash within an acceptable time frame. This activity is only a piece of the whole picture, however; additional services fill out the full set of activities. The security of the transaction, for example, is imperative to the ATM service as a whole, and the security service has its own set of KPIs. Therefore, the entire ATM service to customers incorporates a whole set of KPIs, as illustrated in Figure 3-3. This situation is true for all other component services. Consequently, if the KPIs for the whole service change, you also need to adjust the component KPIs.

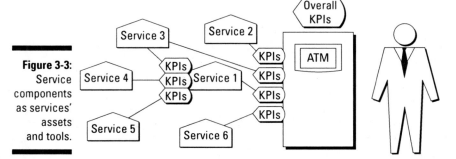

Figure 3-3:
Service
components
as services'
assets
and tools.

To optimize a service, you have to optimize the whole service across all interdependent component services. Optimizing select components out of context isn't enough.

Part II
Getting the Foundation in Place

"We should cast a circle, invoke the elements, and direct the energy. If that doesn't work, we'll read the standards and best practices."

In this part . . .

Standards and best practices have been developed for service management just as they have for many other aspects of IT and business. In this part, we discuss the Information Technology Infrastructure Library (ITIL), which many organizations use as a handy service management reference. We also describe a strategic approach to enhancing and evolving service management capabilities.

Chapter 4

Service Management Standards and Best Practices

*T*he definition of service is expansive, ranging from providing service in a restaurant to delivering cash to a banking customer through an automated teller machine (ATM); it even includes digital services, such as sensors included in many automobiles to aid in repair and maintenance services. That definition provides for a lot of services that need to be managed. Services aren't just hidden within a company's own environment; rather, they have to be managed across everything from the supply chain to the product design partners. Because these services are so important to how well companies run, more and more services are being implemented based on best practices and standards for service management.

Organizations need to control, manage, and continuously improve services without always having to re-create what works and what doesn't work. By leveraging standards and best practices, organizations can manage services more effectively and efficiently than they could otherwise.

In this chapter, we explore the world of service management best practices and standards. We also describe why companies leverage standards and best practices, and we introduce the organizations that create and distribute necessary information about these standards and best practices.

Understanding What Best Practices and Standards Can Do for You

Best practices and standards can help improve quality and control costs. To be clear, here's what we mean by the terms *best practices* and *standards:*

- ✔ **Best practices** are accumulated knowledge that can help people and organizations avoid mistakes that others have made. Best practices range from recommendations for specific coding specifications to descriptions of enterprisewide management processes that have proved to be successful. You can find best practices in many ways, including industry organization and independent books, training materials, Web sites, and blogs, as well as vendor Web sites and consulting practices. (For a few best-practices resources, see "Using Standards and Best Practices to Improve Quality," later in this chapter.)

- ✔ **Standards** are a core set of common, repeatable best practices and protocols that have been agreed on by a business or industry group. Typically, vendors, industry user groups, and end users collaborate to develop standards based on the broad expertise of a large number of stakeholders. Organizations can leverage these standards as a common foundation and innovate on top of them.

Best practices and standards provide a starting recipe, appropriate tools, required ingredients, and some tips and tricks. Just as an experienced chef experiments with and tweaks a recipe, you may find that you need to adapt best practices to fit your situation and requirements. Best practices provide a starting point for planning, as well as a common language and set of concepts that enable you to communicate and coordinate with possibly large teams without having to communicate the basic approach for the task at hand. Being freed from always having to start with the basics, you can focus on the innovation that can transform the current environment into something special.

Making use of standards that other people in your industry have evaluated, tested, and refined may seem to be an obvious approach. Using standards is the best way to cut down on errors and get results quickly — but many businesses don't follow this approach. Some companies are reluctant to implement standards because they see themselves as being unique, with highly differentiated sets of business processes. When your business makes a commitment to identifying processes that are consistent with those of other companies in similar markets, however, you can take advantage of best practices for these processes. This important step frees resources that you can use to improve processes that support areas of *real* differentiation.

Using Standards and Best Practices to Improve Quality

Not surprisingly, many organizations help companies implement best practices. International, national, local, and industry-specific professional associations provide forums for managers to gather and discuss lessons learned and best practices. Here are a few sources for standards and best practices from leading organizations:

- **Information Technology Infrastructure Library (ITIL):** ITIL provides a set of best practices for IT service management. You can find more information at www.itil-officialsite.com/home/home.asp.

- **International Organization for Standardization (ISO):** ISO has developed more than 17,000 international standards, including standards for IT service management and corporate governance of information technology. You can find more information at www.iso.org.

- **enhanced Telecom Operations Map (eTOM):** eTOM is a framework that provides a business process model for the telecommunications industry. Find out more at www.tmforum.org/BusinessProcessFramework/1647/home.html.

- **Control Objectives for Information and Related Technology (COBIT):** COBIT provides an IT framework with a focus on governance and managing technical and business risks. You can find more information at www.isaca.org/cobit.

- **eSourcing Capability Model (eSCM):** eSCM is a framework developed at Carnegie Mellon University to provide a best-practices model for improving relationships between customers and suppliers in outsourcing agreements. Find out more at Carnegie Mellon's IT Services Qualification Center (ITSqc) Web site, http://itsqc.cmu.edu/models/index.asp.

- **Capability Maturity Model Integration (CMMI):** The Software Engineering Institute (SEI) of Carnegie Mellon University developed CMMI along with members of industry and government. CMMI is a process-improvement best practice used to improve processes in a project or overall. Find out more at www.sei.cmu.edu/cmmi.

If you're looking for more information, don't worry. In "Finding Standards," later in this chapter, we give you a list of the details.

One of the greatest benefits of the organizations that provide standards and best practices is that they enable people who have specialized knowledge to exchange information about lessons learned. Therefore, these organizations can provide forums and create documents that are very helpful in preventing mistakes.

As markets and industries change, best practices are updated. Formal sets of documented best practices have input from major universities, product and service providers, commercial consultants, educators, and organizations from every industry sector. When these collections of best practices are published, they provide significant value because they show what many people with different and sometimes conflicting business objectives can agree on.

Why are we talking about this topic in the context of service management? The reason is quite simple, actually: Standardization drives commoditization and changes the focus to innovation and differentiation. When you follow agreed-on industry standards for connecting to networks, systems, and servers, for example, you're free to focus on service innovation. As agreements on standards for network protocols change, the focus of innovation changes to the types of services that travel over the network. This model seems to be very basic but has profound implications for service management. As service management processes become standardized, the focus of innovation turns to service.

On a different level, organizations are starting to see that they can standardize management processes. As this standardization happens, organizations can respond to changing market conditions more quickly without reconstructing all the pieces they may need.

Using standards and best practices alone doesn't guarantee quality results. You need to apply standards and best practices with thoughtful care, experience, and knowledge. You can't assume that your processes will be optimized just because you send the members of your IT team to get certified in their understanding of accepted best practices and standards, for example.

By now, you may be thinking, "I get it. Standards and best practices are important." And you probably have a few questions to ask, such as these:

- ✔ **Why are some companies reluctant to use standards and best practices?**

  Some businesses think that they won't benefit from applying industry best practices for certain projects, even if staff members have been certified in those best practices recently. One common reason for staff members to refrain from implementing standards and best practices relates to the uniqueness of complex standards. Understandably, a business owner may feel that the highly specialized nature of the business makes it hard to benefit from best practices that have been honed in other businesses. Many companies, however, find that they can leverage best practices as a starting point and make adjustments so that the specifics of the business are taken into account.

✔ **Who is most likely to benefit from using standards and best practices?**

Your company! Standards and best practices can become the foundation for implementing service management and help your organization meet expectations.

✔ **How do companies get started?**

If you're a new user, or if you're inexperienced in certain business processes, a standards-and-best-practices approach can be an excellent way to get started. Standards and best practices can provide a framework for you to follow. Also, following standards and best practices helps you check on how well you're doing.

Finding Standards

Although following a best-practices approach may seem to be logical, many companies find roadblocks that keep them from choosing this path. Organizations know that they need to develop a strategy to implement and manage services, but they can easily get sidetracked by concentrating on immediate project needs rather than the big picture. Operations must work in tandem with the business to provide a quality management system for business services, which are critical to business success.

The sections that follow provide an overview of the most widely used service management standards and best practices. ITIL, for example, is the most broadly accepted set of best practices for IT operations. As its use spread, the organizing body increased its comprehensiveness, so ITIL now covers just about everything related to services in general. Other widely accepted best practices and standards are ISO, eTOM, COBIT, eSCM, and CMMI.

ITIL

The Information Technology Infrastructure Library (ITIL) is a set of books that describes best practices for service management. Today, ITIL contributes some best practices — very well-tested practices — that become the frameworks for improving service quality. These best practices are codified in books that can be purchased from ITIL. The most recent version, Version 3, consists of five core books that describe best practices for service management. These books focus on service strategy, service design, service transition, service operation, and continuous service improvement. As you can see by the book titles, ITIL Version 3 takes a life-cycle approach to service management.

ITIL's knowledge gathering and documentation began back in the 1980s, when a group of people working for the United Kingdom's government assessed the quality of government IT services. They found that the quality was not up to their expectations. Although the technology executives were very good at their jobs, it was common practice for them to move around to different positions quite a bit. The resulting lack of continuous leadership led to some major challenges in providing consistent and high-quality results for technology projects.

To improve quality, the UK government decided to outsource many of its IT projects. Using outside consultants had its own challenges, and service quality continued to deteriorate. To keep the outside consultants in sync with the internal IT departments, IT methodically began to record all the best practices surrounding IT strategy, design, development, operations, and maintenance. This very comprehensive set of practices for IT projects became the basis for ITIL. The framework was picked up by government and nongovernment agencies in the UK and globally.

ITIL Version 2 (also known as V2), released in 2001, consists of seven core books that took a processcentric approach to service management. The focus of V2 is on improving processes such as service support, service delivery, security management, and infrastructure management.

Over time, V2 needed revision because best practices changed. Many ITIL projects focused on processes being developed in isolation without a focus on the services to be managed. Service management requires addressing both service and the service management processes to achieve the value that the business needs. Processes shouldn't be viewed as being new stand-alone sets of requirements; they have to be understood in context of the overall business strategy. Version 3 (V3), released in 2007, expands on earlier versions and provides a service-focused approach with an emphasis on integration and producing value from assets.

So whereas the first version of ITIL focuses on managing systems and V2 focuses on management processes, V3 focuses on services and the activities that need to occur throughout the service life cycle to produce the maximum value from all business and IT assets.

One of the fundamental shifts between V2 and V3 makes very clear that if you wait until service delivery to think about managing service levels, you're too late. You need to begin planning for service levels during service design. V3 emphasizes the need for integrating everything — processes, services, people, tools, and information — and the need for collaboration among different parts of IT. Many of the processes and best practices from V2 are still relevant and are covered in V3, but ITIL has matured, and the best practices of V2 are given more of a strategic enterprise view in V3. Also, the relationships between IT and the business are clearer and better defined in V3.

ISO

As you may well know, no global boundaries exist in business anymore. The Internet helped eliminate barriers to entry for tiny businesses in remote locations. Now, as long as tiny businesses have reliable Internet connections and workable e-commerce applications, they can operate on a global level. So it seems logical that representatives from countries all over the world should get together and agree on international standards for business. These standards are the responsibility of the International Organization for Standardization (ISO), coordinated by representatives in Switzerland. National standards institutes from 157 countries send representatives to ISO. Together, the representatives develop and publish international standards from the perspective of both business and public needs.

Whereas ITIL was developed and is maintained by the UK government, ISO is comprised of international body members with voting rights and has many liaison relationships for advice and support. The group isn't a government organization.

ISO has a joint agreement with the International Electrotechnical Commission (IEC) on standards related to IT and computing. These standards are called *ISO/IEC standards*. Although many ISO and ISO/IEC standards are relevant to service management, ISO 9001, ISO/IEC 20000, and ISO/IEC 38500 are the most directly relevant. We cover them all in the following sections.

ISO 9001

ISO 9001 is *the* management system standard for managing both products and services, laying out the requirements that an organization needs to meet if it wants to have a good quality management system. If your company wants a quality management system that is ISO 9001-registered (meaning that it's reviewed by an expert), you should do the following things:

1. Identify the processes required for the production of high-quality services.

2. Determine the sequences and interactions of these processes.

3. Design and document each process.

4. Check and analyze the implementation of each process, and continually improve the effectiveness of the service management system made up of all those processes.

ISO/IEC 20000

ISO/IEC 20000 is an international service management standard that describes a core set of auditable service management principles for a limited set of service management processes. Currently, the ISO and the IEC are revising this standard to provide more guidance for a standards-based approach to service management processes. Whereas ISO 9001 takes a more generic approach, ISO/IEC 20000 provides descriptions of specific management processes common within service providers. Whereas ITIL describes best practices, ISO/IEC 20000 documents a minimum set of service management requirements that every service provider should apply.

ISO/IEC 38500

ISO/IEC 38500 provides a set of principles for the governance of IT services. Due to the costs, human effort, and risks associated with the supply and demand for IT services and IT-enabled business services, it's more critical than ever to ensure that IT is properly directed and controlled. This standard provides guidance to directors and those who advise directors to ensure that IT services are well governed.

COBIT

Control Objectives for Information and Related Technology (COBIT) was first released in 1996 by the Information Systems Audit and Control Association (ISACA) and the IT Governance Institute (ITGI). COBIT's creators have since released many updated versions. In early 2009, COBIT was in its fourth version.

COBIT is known for its focus on governance and on managing technical and business risks. Its popularity and acceptance increased in 2002 after the U.S. government passed the Sarbanes-Oxley Act. But COBIT isn't as widely used as some other standards, even though the publications are available without charge at www.isaca.org.

The COBIT framework includes six documents on management, tool sets, control objectives, and guidelines for auditing. COBIT has been mapped to other standards, including ITIL and ISO, both of which are covered earlier in this chapter. ISACA and ITGI provide globally accepted practices for IT governance (the management system required to direct and control IT) and other valuable guidance.

Maturity model and other models for service management

Another type of best practice is available for service management. All the models mentioned in the "Finding Standards" section of this chapter focus on best practices as things that are either done or not done. This other type of best practice is a *maturity model,* which is a road map that an organization may follow in its service management journey. Each stage of the road map represents a new level of expertise and experience in operational development, as well as the organization's relationships with customers, partners, and suppliers.

The ISO, various universities, and commercial service providers offer versions of maturity models. Carnegie Mellon University (CMU) in particular has established various maturity model best practices designed for assessment and certification. CMU's Software Engineering Institute (SEI) and its IT Services Qualification Center (ITSqc) have both produced sets of maturity-model best practices. CMMI (Capability Maturity Model Integration), also developed by Carnegie Mellon, is a Capability Maturity Model (CMM) for software engineering. The latest version includes both a staged model approach and a continuous model. The staged model is based on improving the overall management capability of all processes collectively, in five stages or levels of maturity. The continuous model is based on improving the maturity of each management process individually. Some processes may be more mature than others, depending on business need.

ITSqc has developed a service management capability model called eSCM (eSourcing

Capability Model). The term *eSourcing* refers to outsourced services of IT-enabled business processes and business services. This model has been developed specifically to certify IT-enabled service providers that recognize their different capabilities. One provider may apply best practices to only one account, whereas another can apply best practices to many accounts. eSCM is different from a maturity model, which is based on the idea that a management capability or process may be done in various levels of maturity, from poorly to well.

The ITSqc Capability Model is focused on recognizing different types of capability. Another interesting aspect of the eSCM is that it recognizes that a service is an active collaboration between provider and client and that value is an act of co-creation. This model provides details on practices that clients should employ to get the most from their sourcing relationships.

In the future, you'll see even more maturity models. It appears that various universities are developing additional service management maturity models, for example. ISO/IEC also plans to produce more service management standards: a maturity model, an incremental conformity model, and a process-reference model standard. With all this activity going on, service management organizations have a great need to understand the models' real value — and where those models do and don't add value to their business objectives.

eTOM

The enhanced Telecom Operations Map (eTOM) is designed to provide a business-process model or framework for the telecommunications industry. eTOM describes enterprise processes required by a service provider. You can analyze them based on their significance to the business. For suppliers, eTOM outlines potential boundaries of software components to align with the customers' needs, and it highlights the required functions, inputs, and outputs that products must support. Like ITIL and COBIT, eTOM contains many concepts that benefit all service providers.

One interesting aspect of eTOM is its view of services as products. This view is aligned with the ISO 9001 perspective on common requirements in quality management system products and services. eTOM provides prescriptive guidance for applying the ISO 9001 concept of a quality management system to a telecommunications service provider.

eTOM, like COBIT and ITIL, is going through continuous improvement. Currently, the TM Forum (the organization that publishes eTOM) is evaluating some of ITIL V3's best practices for inclusion.

Getting Certified

Certification is an important part of any discussion of service management because certification implies a certain level of expertise. Here are a few basic things that you need to know about certification:

- ✔ **Types of certification:** You can choose among three types of certification, according to your needs:

  - • **Personal certifications** validate a candidate's understanding of specific terms and concepts.

  - • **Professional certifications** indicate that a person can prove both knowledge and experience in a topic.

  - • **Organizational certifications** validate an organization's methods, proving that it does something in a reliable way.

- ✔ **Certification versus standard:** You should understand the difference between the certification and the body of knowledge or standard with which it is associated. ISO/IEC 20000, for example, is a documented standard for service management. Some certification schemes are designed

> to validate whether ISO/IEC 20000 principles have been implemented in practice in a service provider.
>
> ✔ **Value of certification:** The value of a certification is tied directly to the value that the market associates with it. The standard or best practice may be very beneficial, whereas a certification may or may not have market value.

Education is one of the most important aspects of getting on the right path to implementing standards and best practices. Many of the standards and best-practices bodies have extensive education and personal certification programs that allow you to become proficient in your understanding of their standards.

ITIL has a very extensive personal certification program. The V2 series of certificates includes the Foundation Certificate, the Practitioner's Certificate, the Clustered Practitioner's Certificate, and the Manager's Certificate. The V3 certification program includes a Foundation Certificate, a choice of five Lifecycle Stage Certificates or five Capability Certificates, and an ITIL Expert Certificate. The certification courses teach you about ITIL's language and terms. The programs provide information about the philosophy of ITIL service management.

The V3 course's target audience includes employees of IT companies who are involved in supporting and delivering IT services, as well as just about anyone else who needs to understand ITIL and service management best practices.

If you're suffering from certification burnout, it's okay to learn the knowledge and just do your job. Also, the IT industry is increasingly expressing interest in professional qualifications that recognize that skills and qualifications are acquired outside the classroom as well. Certifications are good, but certification plus experience is even better.

Getting an ITIL certification isn't a surefire recipe for success. In fact, taking any class on any subject isn't a surefire recipe for success. Many other factors are required for a company to implement standards and best practices for service management successfully. We delve deeper into this topic in Chapter 6 and Chapter 7.

Chapter 5

Implementing ITIL

***

In This Chapter

≫ Using ITIL V3 as a blueprint for enterprise service management

≫ Considering practical matters in implementing ITIL

≫ Understanding how ITIL integrates with other best-practices frameworks

***

So far in this book, we've defined a service, discussed the importance of managing a service, and enumerated the value of best practices in service management. We've also given you a brief overview of some of the important public standards and best practices — namely, best-practices models such as Control Objectives for Information and Related Technology (COBIT) and enhanced Telecom Operations Map (eTOM), as well as standards from the International Standards Organization (ISO). (Refer to Chapter 4 for more information on these models and organizations.)

In this chapter, we explore in detail one of the most comprehensive sets of best practices for service management: Information Technology Infrastructure Library (ITIL). We chose ITIL for this discussion in part because many of its best practices are now being adopted even beyond IT (such as in service provider operations) to help adherents align existing services with business objectives; to identify new service opportunities to support the business; and to successfully address the closed-loop planning, execution, and continuous improvement of these services.

Although ITIL is a set of published guidance books that you can simply download to your computer or view on the Internet (at www.itilsurvival.com/ ITILBooksintheUS.html), implementing ITIL service management best practices in your organization isn't so simple, so we also talk about some practical considerations in implementing ITIL. Specifically, we discuss how ITIL integrates into other frameworks.

ITIL V3: A Useful Blueprint for Enterprise Service Management

In Chapter 4, we introduce ITIL and tell you a little bit about its history and objectives. We explain that ITIL is a library of books that describes best practices for service management. In 2007, the Office of Government Commerce (OGC), a UK agency, introduced the latest version of ITIL: Version 3 (V3). This version emphasizes the importance of building best practices throughout the entire services life cycle because, frankly, if you've waited until your service is delivered to consider best practices, you've waited too long. So ITIL V3 emphasizes the need for integrating everything: processes, services, people, tools, and information, as well as collaboration among different parts of IT.

ITIL V3 consists of five core books that describe these best practices. The five books address each aspect of the services life cycle, from developing a service strategy to designing the service and then rolling out and operating the service. The books also provide guidelines for continually improving your services. Within each of these life-cycle areas, a series of 26 best-practices components guides you through service management. Many of these best-practices processes occur throughout all stages of the life cycle. Wow! This sounds like a lot of information — and it is. We distill it for you in the following sections.

Book 1: Service Strategy

Just as a business needs a strategy, so does IT. *Service Strategy* addresses how to set a strategy to meet customer needs and provide value. Key elements include strategy guidelines, financial considerations, and portfolio and demand management. Here are the highlights:

- **Strategy considerations:** IT doesn't live in a vacuum. To develop a strategy, IT needs to align with business objectives that include understanding customer needs, the market, and the competitive environment; then it must set the vision and direction for IT services in the context of the broader corporate strategy. IT also needs to put together a plan for achieving this vision, listing the services and products that customers expect as well as outlining the organizational and sourcing design for achieving these goals. *Service Strategy* defines the different kinds of service providers, both internal and external, that are required to make these services a reality. Finally, because a strategy isn't complete if you can't measure it, *Service Strategy* provides guidelines for developing key performance indicators (KPIs), which are measurements to help track how well services meet objectives.

- ✔ **Financial management:** Setting a strategy is great, but you need to make sure that you can pay for it, so ITIL V3 also includes guidelines on budgeting, accounting, and charging. It helps you understand how to think about the costs and revenue associated with your services, how to account for the costs, and how you might charge for the services.

- ✔ **Portfolio management:** After you deliver the services, you need to manage them from a financial perspective to make sure that they address business needs. This management includes identifying and validating the portfolio of services, as well as monitoring them to ensure that they continue to provide value. An automated teller machine (ATM), for example, provides several services, but if one of them — say, a stamp-dispensing service — isn't what customers want, keeping the service running may not be financially viable.

- ✔ **Demand management:** Your services are useful only if customers want them and you can provide them. Imagine what would happen if you built a service and found out that consumers no longer demanded it, or if consumers demanded the service but you didn't have the capacity to meet the demand.

Service strategy boils down to a simple concept: Transform assets into value. Value has two aspects:

- ✔ **Assets:** First, the provider needs to derive the most value from his assets in the form of the products and services provided.

- ✔ **Customers:** The second aspect of transforming assets to value comes on the customer side of service management. The most valuable service a provider can offer is one that helps the customer get more value from the assets that the customer owns.

The whole *Service Strategy* concept builds on the core concept of producing value from different types of assets. The ability to turn assets to value — service management — is a critical business asset.

Book 2: Service Design

According to *Service Design*, after you set your strategy, it's time to design your services. This design includes dealing with architecture, technology, processes, information, and organizational issues. Service design also includes collecting business requirements, as well as designing and developing appropriate service solutions, processes, and measurement systems. Consider these seven critical aspects when you're designing services:

- ✔ **Service-catalog management:** To build and operate your services effectively, you need a central registry/repository of information about these services: a service catalog. The catalog includes services that you've already agreed to as well as services requested and provides a view of the services offered to those who want to or need to see them. So a good catalog provides meaningful views of services to multiple stakeholders: customers, users, suppliers, and providers.

- ✔ **Service-level management:** A service needs to meet customer expectations, which means that it needs to meet certain service levels. Banking customers, for example, expect ATM machines to be available 24/7, so a bank needs to make sure that services supporting the delivery of cash and other services to customers meet this expectation.

- ✔ **Capacity management:** If customers desire a service that isn't available because of IT constraints, customer expectations aren't met. Capacity management provides a way to understand whether IT can meet customer needs, and it helps you plan accordingly. The data center servicing ATM machines, for example, may need to be staffed at a certain level to meet service-level and operational-level agreements, so the bank may need to hire and train new staff members, as well as buy new hardware and software to support the data center.

- ✔ **Availability management:** You need to have someone (or a team of someones) monitoring the availability, reliability, and maintainability of all your services, which is what availability management is all about. Ideally, management isn't simply reactive in terms of measuring what's happening to a service; it's also proactive in determining what you need to do to meet expectations.

- ✔ **IT service continuity management:** When your business requires high IT availability, you need a support structure in place to ensure that availability.

- ✔ **Information security management:** Information makes the world go 'round, and securing this information is paramount to effective IT services. This best practice is all about ensuring that you include information security when you design services, which means including information confidentiality, integrity, and availability. When you go to your ATM machine, for example, you certainly expect that all your account information will remain accurate, complete, timely, and confidential.

 ✔ **Supplier and contract management:** You need to make sure that all the suppliers you hire to support a particular service supply the service at the level of expectation the customer needs. If you hire a security company to deliver money to your ATM machine, and the machine is empty, the supplier isn't meeting its obligations, and your customers won't be happy. To make this service happen, you need to manage supplier contracts effectively.

In general, service design integrates service management best practices early in the life cycle. The key concept is that you design and develop a service, not just infrastructure or an application. Service design also incorporates the ideas of service utility and service warranty. *Service utility* refers to what the service does. In the case of IT services, service utility is often close to the key functional attributes of the applications that make up the service. *Service warranty* is the level of service that you offer. What you hand off to operations to be deployed is a *service package,* including both the service utility and the service warranty. You can't wait until service delivery to think about service-level management, availability, capacity, continuity, and security.

Book 3: Service Transition

The next phase of ITIL's best practices involves getting the service package into operation, which is the topic of the *Service Transition* book. This book covers transitioning all aspects of the service: the technology as well as the people and processes.

Imagine that you've built the best ATM machine in the world and all the supporting technology infrastructure to go along with it. If you don't have the armored-truck drivers, data center operators, and all the other people and processes in place to make getting money out of that machine possible, everything is for naught.

Service transition requires transferring the knowledge that goes along with the services to those who operate them. It also includes processes for dealing with any changes that might occur in the service.

Service Transition includes the following best practices:

 ✔ **Change management:** It's okay to make a change in a service, but before you do, you need to make sure that certain things happen. If you want to change the way that deposits are made at an ATM machine, for example, you need to evaluate and authorize these changes. After you authorize the changes, you need to record them, and you should also test and validate them to make sure that nothing goes wrong down the road. Standard processes are key; otherwise, you'll never be able to keep track of anything.

- ✔ **Service asset and configuration management:** A lot of IT and non-IT assets make up an overall service, and you need to identify and control all those assets. Configuration information is the basis for managing any service. The best-practices approach is to have an integrated asset and configuration system to provide service configuration information to all other service management processes. This information enables service management to manage both the technical and financial aspects of services effectively.

- ✔ **Knowledge management:** Knowledge management ensures that people get the information they need to do their jobs correctly. A service knowledge system is required to make the service management system effective. People and tools need complex, integrated information to manage services. If the data center personnel at the ATM data center don't have the right information to do their jobs, for example, the jobs won't get done efficiently or effectively.

- ✔ **Release and deployment management:** When you deploy a new service or release a new version, do it in a controlled manner, within agreed-on service-level constraints, to prevent service incidents.

- ✔ **Service evaluation:** Evaluate services to ensure that they're useful.

- ✔ **Service validation and testing:** As you deploy services in the organization — or if you change them — you need to test those services to make sure that each one works effectively by itself and with other services. An ATM's new stamp-dispensing service may work well by itself, but if it hasn't been tested with other services, it may interfere with subsequent transactions, such as withdrawals.

Service-transition processes balance the need for stable operations with stakeholder and customer requirements for innovation and change.

Book 4: Service Operation

The rubber meets the road in *Service Operation,* where customers begin to receive value. When services are up and running, make sure that they continue to provide value to customers. *Service Operation* describes several best practices to ensure this outcome while you deal with balancing factors such as quality of service versus cost of service.

Service Operation describes five key components:

- **Event management:** An *event,* according to ITIL, is a change of state that may indicate that something has gone wrong. An ATM machine experiences an event when it runs out of paper and can't generate a receipt, for example. This event is noted, and it may lead to an incident or problem (discussed later in this list) or even a change in the system. The essence of event management begins with noticing these changes of state, and it continues with filtering and correlating to isolate the events that you must address to maintain agreed-on service levels.

  Event management is a critical bedrock operational process. Without event management, you're relying on customers or staff members to notice events. Detecting events before customers discover them — and before agreed-on service conditions are breached — helps control both the quality and the cost of service.

- **Incident management:** An *incident,* according to ITIL, is an unplanned interruption in an IT service. The purpose of incident management, then, is to restore the service. When an ATM runs out of paper, for example, the incident management follow-up may be to call suppliers that can install the receipt slips at the ATM machine. You need to detect, log, analyze, resolve, and close all incidents. You need to record all incident activity because the record provides a basis for problem management analysis (discussed later in this list).

- **Request fulfillment:** According to ITIL, a *request* can be for a change, information, or access to an IT service. This request can come from any user. In the data center servicing deposits and withdrawals at an ATM, for example, a request may be made for a report detailing ATM activity.

- **Problem management:** A *problem* is a condition with an unknown cause. If someone takes $100 out of an ATM machine and is debited $200, for example, ABC Financial needs to investigate this problem. Problem management studies past incidents and other information to identify opportunities to prevent future incidents. By analogy, if incident management is a firehouse responding to fires, problem management is the city planner's office, which studies all past fires and makes change requests for new city ordinances to prevent future fires.

- **Access management:** *Access management* ensures that information is provided only to authorized users. Only properly identified users with proper access authority can see client activity at a given ATM machine, for example. Access management also addresses entitlement management, which ensures that users have access to services that they're entitled to access and prevents them from accessing services that they aren't entitled to access.

Book 5: Continual Service Improvement

You can run as many services as you want, but if you aren't monitoring those services to maintain and improve them, chances are that you won't be successful. Remember those KPIs that we discuss as part of developing your strategy (refer to "Book 1: Service Strategy," earlier in this chapter)? Well, *Continual Service Improvement* describes how to collect and analyze this information via a seven-step improvement process that puts these KPIs into practice. Additionally, the book provides information on the following aspects of service improvement:

- ✔ **Service measurement:** The section provides guidelines on monitoring and measuring your services.
- ✔ **Service reporting:** This section provides guidelines on the kinds of information that you should present in reports to help readers understand how well the service is performing. The reports can also help you predict what issues the service may face in the future.

Continual Service Improvement also discusses several important tools and techniques for measuring and improving both processes and services.

Practical Considerations in Implementing ITIL

As we mention earlier in this chapter, you can't simply load ITIL onto your computer and claim a service management victory. ITIL is about technology, people, and processes. If you leave any one of these ingredients out of the mix, there's a good chance that you'll fail. We discuss how to get started implementing a service management strategy like ITIL in the next two chapters. But before we do, we want to point out some practical considerations regarding implementing ITIL.

Surprise! Industry pundits have noted some major failures by organizations undertaking ITIL implementations. You certainly don't want to have one of those failures. In most cases, failure is due to the fact that organizations jump onto the ITIL bandwagon with unrealistic expectations and unclear goals. Here are a series of questions you should ask about your company before embarking on ITIL:

- ✔ Do we have well-defined business drivers?
- ✔ Do we have well-defined business requirements?

✔ Have we set our priorities?

✔ Have we thought about the right-size project to get started with?

✔ Do we have committed sponsors?

✔ Does good communication exist between business and IT?

✔ Do we have effective project management capabilities?

✔ Have we thought about governance?

✔ Do we have good vendor relationships?

Aside from the five core ITIL books and a willingness to succeed, companies should consider the assets and skills they have at their disposal. Successful companies also need to have prioritizing and diagnostic techniques to help plan and assess where they are and where they want to be with ITIL. In addition, they need an improvement approach and a governance model. Rather than focusing on implementing ITIL, organizations should focus on implementing business-driven service management improvements.

It's best to implement service management improvements with clearly defined phases and milestones — and not bite off more than you can chew. Some companies have found it beneficial to work with outside experts to help them get started in ITIL. These experts can help educate the team, find out where the organization stands in terms of ITIL, and provide tools and techniques to help with the ITIL journey and ITIL goals.

The first book in the ITIL V2 library is *Planning to Implement Service Management*. The first book in the ITIL V3 library is *Services Strategy*. The International Standard for Service Management's ISO/IEC 20000 says, "Service management shall be planned." The first best practice for service management is clear: Start with strategy and a plan for how you'll produce business value through service management improvements.

How ITIL Integrates with Other Best-Practices Frameworks

Sometimes in service management, "Is it ITIL?" discussions get more attention than business objective discussions. Deploying a best-practices framework should be about business objectives, leveraging ITIL, and anything else that's appropriate to help you achieve your goals, such as some of the other standards we mention in Chapter 4.

Any organization can use ITIL, but no organization should use it without considering other bodies of knowledge. ITIL says that taking an integrated approach to leveraging many sets of best practices and standards is itself a best practice.

ITIL documents are accepted best practices for executing service management. Some people call them a "code of practice" for people who perform service management activities.

Following are some other common best practices for service management that integrate well with ITIL (for more information on all of them, see Chapter 4):

- ✔ **COBIT:** Provides excellent guidance for a system of management control. Organizations that adopt service management frequently adopt COBIT controls as well.

- ✔ **eTOM:** Provides accepted best practices for telecommunications service providers. eTOM gives service providers descriptions of common business processes, which they can use to manage commercial business services. eTOM users also leverage ITIL. ITIL and eTOM users have many common interests.

- ✔ **ISO/IEC 38500:** Provides valuable guidance for directing and controlling IT services. This standard, created by the ISO and the International Electrotechnical Commission (IEC), guides directors in approaching the very real and very high business risks and costs associated with IT services. It provides guidance for directing, evaluating, and monitoring the governance of IT services.

- ✔ **ISO/IEC 20000:** Provides guidance for the auditable service management practices. Ideally, you use this standard in conjunction with ISO 9001 to provide a standards-based audit of a service provider's service management system.

It's pretty obvious how important service management and a framework like ITIL are to our example ATM machine. A best-practices approach to service management will help ABC Financial decide what services it wants to provide through the ATM in the first place; how to design, build, and implement those services effectively; and how to make sure that it continues to provide its customers value.

An ATM machine isn't just a piece of technology; it's also a system of services that includes people, processes, technology, and information. The ITIL framework provides guidelines to help IT build, operate, and improve the ATM machine so that it meets — and ideally exceeds — expectations.

Chapter 6

Implementing a Service Management Strategy

*I*f you've read the preceding five chapters of this book, you should have a good idea of what service management is and the role it can play in helping your organization respond to customers and manage change.

In this chapter, we delve into what it means to implement service management. We give you some examples of working across all aspects of business operations in an integrated way and show how you can use this approach to improve and extend the value of your company's brand.

Seeing What Service Management Can Do for Your Organization

A service, in many instances, is a way of delivering value to a customer by facilitating the customer's expected outcome. Effective service management is a way to ensure that outcome. It's also a way to prepare your company for disruptive change.

You're probably asking, "What does that mean — preparing your company for disruptive change?" Well, this isn't your father's (or mother's) service delivery world. In the old days, the service provider might count on minimal change in the services that it delivered. In today's markets, for most businesses, such market stability is absent. Consequently, service providers have to think differently. They have to think about how to leverage their assets and, perhaps, augment or integrate them to adapt for volatile market conditions and rising customer expectations. Service has become an area in which companies leapfrog competitors when they take new and innovative approaches to producing value from their existing assets. By enabling this services approach, they can help their customers get more value from their own assets. Service management is strategic.

Considering a real-world example

Remember when video stores dominated the way customers watched movies? When you wanted to watch a movie, you went to a video-rental retail outlet; browsed the selection of movies on the shelves; and, if you were lucky, got to take home an enticing movie. This process was the normal process of video distribution for years. Companies that survived in that competitive market did the right things. These companies were pretty smart. They realized that they needed to have the right number of copies of the most popular releases. Some of them also offered guarantees: If a movie wasn't in stock, the customer could pick something else free of charge. They broadened their product range by renting related products such as videogames and even the game systems; they also sold candy, popcorn, soda, and other merchandise. In other words, they worked hard to improve the customer experience and to exceed customer expectations.

Then something unexpected happened. A company called Netflix introduced an alternative way of distributing movies, based on an innovative use of emerging IT that allowed the company to measure and optimize the customer experience. Rather than visiting a video store, Netflix customers can order their movies online for shipment within a few days. The company makes it simple to order, receive, and return movies. Netflix also provides a simple way to queue up for the most popular movies when they're first released. Needless to say, this company had a dramatic impact on customer expectations, although most competitors originally paid little attention and focused on business as usual.

Netflix didn't rest on its success; it built on it. In addition to sending physical discs through the mail, it decided to further leverage the Internet by giving customers the ability to watch movies on their computers or gaming systems in real time. Now customers don't have to wait for the mail or wait in line for the movies or TV shows they want to watch; those products are available on demand in the home.

Relating the example to service management

How does this example relate to implementing service management? It shows that by monitoring and optimizing the services you provide your customers and stakeholders, you're in a position to make changes in your business model that set you ahead of the competition. By implementing service management techniques, you have more time and resources to devote to keeping up with market and technology changes. Also, if you've built a system that is flexible enough to allow for change, you should be able to respond to those market and technology changes by offering more innovative services.

The important thing to understand in this example is that the service that is ultimately delivered is the same in all distribution methods: The customer gets to enjoy watching a movie. The movie provider that was most successful, however, provided the service in the way that customers preferred.

When Netflix entered the market, it took an established idea and innovated on the delivery of the service. It replaced the traditional retail store with an online approach — an IT-enabled service. In many ways, the business service of getting movies into customers' hands requires similar business systems in the back office, whether the distribution is through traditional retail stores or online. Both types of organizations need systems to record customers' requests, both for billing and stocking purposes. They need an inventory system and quality control, along with the traditional set of back-office systems such as finance and human resources. When Internet technology evolved to the point at which streaming video to the household was possible, Netflix was able to change its business model again to take advantage of changing dynamics and technology evolution. Because of its ability to change dynamically, the company established strategic control of its service delivery.

Starting with the Service Strategy

To prevent confusion, we need to distinguish between a service strategy and a service management plan. For right now, we'll just say that a *service strategy* is your road map for the future, based on your business goals. After you figure out your strategy, you need a *service management plan* to execute that strategy on a tactical basis (see the following section). The two concepts may sound like they're the same thing, but they're just close friends.

Creating a service strategy

When a company offers a distinctly new and different service or product, it can't know for sure whether its customers — or potential customers — will want it. If you start with a known desired outcome and work backward to determine how to achieve that outcome by better leveraging all existing assets, however, you have more assurance of success in the new service offering.

To continue the Netflix example, when the company decided to offer its customers a new service — streaming video — it went beyond trying to satisfy known customer demand for certain movies in certain formats and in certain capacities. The company moved to a plan to provide the desired outcome in a way that better leveraged all existing capabilities and resources. Many customers now have Internet connections with networked devices plugged into their TV sets at home, for example. Because the desired outcome is to enjoy a movie at home, the provider considers what assets it has and what assets the customer has, and then determines how to integrate everything in a new configuration to provide a new service.

Finding out what customers really want

Companies aren't always shooting in the dark. They leverage market research involving surveys and focus groups, and they have a pretty good idea of what customers think they want. Even so, it is entirely possible for any new product or service to be rejected — even by customers who, when asked, were convinced that they wanted or needed it.

Be aware of the difference between what customers ask for and what they really want. Consider Henry Ford's experience in creating his horseless carriage. Ford's customers may have asked for horses that ran faster, ate less, and required less training and maintenance, but focusing on a desired outcome instead gave him more assurance of success. Customers really wanted to travel to certain destinations that were connected by roads or paths; they wanted to steer; they didn't want to walk; and they liked bringing other people and things with them. A good horse-and-cart combination was one route to the desired outcome, but a technology-enabled alternative was another.

Getting a plan wrong is expensive, and getting it right begins with a service strategy: a provider's plan for the services it will offer to customers and for delivering, marketing, and selling those services. One part of the Netflix service strategy, for example, is providing streaming video service to its customers.

Creating a Service Management Plan

In contrast to a service strategy, a *service management plan* defines how the provider will manage the services in the service strategy and road map. This plan is more complicated than it may sound. In the real world, companies typically work in *silos* (isolated implementations of services). IT operations in one division may have a separate service management implementation for a group of servers. Although silos and organization charts are convenient for internal order and control, they don't serve customers — and very often generate internal friction in the company that prevents customers from getting their desired outcomes.

Business management staffers use the data available to them to think great thoughts about the business and to formulate products and service strategies. They operate business units to provide — profitably and efficiently — products and services that will keep customer and stakeholder expectations satisfied. They plan for the future because they know that they'll need to innovate with new products and services. They also understand that they need to provide better management of the products and services they already offer. Their plans include how to get more value from all their capabilities and existing resources.

On another floor somewhere, IT management has its hands full operating the physical and virtual world of servers, applications, security, and the like. The typical IT organization sees itself as a systems support operation. (The same problem may occur in other aspects of enterprise operations.) But is this approach good enough? You probably anticipate at this point that the answer is no. Correct.

In the brave new world that has emerged, it isn't wise for business and the various flavors of enterprise and IT operations to operate as separate silos. They need to align better. Better alignment of all operations with the business always has a twofold meaning: Operations can help drive the cost out of business products and services, and it can help differentiate the business from its competitors. Technology-enabled services, for example, can reduce cost, improve quality, and help achieve specific business objectives. Technology improves a production line's efficiency and reduces costs at the same time that it helps the research-and-development department innovate. In fact, business and operations need to expand the scope of alignment to levels we've never seen before. Just look at the Netflix example. Is its business about enabling people to watch movies, or is it about service management? Is service management the supporting actor, or does it play a lead role? A business needs to provide new, innovative IT-enabled services, and at the same time, it needs to manage the cost and quality of those services so that the price and reliability provide a desirable outcome.

In many businesses nowadays, service management needs to have a leading role. Where would Netflix be as a company if it didn't monitor, measure, and optimize the way it offered its service to customers? Where would it be if it couldn't support its innovations? Probably out of business.

Defining a Service Management Plan

In the general sense, all service management plans should point in the same direction. The goal is for all facets of operations that play a contributing role in business services — IT, facilities, plant operations, network operations, and beyond — to align with the business more effectively.

You may think, "I've heard that cliché a million and one times. IT has been trying to align itself more effectively with the business since Adam got his first computer." So we'd probably better explain.

Figure 6-1 illustrates exactly what we mean. You start with managing the physical systems — be they systems of enterprise assets, smart assets, or IT assets. Then you focus on managing how all these systems relate to one another. Finally, you manage how these interconnected resources actually perform the series of processes required to satisfy the business goals.

In most organizations, the focus is on the management of systems — systems that individually don't serve customers. The services that customers value typically are complex configurations of capabilities and resources that span business and operational lines, all of which must work together to provide a desirable outcome before the customer sees sufficient value.

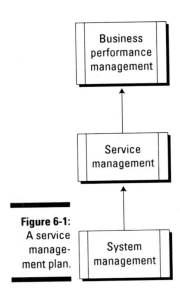

Figure 6-1:
A service management plan.

To fully align with the business, all flavors of operations must evolve to the point where all their respective activities focus on business performance management. The final goal is managing business performance effectively. Companies take different approaches to managing performance, depending on industry dynamics and potential innovation. To reach that goal, operations as a whole first has to evolve to the point where its activities can be accurately described as service management — where operations no longer focuses only on managing systems, but also focuses on managing the services that contribute to business performance.

That concept sounds simple — a two-step program from here to there. If that program were all that was involved, we could finish the book here. But service management is a little more complicated, as we describe in the rest of the chapter.

Understanding Service Management and Governance

The scope of service management is broad and deep. Therefore, you need to have oversight of all the management processes and services, including how they work and what they actually do. You have to implement governance in the context of service management.

No matter how you organize a business, you end up with groups of people who have to collaborate and tools that have to integrate to serve the customer. Because these groups need to work together to serve customers, you need some mechanism beyond the internal controls within each group to provide the overall direction and control to ensure that the services meet customer and stakeholder requirements. You need to establish clear decision rights and accountability chains (who is allowed to make what decisions under what circumstances) for each management process and each service. Good service management requires clarity and transparency in the decision rights and accountability chains for directing, controlling, and executing each management process and service. Without this clarity and transparency, human behavior and decision-making within the service provider don't lead to outcomes that customers and stakeholders desire. The greatest risk that every service provider faces is human behavior and decisions that are out of alignment with stakeholder requirements.

We could continue to discuss the matter in this vein, but we can be a little simpler and refer to the models that we've already described. *Service management* is the set of management processes required to manage services. To explain what we mean, first we'll remind you what a service is and how it relates to service management.

Suppose that an organization creates a service that calculates the tax rate for an order. We'll call it the tax rate service. *Service management* is really the business manager, the controller, and the auditor combined. A piece of software ensures that the service calculates the order total according to company and government rules and then executes in an efficient manner. Although it would be nice to think that the company could use this automated program without any oversight or intervention, that scenario isn't possible. Service management, therefore, must involve people, standardized processes, and tools to manage the service across traditional operational boundaries to support a comprehensive business service and all its moving parts. Indeed, in discussing the Information Technology Infrastructure Library (ITIL) in Chapter 5, we outline a set of standardized IT-centric management processes that support one major operational constituent with a vested interest in business-aligned service management. On the road to success, however, all constituents — not just IT — must have a vested interest in the success of the business, and must govern and measure across operations to ensure the integrated management of business services.

Service management, like any other management discipline, requires measurement. The old axioms "What gets measured gets done," "Inspect what you expect," and "You can't manage what you don't know" still hold true. For every management process and every service, the provider needs management information. Key performance indicators (KPIs) track the agreed-to activities. Key goal indicators measure the progress made toward business objectives. Key cost and quality indicators also have to be measured; otherwise, the service provider is flying blind. Without some automation, managers would be up very late at night trying to figure out how everything is working!

Automating Service

Effective automation is critical for managing service cost and quality, as well as for providing the information that you need for effective direction, control, and execution of services and service management. In most organizations, service management automation is poor; consequently, the management information just isn't available.

Figure 6-2 illustrates the service automation path that an operational department needs to traverse. It begins with automation, consisting of a set of fragmented services. Many IT departments find themselves in this situation. The next step from there is standardizing the foundations of service automation so that all service automation systems can talk to one another in a comprehensible way. That standardization establishes a basis for the integration of all services that contribute to the next step: overall service automation. The final step is optimizing across all those services.

Figure 6-2:
The evolution of service automation.

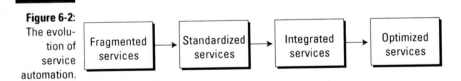

That process seems to be simple: Assuming that you start with fragmented services, you simply follow a nice three-step process. If you're dealing with a tax collection service, you might make sure that it works effectively and does the right thing. So far, so simple. Don't forget, however, that this process becomes part of a service management plan, which complicates the matter.

Luckily, this situation translates into a pretty picture. Figure 6-3 illustrates the simple fact that the service management plan and service automation need to work together. The graph shows 12 areas of automation mapped against overall strategy. An organization can sit in any of those 12 areas. It may have highly developed service automation to the point of delivering an optimized service, yet any one operational team (such as facilities, plant operations, or network operations) may have limited vision in terms of its role in service management. The IT department may do nothing more than systems management, for example. Similarly, the company could have fragmented service automation but be fully focused on business performance management.

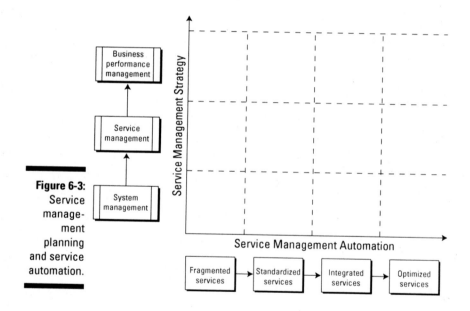

Figure 6-3: Service management planning and service automation.

The usefulness of Figure 6-3 is that it helps with service management planning. It helps you define what management capability your organization needs to work on next.

When we refer to *service automation,* we're referring directly to software. By contrast, service management also includes skilled staff members and standardized management processes. Both services and service management benefit from automation. Automation reduces human effort and labor costs. Reducing human effort also reduces human error that can hamper quality. Automation helps reduce cost and improve quality of service.

A service strategy needs to include a service management plan. The service strategy sets the business context for the service management plan, including the three interwoven strands: people, standardized processes, and tools that deliver automation.

Planning Service Strategy and Service Management

When you're planning for implementation, here are five sets of questions that you should be able to answer about your road map:

- With the changes happening in my industry, how agile is my approach to managing my physical and virtual assets? Can my company change quickly enough while protecting the integrity of oversight, if it needs to?

- Can I manage my world if and when change comes? Does the organization see sufficient collaboration across groups and divisions? How is this collaboration exhibited in terms of people, processes, and automation?

- Can I direct and control changes in my services if the inputs and outcomes are different? Do I have the right level of visibility and control?

- Do I understand my management processes today? Can I adapt those processes to new business demands? Can I integrate those processes across the organization so that I get a complete view across my value chain? (A *value chain* is the sequence of business activities that links all important contributors to the company's success, such as suppliers and customers.)

- Do I have a standards-based approach to service management to enable greater collaboration, not only across my own management domains, but also with my suppliers and customers? Do I have sufficient clarity and transparency in decision rights and accountability chains that I can change and innovate? Can I direct and control service management?

Finding Out How Your Organization Measures Up

The vision of service management laid out in the service strategy can be daunting for many organizations. You have to worry not only about keeping the lights on and the processes operating efficiently, but also about keeping customers happy and preventing competitors from gaining an advantage. How ready are you to change, innovate, grow, and compete? This question isn't easy to answer, because it requires a certain level of assessment to determine the readiness of your organization. We lay out the framework for this assessment in Figure 6-3, earlier in this chapter, but the framework also includes the assessment of skills and standardized processes. As part of this assessment, you should ask the following sets of questions:

✔ Where is the business value within my organization? Which assets (sets of capabilities and resources) produce my company's unique differentiation: my information, for example, or my distribution network? Can I measure these assets in terms of how they're designed to service customer needs?

✔ Do I have a service management capability that enables my organization to change services quickly when the market demands innovation?

✔ How well does my service management capability prepare me to control costs and quality while providing customers what they need? Do I have the technology in place to measure the customer's view of the value I'm offering and provide the detailed management information I need?

✔ Do I understand both my service and service management gaps — areas where I lack the systems that can address problems but can't provide that capability? When I know where the business needs to be, can I direct and control the capabilities and resources required to get there?

This type of assessment is critical to your organization's ability to move forward. No organization should move to the adoption phase without a good, honest assessment of the current state of service management. The quickest route to ruin is acting without forethought.

Seeing What Service Management Will Look Like in Your Organization

Service management isn't a project or a product. You might say, "I really just want to go out and buy something and be done with it. I'm ready to manage change and become an agile company." If only life were that simple! Service management is a journey.

As we've discussed so far in this chapter, service management is a combination of vision, scope, and assessment. When you figure out where you are, you can begin to plan for where you want to be.

Putting the focus on business performance

Unlike systems management, service management is about looking at business performance rather than just server or data center management. In a typical systems management scenario, you may look at an incident. You log the incident, work to figure out what caused that problem, and come up with either a work-around or a patch to repair the problem. You're done!

If you look at this same issue from a service management perspective, however, you're looking at the incident differently. You have to ask what the incident was all about: what type of incident it was, whether it was isolated to a particular piece of hardware, whether a critical service wasn't working properly, or whether the incident involved a network router or a potential disruption of a service.

Organizations need to think differently about how they deal with service disruptions. They need a combination of good tooling, skills, and information to manage services in context with the business problems that they're addressing.

To continue the Netflix example, suppose that the company is unable to stream a popular movie to its customers' computers or game boxes. The company needs to ask itself a variety of questions, such as what impact the incident will have on customer expectations; which services were affected (or potentially affected); and whether the organization has the process, skills, and tools required to manage this situation and others like it.

When planning a change, management needs to understand which services are potentially affected and what the business outcome will be, as well as whether the company has the service configuration information required to assess the effect of the change. All of a sudden, the challenge is very tangible and fundamental: How should these services be managed? In other words, the organization needs to look at manageability from many perspectives with the right business context. It needs well-constructed strategies for managing customer expectations in context with costs, competitive conditions, and operational effectiveness. All these issues require skills and good judgment.

Understanding service oriented architecture

To really understand service management, you also should understand service oriented architecture (SOA). We strongly recommend that you take a look at another book, *Service Oriented Architecture For Dummies,* 2nd Edition

(Wiley Publishing, Inc.). (Yes, our team wrote that book too.) Why are we complicating things by bringing up SOA? We're not. We're trying to clarify the situation. We define *service oriented architecture* as a software architecture for building applications that implement business processes or services by using a set of loosely coupled, black-box components orchestrated to deliver a well-defined level of service.

Admittedly, this definition doesn't flow trippingly from the tongue, but from it springs a sustainable, reusable, extensible approach to business and technology that is already providing huge competitive advantages to organizations around the globe. Here are some of the principal characteristics of SOA that are important for service management:

- **SOA is a black-box component architecture.** SOA deliberately hides complexity wherever possible, and the idea of the black box is integral to SOA. The black box enables the reuse of existing business applications by adding a fairly simple adapter to them, no matter how they were built.

- **SOA components are loosely coupled.** One component passes data to another component and makes a request; the second component carries out the request and, if necessary, passes data back to the first. The emphasis is on simplicity and autonomy. Each component offers a small range of simple services to other components.

  A set of loosely coupled components does the same work that tightly structured applications used to do, but you can combine and recombine the components in myriad ways to make the overall service infrastructure much more flexible.

- **SOA components are orchestrated to link through business processes to deliver a well-defined level of service.** SOA creates a simple arrangement of components that collectively can deliver a very complex business service. Simultaneously, SOA must provide acceptable service levels. To that end, the architecture embodies components that ensure a dependable service level. Service level is tied directly to the best practices of conducting business, commonly referred to as *business process management.*

Because so many of the business applications that you have to manage are now built in this loosely coupled, modular fashion, service management needs to walk hand in hand with SOA. SOA becomes part of the architectural approach required to make the pieces of business services, processes, and operations work in coordination.

Getting to the Desired End State

We've given you a lot to think about in this chapter. Your organization will have to take many steps in its journey toward a well-structured and well-managed service-based organization. Before you consider the goal of having a good handle on your managed services environment, however, you have to come up with a plan. You have to understand what makes your business and industry operate today and how those factors may change.

Achieving your goal of having a well-orchestrated, well-governed organization requires you to start with a vision of your end state and work backward. You have to understand what business you're in, how that business works today, and how it will change. You can start to understand your business as an eco-system — more like biology than a series of steps. In biology, you work with sets of interconnected systems. Something that goes wrong in one system may affect the overall set. When you understand this philosophy, it's a lot easier to move away from looking at management as a set of independent steps.

In the next chapter, we provide some ideas for implementing a service management plan. Where you start depends largely on what you already have in place and how well coordinated you are on both the technical and management level. A service management plan has the potential to take your organization to a whole new level of sophistication. It requires some work in areas such as education, strategy, assessment, and design.

Chapter 7

Launching into Service Management

*W*e hope you understand that service management isn't just an operational issue; it's also a business issue. In Chapter 6, we discuss how a service management plan supports the actual service strategy. The types of services that your organization needs to manage are much more diverse than ever before. To get started with service management, you need to take a holistic approach. You need to understand that just about every asset under your control — be it physical or virtual — must be managed in a way that allows you to integrate all your capabilities and resources so that you can direct and control the costs, quality, and value of your services.

In Chapter 6, we also talk about some of the hard work involved in setting a new direction for service management, including education, strategy development, assessment, and design.

In this chapter, we give you some ideas of how to put your service management plan into action. First, however, here are two key things that you *shouldn't* do:

✔ **Don't think of service management as being just an IT operations problem.** In other words, you shouldn't begin by sending the IT staff to get best-practices certifications and assume that certification alone will help you deliver a successful service management plan. Before you send anyone for training, make sure that everyone in the organization understands the business goals of service management, as well what service management is and why it's imperative to the company's long-term success. You need to start by recognizing that the strategy of the business needs to be continually reevaluated in harmony with the service strategy and the service management plan. Your service management strategy will involve a collaboration among the chief executive, operations, and information officers because it involves strategy, business operations, and IT.

✔ **Don't try to do everything at the same time.** You need a vision for the future and an incremental road map that describes how you'll travel from where you are to where you want your services to be.

In this chapter, we offer some suggestions about how to optimize your business through service management. We talk about some key components of service management, including education, strategy development, needs assessment, and strategy design. We also talk about another key component of a service management plan: the need to measure, monitor, and optimize your approach to achieve the business outcomes that your business needs.

Four Key Elements to Consider

The most important thing to keep in mind is that not every company is at the same place in its journey toward service management. Therefore, your company may have a different entry point from another company, based on how much your company has already done.

In the following sections, we discuss four key areas that you need to consider when you're actually implementing service management.

Education: A crucial component

Education is crucial because one of the biggest limiters of service management is human understanding of service management. Educating the team is at the heart of getting started.

The best starting point for education is making sure that everyone understands the foundation of the business itself. Employees should understand the following aspects of the business and be able to answer the following questions:

✔ **The company's industry:** Is your company in transportation, hospitality, or manufacturing, for example?

✔ **Customer expectations:** Do you understand how to provide value to your customers? What is the customer experience of working with your company like?

- ✔ **Logical components:** What are all the pieces that are necessary to make your business work well?

- ✔ **Most critical services:** What business services and supporting IT services are most critical to your customers and stakeholders?

- ✔ **Biggest contributor to the cost, quality, and value of the business services:** What are the most expensive aspects of your business services? Are they important to overall quality and value for your customers and partners?

This process may not sound like rocket science, and it isn't! Everyone in the company should have this knowledge, which takes on a new sense of urgency in the service management area because you're on the front line in terms of ensuring that your company understands its goals, objectives, and customer expectations.

Certification classes in industry best practices and standards can help operations get ready for a service management approach. In addition to the classes, you can find armloads of the books associated with the certification programs. Couple these programs with a focus on your service strategy, which is driven by the business strategy. Classes in best practices taken in isolation won't help you reach your business objectives. If these best practices are going to be meaningful, everyone in the business needs the same level of understanding of what these best practices will be applied to.

Creating centers of excellence

In addition to formal courses, organizations can expand knowledge across business and technical leaders through centers of excellence. A *center of excellence* is a process of bringing together key people from all areas of the business and operations to focus on best practices. A center of excellence provides a way for groups within the company to collaborate. This group also becomes a force for change, as it can leverage its growing knowledge to help different business units learn from experience.

Establishing a center of excellence is one way that your organization can improve a corporate culture that has become stagnant. You want to make sure that your corporate culture supports your ability to change. Also make sure that you view cultural issues as being core to the business and service strategy, and incorporate these issues into your educational plan. You can use a center of excellence to explore corporate-culture issues, as well as to set an agenda for change to ensure that people at all levels of the organization — from senior management to entry-level assistants, customer-service representatives, and operations staff members — have a holistic view of the mission and goals of the organization.

Service strategy: The driver of the service management plan

One of the most important requirements for service management is putting a strategy in place, which involves understanding what your business looks like today and how it may change in the future. The first thing to do is establish objectives. You need to ask yourself, "What do I really want to achieve?" Remember that your service management plan is based on the service strategy and needs to support changing business conditions and customer expectations.

Remember our example bank, ABC Financial, from earlier chapters? Although the bank is well established in its ability to provide automated teller machines (ATMs) to its customers, it needs to plan for a future that may be different from the present and the past. It needs to understand the expectations of its customers and anticipate how those expectations may change.

ABC Financial has a fundamental business goal of accepting deposits and providing cash to customers through its system of ATMs. Various key performance indicators (KPIs; see Chapter 5) are associated with this goal: Cash must be available for customers 24 hours a day; each ATM must be fully functioning 99 percent of the time; and at least one ATM must be functioning within a specific geographic radius. The operations team at ABC Financial initiates a cost-cutting initiative, expecting to save $800,000 in annual maintenance fees on the company's ATMs. This plan was put in place based on company goals for cost cutbacks. The operations and ATM-services divisions, however, didn't collaborate on plans for this new project. Each division had real goals to achieve but didn't evaluate the impact of the cost-cutting measures on customer expectations.

The new ATM maintenance plan didn't actually save money for the bank; the downtime was so great that it destroyed previously strong customer relationships. Customers moved to competitors, and the resulting losses to the bank were far greater than the dollars saved from the cost-cutting measures. Lesson learned: The overall goals for the business need to be evaluated in context with one another, and everyone in the company needs to understand what these goals are before any decisions about service management are made.

Companies that are prepared for the future have well-articulated corporate goals that are understood and followed throughout the enterprise. An understanding of corporate goals becomes part of the business fabric of the organization.

Service management begins with the business. Good service management requires leadership so that employees understand their responsibilities within the context of the broader business goals and objectives of the enterprise. Inherent conflicts are likely to arise between divisions or departments that are trying to achieve specific KPIs. These conflicts need to be anticipated and planned for at the enterprise level to create a service management plan that produces consistent results.

Assessment: Where you are today and where you want to go

When your company's service strategy is in place, it's time to do an assessment. This assessment includes a step-by-step approach to understanding the business you're in and developing a vision for the future. You need to specify what services your business offers and what the company needs to achieve your vision. When you know what your objectives are, you can assess your current service management capability around those particular goals. At this time, you can find the gaps in your service management capability and develop a plan to deal with those gaps. It's important to evaluate what you have if you expect to be able to locate and close the gaps and achieve your strategy.

An organization can't thrive in a competitive market unless everyone on the technical and business sides knows the company's objectives, which includes understanding the definitions of the business and the customer and knowing how the company plans to meet its objectives. A member of the IT staff who's responsible for keeping company servers up and running, for example, must understand his responsibilities in the context of the IT-enabled business services that the individual servers are part of. Just understanding the technical requirements for managing the servers isn't sufficient; the staff member also needs to have a realistic understanding of the business implications of downtime and the relative significance to the business of the different applications running on those servers.

Assessing where you are today is really about evaluating your technical and organizational readiness for implementing your service management plan. You may already have many of the technical components required for a well-integrated infrastructure, but you may maintain them in a siloed manner (see Chapter 6). By evaluating your infrastructure from the perspective of an integrated enterprise, you may find that you don't need much in the way of additional technology. You may determine, however, that you do need a center of excellence (refer to the "Creating centers of excellence" sidebar, earlier in this chapter) that empowers business and IT to leverage the technology at hand to reach new levels of integration and success.

Here are some questions you may want to ask during the assessment process:

- Do you have a consistent way to manage assets across your organization?
- Do you have a process for change and configuration that ensures that all members of the organization have reliable access to the service configuration information they need to perform their responsibilities?
- Can you ensure that business services created and maintained by one division are made available in a consistent manner across other areas of your organization?
- Will these business services help you reach your goals when they're adapted to the various divisions of the company?
- Do you have a process for assessing whether your technical and business divisions are performing at the right levels to keep customers satisfied?
- Have you developed a process to identify business services and encourage sharing across the enterprise where appropriate?
- Can you monitor and measure the effect of your strategy on demands for security, storage, and hardware?
- Are organizational structures in place that support creative knowledge sharing across business and IT teams?
- Have you identified roadblocks — such as outdated or inflexible business processes or people who place personal power ahead of delivering value to customers and business stakeholders — that may hamper your success in a collaborative business/IT world?
- Does your corporate culture support processes that help balance the management of individual components against the broader needs of managing customer experience?

Service management plan: A road map for moving forward

When you understand the gaps, you can start to design your service management plan. Because you've done (or will do) an assessment, this design isn't a matter of everyone just grabbing a hammer to build a house; the design needs to be well thought out. You need to understand and plan for service-level commitments when you're designing solutions and services. If you wait until services are delivered to figure out service levels and other management issues, you've waited too long. How will you make sure that you have the capacity, security, and financing available?

We mention reusable components in Chapter 6, and you certainly should consider this concept to be part of the design process. The discovery of services shouldn't be confined to one department or even confined to your company; you also need to look at your broader ecosystem of partners, suppliers, and customers. You aren't discovering just pieces of code, for example; you're also discovering what business processes exist in your company and what resources they need to access or integrate with. Look for overlapping or contradictory business processes, and fix them before they cause serious business problems.

An essential ingredient of a successful approach to service management is a well-defined, rationalized, and integrated approach to infrastructure. It's particularly important to ensure that you have a well-integrated architecture to support the intersecting physical, virtual, and IT worlds. This area is where service oriented architecture (SOA) may be very helpful. (See Chapter 6 for some basic definitions of SOA.) If your service strategy centers on the development of a stand-alone data center, your infrastructure requirements may not require a SOA approach. Your top priority, however, should be to create a road map that lays out where you are today and defines your steps to the future. A road map helps by ensuring that you take a measured, step-by-step approach to developing and defining your infrastructure. You shouldn't plan to do everything at the same time.

One reason why moving too quickly can be a problem is that you may be tempted to skip some of the details. Throughout the process, details matter. You must pay attention to details such as fine-tuning your configuration, looking at the dependencies among services, and considering how the pieces fit together in context with customer expectations and change.

Don't Forget to Measure, Monitor, and Optimize

You've educated your team, assessed your readiness for service management, and designed your service management plan. Do you sit back in a comfy chair and wait for the profits to roll in? No! Your business and operational strategies are never static. You always have more work to do because the business environment changes constantly. (Refer to the Netflix example in Chapter 6. That company was able to challenge traditional video stores by changing to a technology-driven business model.) Technological and business change happens so quickly that you can never assume that your strategy is complete.

The processes you create to measure, monitor, and optimize your results are critical components of any service management plan. Thinking about the measurements you need as you begin developing your service management plan is important. These measurements should be designed to help you meet your objectives. Your business doesn't operate in a static environment; therefore, your capabilities for monitoring and measuring must always be active. You need to monitor and measure against your service objectives on an ongoing basis to ensure that you understand how your business is performing on a day-to-day basis and optimize your future outcomes.

To continue the ABC Financial example, suppose that one division of the company decided on several business objectives to help measure and monitor results related to ATM services. Unfortunately, ABC Financial's monitoring process was based on a series of KPIs that were inconsistent across the company. The company didn't have its eye on the ball during a crucial economic period. Customers expected high (99.9 percent) availability at ATMs and wouldn't be satisfied with anything less. ABC Financial let cost-cutting measures interfere with its ability to meet its KPI for ATM availability. The company suffered because it didn't measure and monitor the right outcomes.

The monitoring-and-measuring process must be designed to make allowances for evaluating changes in quality relative to cost. As ABC Financial adjusts its service strategy, for example, it has many trade-offs to consider. In its desire to improve customer satisfaction, it may decide to include several high-quality new products that customers want but that are very expensive to maintain. As it turns out, the value of these products is high for only a small segment of the customer base, and the cost of producing and maintaining these products is high. It's unwise to optimize a subsystem (such as new ATM services) at the expense of a service management system. The result can be an unmanageable cost structure.

Part III
Service Management Technical Foundation

The 5th Wave   By Rich Tennant

I told Russel he should data model before we go any further.

May I speak to Kate Moss, please.

In this part . . .

This part is where we get a little technical, defining the service management universe, what it contains, and how it's governed. We identify the technical foundations of service management, particularly the data that it uses and the primary service management processes that create and maintain that data.

Chapter 8

The Service Management Universe

*I*n earlier chapters, we mention that service management is a big field that covers information technology of every conceivable kind and also involves understanding how to organize staff to manage that technology, not just to make it run, but also to make it run effectively and (ideally) in highly optimized fashion. Service management also embraces the governance of IT, best practices, the alignment of IT with the business, the integration of all the technology, and the monitoring of both business key performance indicators (KPIs) and IT KPIs.

We confess right now that this book doesn't give a detailed explanation of every service management process, underlying technology, and tactic that you can adopt to provide effective services. Luckily, that isn't the goal of this book. What we intend to do is give you an all-round appreciation of what service management is and how to deliver it successfully in the context of a living, breathing organization.

In this chapter, we present service management in overview, making the link between service management at the business level and at the IT level. We provide a way of looking at the whole service management process and also tackle the question of the value of service management within an organization.

Viewing Service Management in a Business Model

You may wonder why we haven't yet defined precisely what falls under the heading of service management from a technology perspective, so we'll do that immediately. Consider the simple diagram in Figure 8-1. This figure depicts the fact that from an external perspective, an organization can be viewed as a collection of business services performed directly or indirectly for the benefit of customers. Within that model, from an IT perspective, many elements of the various business services involve IT business applications. Those business applications operate effectively (if they do) because of the technologies, processes, and skills that collectively make up service management.

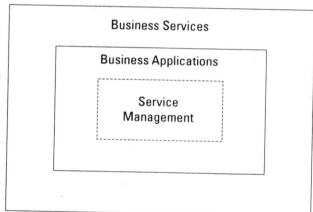

Figure 8-1:
The contribution of service management to business services.

If you consider IT from an external perspective, you can think of service management as being mainly invisible. The IT applications provide automation to various parts of the business processes that run through the organization, and they need a variety of resources to deliver their benefits. Service management monitors those applications and sometimes also monitors the business processes that they serve.

Perhaps to a businessperson, service management is mainly invisible, limited to the voice at the help desk and a relationship manager to negotiate service-level expectations and costs.

A simpler way to look at service management is to divide it into layers, as we do in the following section.

Understanding the Six Layers of Service Management

Service management is carried out with a variety of applications. Business applications consist of software and data; they run on computer hardware; and they have users. Given just those facts, you have four distinct layers to think about: software, data, hardware, and staff.

Now add the fact that all these business applications and the computers involved in running them need to be housed somewhere, either on desktop computers or in specially built data centers. That fact correlates to a foundation layer.

Finally, you need to acknowledge that in one way or another, some service management activities may be delivered as services. Some help-desk activity could be outsourced to a call center, for example, or some of the facilities provided to run applications could be delivered by a service provider. This fact gives you a sixth layer. Figure 8-2 shows all six layers.

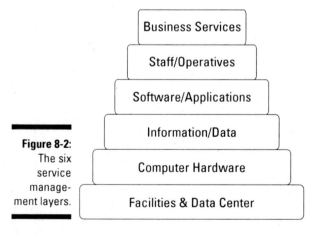

Figure 8-2:
The six
service
manage-
ment layers.

Defining the six layers

In the following sections, we describe these layers one by one.

Facilities and Data Center

Most companies have one or more data centers where all shared computer resources are kept. With the current state of technology, even medium-size organizations have a clear need for data centers, because computers require specialized electrical power, physical security, atmospheric control (usually, a dramatic amount of air conditioning), and communications. A data center may also perform specialized activities, such as printing, scanning, or creating DVDs. Data center space is very expensive because of its specialized nature, and a data center can't be expanded easily and simply.

Organizations that are geographically distributed may have multiple data centers, of course, and there may even be multiple data centers just for the sake of disaster recovery. The distribution of client computers around an organization should be considered to be part of the Facilities and Data Center layer, which is all about the accommodation of computing and communications resources. Ultimately, that means that all areas accommodating network access devices, such as automated teller machines or kiosks in shops, are part of this layer.

Computer Hardware

As in all other areas of IT, an organization has to make choices about the sizes of the computers it buys and about how those computers are managed as a collective resource. Sometimes an application has to be implemented on a specific item of hardware, but usually, some flexibility is available. The direction of technology is toward greater flexibility, with the idea of an application being able to run on almost any hardware platform.

Naturally, organizations attempt to optimize their use of hardware in whatever ways possible, such as by establishing purchasing and replacement strategies. They're likely to have different strategies for data center computers, desktop computers, and the full variety of mobile devices.

Information/Data

Application data presents several problems apart from how it needs to be used in applications or shared among applications (which isn't the problem of service management). Primarily, data has to be located in a convenient place; secured against theft; and backed up so that it can be restored in the event of hardware or software failure and, probably, just to meet auditing/compliance requirements. This requirement naturally extends to desktop devices and mobile devices; hence, the fairly simple needs for availability, security, and recovery alone can become complex.

Application data isn't the only kind of data. A whole set of data is created and used in service management activities, such as log files, asset data, and management data of all types.

Software/Applications

Software has the same characteristics as data in some ways because it's stored as data, so everything we note about data also applies to software. In addition, software needs to be configured for use, and management of the configuration of thousands of software components in a large network is itself a complex activity.

Also, software — whether it's application, operating-system, or management software — has a life cycle that also demands management.

Staff/Operatives

All service management activities include manual elements and demand a certain level of skill from staff members. Many of these activities are structured according to experience with the task, built up over years, or implemented from best practices based on some authority. Collectively, the staff (including all its management elements) can be viewed as being the presiding intelligence of service management.

Business Services

All service management activities are internal business services of one sort or another whose function is to support other business services, including — most important — those services that are provided to customers. Some of these business services can be outsourced. Indeed, some organizations have taken the rather drastic step of outsourcing the whole of their operational IT activities. Thus, in those instances, almost all service management activities have been outsourced.

The point is that you can think of service management activities (business services) as being assembled and constructed from the combination of the resources in the five layers below them (Staff/Operatives, Software/Applications, Information/Data, Computer Hardware, and Facilities and Data Center).

Recognizing the dynamic nature of the six layers

We present this six-layer model to draw attention to a couple of facts: Each of these layers can be considered in isolation, and various policies or broad guidelines can be created for managing each layer. More important, however, is the fact that these layers are not at all static. Everything keeps changing, which makes managing the whole ensemble difficult.

In the following sections, we discuss the layers one by one again, but this time, we discuss them from the perspective of change.

Changes in the Facilities and Data Center layer

If you look back over the past 15 years, you see huge changes in the nature of the typical data center. It went from catering to tens of servers to hundreds of servers or (in some companies) thousands of servers. As the data center grew dramatically, the parameters for air conditioning and cooling changed, and so did the power requirements.

Now consider other computing devices. Laptops have replaced desktops for many people, and smartphones are replacing mobile phones to some degree. If those changes weren't enough, we're slowly moving to a world of embedded processors and radio-frequency identification (RFID) tags attached to anything that moves. Therefore, any facility or space is potentially a computing facility and connected to the corporate network in some way.

Changes in the Computer Hardware layer

Regular dramatic changes in the capabilities of computer hardware have been the rule rather than the exception for decades now. These changes have been driven by Moore's law, which not only affects CPUs, but also confers its gifts on memory, switches, disk speeds, and just about every other component of a computer. Consequently, no fixed approach to computer and network architectures is possible. The parameters keep changing, making hardware configurations that were once impractical quite viable. All disk files used to be local to the server running the application that used them, for example. Then came file servers, storage area networks (SANs), and network attached stores (NAS). Applications that used to run on a single sever are now spread across multiple servers.

Changes in the Information/Data layer

At one time, all data was structured data, held in files or databases. The advent of document management and text mining tools added less-structured data to the mix. Then came sound, images, and video. At the same time, the volume of data grew. Companies that once stored megabytes of data began to preside over gigabytes and then terabytes — and recently in some companies, data volumes have grown to the petabyte level.

Changes in the Software/Applications layer

Naturally, the growth in computer power has been accompanied by a growth in the number of useful applications that businesses can exploit. The advent of the Internet connected most of the computers in the world and subsequently delivered new ways of carrying out many business activities, from buying airline tickets to disposing of unwanted inventory. The Internet has continued to ramp up the speed of change in terms of new applications, and change will only get faster as smartphones displace less-sophisticated mobile phones.

This situation has unwelcome aspects, particularly in the area of IT security, where investment in software is necessary for self-protection. To add to the complexity, all software — whether it's infrastructure or application software — goes through regular revisions and enhancements, so nearly all the software that an organization runs changes over time. These changes make managing the Software/Applications layer very difficult, because incompatibilities and errors need to be prevented at all costs.

Changes in the Staff/Operatives layer

As the technology continually changes in every layer, the skills required for understanding how systems function also change. This situation can cut both ways. The complexity of operating and managing technology sometimes increases and sometimes diminishes. As a result, the people who are in charge of managing a complex network of computers need to be retrained regularly, and they need to be familiar with technology developments in the industry.

Changes in the Business Services layer

The service levels that customers or IT users expect from business services evolve all the time. A company in a particularly competitive market may decide to improve its level of service dramatically so that no competitor can match its performance, for example. In general, however, as technology sophistication improves, customer expectations of service grow, and as customer expectations expand, IT has no choice but to meet rising expectations.

This situation is precisely what happened when e-mail became an increasingly important corporate service. At one time, e-mail users — including employees, customers, and partners — may have been satisfied with 99 percent availability. That level of availability, however, meant that the e-mail service would be unavailable 3.65 days a year, which would translate into 15 minutes of downtime every day. We don't know many companies that would put up with that performance level now that e-mail has become part of the business fabric. Such changes in service demand are difficult to predict and can't be met without investments of one sort or another.

Determining the Value of Service Management

How do you decide on the value of service management? This question is such a good one that we're not sure why we haven't mentioned it before. Unfortunately, it's not an easy one to answer. We're going to take a stab at answering it, though, because chapter after chapter of this book discusses the benefits of service management. Service management isn't free . . . or cheap. So unless you have an infinite budget — and we suspect that you don't — examining the value of service management is important.

So far in this chapter, we've discussed service management in terms of layers. Keeping these layers in mind, we turn now to looking at service management in terms of costs. We consider costs in the following areas:

- Support
- Optimization
- Risk
- Change

These different strands of service management deliver benefits in distinctly different areas, and we discuss them separately in the following sections.

Support costs

Just for fun, we'll start by getting all mathematical and proposing an equation, which we'll call Equation A:

App cost = Cost of app resource + cost of SM resource

This equation shouldn't scare you, because it's very simple. Just think of any business application; its cost consists of all the resources it uses directly plus all the management support it requires (service management, represented in the equation as *SM*). Look at it this way: You could buy the application and all the resources it needs to run, including operators (if any), and then you could just run it.

If you did that without considering the service management component, however, the service that the application provided would degrade quickly. Various hardware, software, and even user errors would occur over time, and someone would need to handle those errors to keep the application healthy. Support costs are inevitable for all applications, and service management processes deliver the support.

Support cost is what an organization pays to deliver the acceptable service level for a particular application over a targeted life span, and that service level is determined by the organization's demands. If you look at service management this way, you also need to distinguish between the operational personnel who run the applications and the support personnel who manage the service.

Optimization costs

Here, we introduce another equation, Equation B:

Total facility costs = Σ Cost of app resource + Σ cost of SM resource – Σ SM savings

This equation also is quite simple. It suggests that the costs of the whole IT facility are equivalent to the sum of the costs of all applications and the costs of SM activities minus (excluding) the amount of savings that the SM activities achieve.

For each of the six layers we describe in this chapter (refer to "Understanding the Six Layers of Service Management," earlier in this chapter), you can achieve economies of scale simply by managing the entire layer as a single entity. You can manage the Facilities and Data Center layer as a single entity, the Computer Hardware layer as a single entity, the Information/Data layer as a single entity, and so on. This practice has many aspects. Negotiating intelligent contracts with hardware and software vendors can reduce unit costs; virtualization strategies may reduce the square footage required in the data center; and common data backup procedures may reduce the cost of backup and recovery. All such activities fall into one layer or another.

Equation B, therefore, states that you can use service management technology and processes to optimize many aspects of the IT operation, and when you do so successfully, you bring down the costs.

Risk costs

Suppose that your organization has a service level of 99.95 percent availability. What does a service level of 99.95 percent availability actually mean? No doubt it means that the IT department will do what it can to ensure that an application is available almost all the time, to the extent that it is unavailable for four hours or so every year.

That availability level is only a target, however. In reality, ensuring such a high level of availability is very difficult, and you have no hard-and-fast way to ensure meeting such a target. All you can do is ensure the probability of meeting the target.

Think in terms only of simple failures, and you realize that this statement must be true. An application may fail because of hardware or network failure, and although you can put a great deal of redundancy into the computer architecture to make failure unlikely, making failure impossible would be very expensive. To complicate this example beyond simple failure, consider the possibility of operating-system errors, errors in other fundamental software, or bugs in the application itself. You can also include mistakes made by staff members, and just for good measure, you can add unavailability due to security breaches, which have been known to bring down whole networks.

When you look at this situation this way, you realize that you have no simple way to ensure any specific level of availability. All you can do is manage the risk that the system will become unavailable.

When an application does become unavailable, a definite cost is involved, and this cost can have three elements:

- **Lost business:** This cost is the direct cost of sales that never happened because of the system's unavailability.

- **Brand damage:** This cost is the drop in customer confidence caused by the service failure.

- **Repairs:** This cost can be small or perhaps even nonexistent, but in the case of a security breach, it can be very high indeed.

This situation presents quite a conundrum, because you can always sink more money into various areas of IT to deliver better service levels. Also, to a certain degree, service levels are points of competition. Underinvestment in high service levels may lead to loss of business, whereas overinvestment surely leads to unnecessarily high costs. We can produce a mathematical formula, Equation C, to express the situation:

SM cost = Probability × (Cost of lost business + cost brand damage + cost of repair)

The point is that it's unwise to invest any more in service management than is necessary to improve service levels or justified by the cost of failures. In other words, you shouldn't invest any more than customer expectations require.

The obvious exception occurs when a company deliberately raises its service level as a competitive move. In this situation, the expense is related to a business decision — not a technical decision — and in the end, that business decision may be the secret to a great service management strategy.

Change costs

Finally, we come to investment in service management that is implemented specifically to manage change. The problem with the factor of change in IT is that change comes in two flavors:

- ✔ Predictable
- ✔ Disruptive

Under the heading of *predictable* change come all the factors that can be measured and tracked: the cost of computer hardware, the cost of software, the growth of data, the number of users, the number of customers accessing systems, the variety of transactions being supported, and so on. The growth of these factors can be predicted with reasonable accuracy over time. Then this growth can be combined with corporate plans for new products and services to determine future investments in service management and new IT applications.

The more difficult problem is *disruptive* change. By definition, disruptive change is unpredictable, and it can demand unexpectedly high levels of investment simply because a business has no easy way to prepare for it. Legislative change, such as that imposed by the Sarbanes-Oxley Act of 2002 in the United States, can be disruptive. Exploding security problems are an example of disruptive change in the technology world. Sudden economic changes, from currency swings to stock-market crashes, also can be highly disruptive. The best preparation for dealing with disruptive change is having a service management system that is coherent and flexible.

If you've been following this discussion closely, you probably wonder what we mean by a *service management system.* That's the topic of the next chapter.

Chapter 9

The Technical Foundation of Service Management

*P*eople don't find computers to be as mysterious as they once did. You can blame the PC for that fact. As PCs became ubiquitous, just about everyone came to understand roughly how a computer works. Very few people knew exactly how a computer works down at chip level, but most people know that a computer itself has electronic circuits (hardware) that execute instructions (software) and store the results (data).

Before that time, it was credible to write science-fiction stories about a computer that had exceeded the intelligence of man and was about to take over the world, exterminating those pesky humans in the process and then playing 3D chess with itself for eternity. After the PC proliferation, the story lines became a little different. The superintelligent computer still tried to take over the world, but just as it was about to send the robot armies out to exterminate us, it suffered a blue-screen event and died.

This scenario is where service management comes in. If IT professionals get things right, they reduce the possibility that this computer will suffer a blue screen, and if it does, they ensure that another one is ready to step up and take its place. But don't blame the members of the service management staff if it happens. They don't program the computers; they just try to ensure that the computers deliver an acceptable level of service.

Understanding the Relationships in Systems

Although we have mentioned computer systems many times already in this book, we haven't yet defined the components of a computer system and the relationships among those components. This section is a good place to do that, because now you're ready to explore the foundations of service management technology, which means that you need to have a practical view of what computers and networks are.

Computers and computer networks

In Figure 9-1, we represent a computer system in a simple way that even a casual user can understand. The system consists of hardware, software, data, and users.

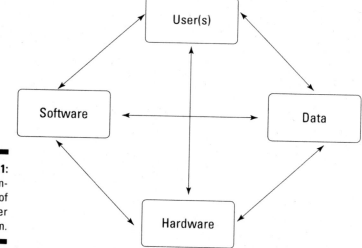

Figure 9-1:
The components of a computer system.

All the elements of the system relate to one another, as indicated by the arrows:

✔ The user interacts with hardware (keyboard, mouse, and screen).

✔ The user interacts with software by running applications.

✔ The user employs applications to create data.

✔ The software (applications) creates, changes, and deletes data.

✔ The software runs on hardware.

✔ The data is stored on hardware.

These components are not as simple as they look in this figure, however. The computer hardware has many components; the data files on a computer are many and often complex; and the software is unlikely to be just one application but many applications (including the operating system) that carry out a wide variety of tasks.

Figure 9-1 depicts a single computer. What about a whole network of computers? Well, this figure works for that purpose too, because computer networks consist entirely of users, software, hardware, and data. The importance of this diagram is that it shows, in a very simple way, everything that a computer network consists of and all the relationships involved.

Service management systems

Now we'll step back for a moment and consider the nature of service management. Service management is about supporting and ensuring the business services that an organization provides; it involves supporting and ensuring all the business applications that an organization runs. You can't do that unless you know where all the applications are, who is using them, which machines they run on, and what data they create and use.

As far as computer systems and computer networks are concerned, the fundamental service management system is the one that captures, organizes, and stores all the data that allows all other service management processes to run. It's the system that captures and organizes all the data about users, software, data files, and hardware.

As you read this book, you see that service management involves a large number of distinct processes. Here's a short list: application management, system management, performance management, service desk, network management, database management, desktop management, mobile device management, IT security, voice and communications management, and provisioning.

Most of those processes have software capability that implements them, and each element of software needs to store information that relates to users, software, data, and hardware. Where is that information going to be stored?

If you answer this question by saying, "In the configuration management database," we'd have to respond, "Well, actually, no, but you're kinda half right."

To explain this answer, we have to explain what we mean by a configuration management database.

Working with a Configuration Management Database

Various service management processes need to store data about the IT environment, including people, software, data, and hardware, as well as the relationships among them. The *configuration management database (CMDB)* is the database that holds this information.

Imagine that you have 30 software applications, and each one stores its own data in the format that it needs that data to be in. This example seems to be rather straight forward until you realize from experience that these 30 applications are going to have real problems coordinating with one another. It would be much better if all 30 applications used the same data standards and shared a database that was the single source of the truth.

That idea is a nice one, but it belongs in Cloud Cuckoo Land. The problem is that those 30 applications will come from different vendors; some may even have been written in-house. The applications will disagree in various ways, from data structure and definitions to security to hardware configuration. To make matters worse, technology keeps changing, so even if hard-and-fast data definition standards were available, keeping them in step with the changing world would be a task and a half.

If you investigate the business applications in an organization of any size, you quickly discover that they, too, have a mess at the data level. The situation is no different with service management applications.

What can you do? The only viable solution is a federated one in which you have multiple data sources that can be coordinated so that they agree as much as possible. A picture is worth a thousand words, so see the diagram in Figure 9-2 for more details.

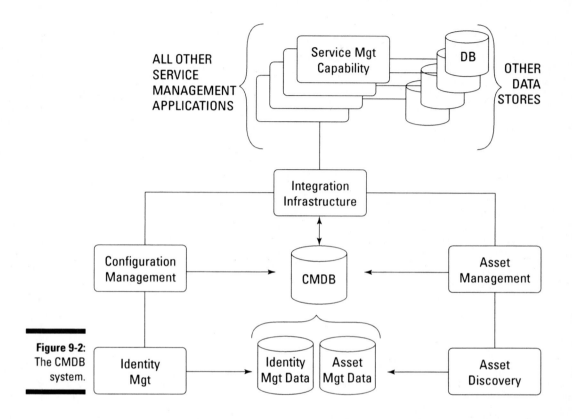

Figure 9-2:
The CMDB system.

In the following sections, we explain the major elements of Figure 9-2.

The important thing to understand about a CMDB system is that it records all the data it can about all the people, hardware, software, and data sources in the organization's collection of IT assets and keeps that data up to date so that it can be used to support service management activities.

Integration infrastructure

Figure 9-2 contains too many elements to explain in one go, so we discuss them piece by piece, beginning with the integration infrastructure (see Figure 9-3).

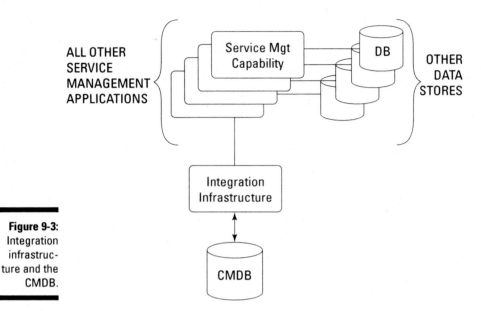

Figure 9-3:
Integration
infrastruc-
ture and the
CMDB.

The *integration infrastructure* is a process that allows any service management
capability to access the entire service management data resource (which
we're calling the CMDB). The integration infrastructure is made up primarily of communications capabilities and interfaces that enable a diverse set
of data resources to appear as a single coherent resource (such as a single
database).

The idea is that any service management application, or any person who is
part of a service management process, can request information through the
integration infrastructure and then retrieve the information.

As Figure 9-3 indicates, service management applications normally maintain
their own data. Unfortunately, the processes that those applications serve
may need access to other information. When members of the network management team are considering network changes, for example, they may need
to know more about how applications in particular areas of the network function than they can find out simply from network management and monitoring
software.

With the current state of technology, you can't buy any product that constitutes service management integration infrastructure in a box. If we'd wanted
to, we could have written "here magic happens" rather than "integration
infrastructure." Don't be deterred, however, by the fact that technology

hasn't yet reached the desired level of sophistication. Usually, when an over-riding need exists, it's possible to find ways to share service management data by using some form of data replication. The important point is to understand that service management will be better automated and better served when the sharing of service management data can be automated reliably.

Asset management and discovery

Asset management is another IT term that can be applied to many things. In its widest definition, it can cover financial, contractual, and inventory functions covering the life cycles of all software and hardware components. It can embrace license management and even such diverse activities as technology evaluation and capacity planning. We won't discuss that topic here, however, because we're interested in the activities involved in collecting all the data that service management activities require.

Figure 9-4 shows the service management applications that are involved in these activities. Taken together, asset discovery and asset management constitute an indispensable part of the foundational capabilities of service management.

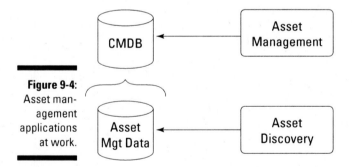

Figure 9-4:
Asset man-
agement
applications
at work.

Asset management application

The application in the top right corner of Figure 9-4 is the traditional IT asset management application, which allows you to record all the information you have about hardware and software. Most such applications also allow you to capture cost information, license information, and so on. Some applications of this kind even have the capability of exploring the network and may gather some information directly. If any application captures most of the basic information that needs to be held in the CMDB, it's the asset management application.

Asset discovery application

IT networks used to be reasonably static, with data about new devices and software being captured as it was added to the network via the asset management application. Today, with the advent of wireless networks and cloud computing, the network can grow and shrink dynamically in terms of both the hardware it contains and the software it runs. Asset discovery software permanently listens to the network to detect changes, such as new devices, and then records those changes for use by other service management applications.

After an asset discovery application discovers new devices, authenticating those devices ought to be standard procedure.

Identity management

Identity management, as the words suggest, is the management of user identity information within the IT network. Identity management systems are relatively new. Before they existed, computer users simply had access capabilities that were tied to their names and passwords. Users never had formal identities, and their access capabilities limited the applications that they could use on any given computer. A user might have *single sign-on* capability, in which his login gave him access to various computers on the network. In identity management systems, users have applications provisioned to them directly, and the identity management system looks after all the underlying logins. In that sense, identity management forms a bridge between single sign-on and the appealing idea of *application self-service,* in which users can select applications to use from a catalog.

Identity management can be regarded as the foundation of a good deal of IT security, as it naturally ties in with user authentication and user permissions. To learn a lot more about security, see Chapter 16.

For purposes of this discussion, however, we're interested in identity management from a different perspective. Identity management is the single source of truth with respect to user information; thus, the data it stores becomes the best point of reference for service management applications that need user information.

In Figure 9-5, identity management data is shown as being an important part of the CMDB. Most of the data that an identity management system gathers is related directly to the applications that users (or customers) use. In some advanced implementations, the data is also directly related to the access devices (desktop computers, laptops, and mobile phones) that people use.

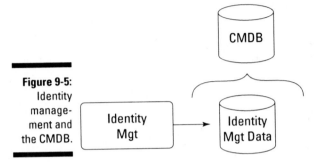

Figure 9-5:
Identity management and the CMDB.

Unfortunately, many organizations don't have full-fledged identity management systems, so they need to assemble much of the information that they need about users from directories and authentication systems. In those circumstances, it becomes difficult to establish a networkwide view of exactly who is doing what with any specific application. For security purposes and for calculating the cost of any given service, the ability to know exactly who is using what hardware and software assets for what purpose is becoming a requirement.

Configuration management

In addition to collecting information on people, hardware, software, and data, an organization needs to know as much as possible about the relationships among those elements to provide better service management. Luckily, it also needs to know most of this information to configure applications to run.

Configuration management data can be gathered by dependency mapping software that automatically parses the job control data that specifies how a given workload will run. This software identifies the data files and databases used by an application and can identify some of the dependencies among applications — at least, with the traditional application silos that have been deployed in data centers over the past decade. Configuration management software products normally go further than that, not only defining all workloads fully, but also tracking all changes made to any workload. As illustrated in Figure 9-6 and as their name implies, such products are often the prime source of information for the CMDB.

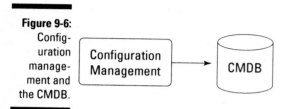

Figure 9-6:
Config-
uration
manage-
ment and
the CMDB.

The complexity of configurations became a little more complicated with the advent of enterprise application integration (EAI) technologies, which made it possible for applications to interact directly in ways that wouldn't necessarily be visible in workload. Then the situation deteriorated even further with the advent of service oriented architecture (SOA). In an SOA, details of services (which means application capabilities) are held in the SOA registry. Consequently, SOA dependency mapping also involves accessing that registry to determine some of the dependencies among applications.

For more information on SOA, see Chapter 6. Alternatively, if you're a real glutton for punishment, check out *Service Oriented Architecture For Dummies,* 2nd Edition (Wiley Publishing, Inc.), which we also wrote.

Federating the CMDB

You may notice that we present an incomplete picture in the preceding sections. We don't explain how every single bit of the information that defines all the users, software, data, and hardware in a computing environment is assembled in a CMDB. All we do is identify the primary sources of important information that needs to reside in the CMDB. We do explain that the data the CMDB is supposed to contain is really distributed across multiple management databases that are used by a wide variety of service management applications. For that reason, we can really think only in terms of a federated CMDB.

In particular, we say very little about defining the inventory of data files that are held within any network. The truth is that the identity of data resources is in its infancy. Some applications, such as document management, define some data items very rigorously, and some important compliance rules involve certain kinds of data. But no service management application specifically gathers a comprehensive set of information about all data files.

The processes involved in populating and maintaining the CMDB are illustrated again in Figure 9-7. Aside from their other functions, the goal of these activities is to make a comprehensive, accurate set of data available to all current service management applications (including any that may be created in the future) and to staff members. With the current state of technology, this process isn't well automated, so you can expect to see significant improvements in this capability as time passes.

Having said that, it may help if we now take a brief look at how the CMDB fits into the strategic evolution of the data center and service management maturity as a whole.

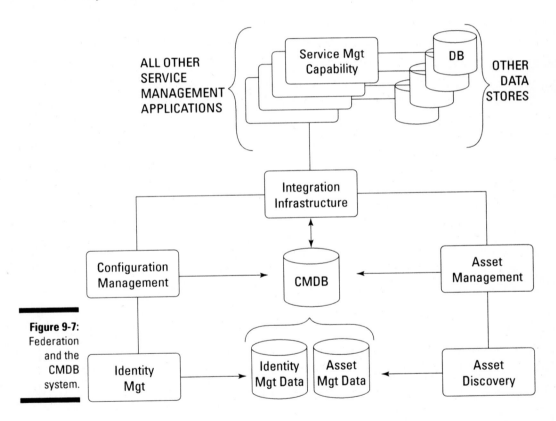

Figure 9-7:
Federation
and the
CMDB
system.

Strategy

The general strategic direction of service management, as we discuss in Chapter 6, is evolution from systems management to business service management. Most organizations today still focus on systems management, although many enlightened organizations are beginning to align the goals of the business with both service management (to manage application services) and business service management to focus on management's needs.

An effective CMDB is necessary for business service management to be possible at all, because it requires comprehensive, up-to-date information about what is deployed.

Strategically, the CMDB is important because it's the platform for all other service management applications. Therefore, improving this capability is a priority. Unfortunately, very few approaches to establishing and managing a CMDB have proved to be effective and have paid for their investment. The value of identity management, for example, lies in the improvements it makes in provisioning and IT security. The value of asset management is in the life-cycle management of those assets. The value of configuration management is mostly in change management and in problem resolution. The fact that they can all improve the coherence of the data available to the CMDB is a welcome side effect.

Maturity

In Figure 6-2, in Chapter 6, we define the maturity of service automation in terms of this progression:

> Fragmented services➪Standardized services➪Integrated services➪
> Optimized services

As we state earlier in this chapter, an integrated CMDB isn't technically achievable right now, so in terms of maturity, the primary and practical goal is likely to be a move toward standardized services.

We think that the first step is implementing those service management applications — asset discovery, asset management, identity management, and dependency mapping — that haven't been put in place or aren't comprehensively implemented. IT also has to develop an effective integration infrastructure to support bringing these pieces together. Such an infrastructure may involve communications products such as enterprise service buses

(ESBs) and messaging products, as well as a protocol to enable interaction among disparate service management processes. We're not aware of any commercial products that do it all.

Key performance indicators

With the CMDB, what matters most is to assemble data that can be shared among all service management processes. No specific key performance indicators can be applied simply to measure the level of data integration. Indeed, integration itself is difficult to measure in almost any context. It is more productive simply to note the level of disruption that the lack of integration imposes on service management and to work toward reducing such disruption.

Chapter 10

Governing the Service Universe

You can't implement effective service management unless IT takes a holistic approach to automation, oversight, and comprehensive asset management across the organization. How can you do this? We recommend establishing a strong IT governance program that can provide the framework to make this happen.

IT governance in service management requires carefully combining rules for IT and business processes. You need governance rules for everything from IT security to general policies about service levels. In essence, think of a life cycle of business processes that focuses on the goal of improving service quality and business agility. Governance from a service management perspective requires that your organization apply sound business and technical judgment. You have to make trade-offs. At times, you need to allow one service to degrade in favor of a more-business-critical service.

This chapter describes the importance of monitoring and measuring service performance, and discusses why IT governance requires companies to take a composite view of all the components of service management.

Understanding the Roles of IT Governance

IT manages a complex infrastructure of hardware, data, storage, and software environments. The data center (some of the largest organizations have many data centers) is designed to use all assets efficiently while guaranteeing a certain level of service to the customer or end user. A data center has teams of people responsible for managing everything from the overall facility, workloads, hardware, data, software, and network infrastructure.

To understand some of the complexities of service management from a data center perspective, we recommend reading Chapter 11.

In addition to the data center itself, your organization may have remote facilities with technology that depends on the data center. IT management has long-established processes for managing and monitoring individual IT components, which is good. What's been a problem for many organizations is finding a way to monitor performance across all components in a way that reflects the overall impact of IT performance on the business.

Helping the organization meet its goals

You should direct IT governance at individual IT infrastructure components within the context of the larger challenges and goals, as well as within the company's overall performance objectives.

IT governance is intended to help you meet the company's overall performance indicators.

IT governance is supported in two ways:

- ✔ **Understanding the compliance and risk measures the business must follow:** What does your business require to meet IT, corporate, industry, and government requirements? IT can support these requirements through technical controls; automation; and strict governance of processes, data, and workflows.

- ✔ **Understanding the performance goals of the business:** You may measure your business performance in terms of sales revenue, profitability, stock price, quality of product or service provided, and time to delivery. Your IT performance measurements should focus on delivering IT services consistently and accurately so that the company gets to optimize its business performance.

Providing a view from the top

What's one of the key benefits of taking a holistic approach to IT governance? When you have a comprehensive view, you can manage and deliver IT services more proactively. Imagine a chief information officer (CIO) who is frustrated by urgent calls from the company's retail stores when terminals are slow or credit machines are unresponsive. The urgent calls always seem to come at the worst times, such as in the middle of a sale. Installing a remote service management system, however, would allow the CIO to do the following:

- ✔ Monitor the performance of all IT services in the retail environment
- ✔ Understand the relationships among those services
- ✔ Notice service degradations so that problems could be fixed before stores had to make emergency calls

In this example, the remote monitoring system enables IT to create a more balanced approach to delivering services based on business objectives and regulatory requirements. The CIO can develop a better understanding of the priorities involved when he makes decisions about service management issues for the retail stores. Many companies have started using an overall business service management strategy as a technique for managing services from a unified business perspective.

We give you a lot more detail on business service management in Chapter 17.

Improving efficiency

Each industry has a set of governance principles based on its regulatory and competitive environment. The most important governance requirement in retail, for example, is for the sales process to be both efficient and accurate. What can happen in retail that becomes an IT governance challenge? Consider another example: Store operations management would like the data center to promise 100 percent uptime supported by fully redundant servers to protect against any service slowdown, but the CIO has cost restraints.

The CIO compromises with the business. Business management and IT management agree that customers shouldn't wait more than three minutes to complete a transaction and that the sales kiosks must be up 96 percent of the time. In addition, they agree that all customer data must be fully encrypted and protected against unauthorized access by anyone at any time.

If the CIO later discovers that performance slows so dramatically that customers leave stores without buying anything, IT governance has failed. If consistently slow credit machines cause sales clerks to make credit card sales without using the automatic credit check, the business is put at risk, and IT governance has failed. On the other hand, if performance is excellent but customer data isn't protected — you got it — IT governance failed again.

An integral part of IT governance is juggling various tasks: meeting customer expectations, optimizing business goals, recognizing resource constraints, and adhering to rules and requirements. We discuss this balancing act in more detail in the following section.

Balancing IT and Business Requirements

IT governance is a combination of the following:

- ✔ Policy
- ✔ Process
- ✔ Controls
- ✔ Consistent data about IT services
- ✔ The means to control those services

The role of IT governance is to do the following with service management:

- ✔ Implement
- ✔ Maintain
- ✔ Continuously improve

IT governance, therefore, has to include the techniques and policies that measure and control how IT systems are managed.

Defining your IT governance strategy is a balancing act. On one hand, it must focus on the key performance indicators of the business. On the other hand, it must balance all the components of the IT environment. You have to look at the relationships among IT and business components to fully appreciate the level of risk to your company.

Although at first glance, IT governance may seem to be a contained approach to providing oversight of IT resources, the range of issues that you must manage and plan is actually much broader. IT governance must be tightly woven with business goals and policies to ensure that services are optimized for customer expectations. As we point out in Chapter 1, however, everything in your business is really a service. Therefore, it isn't surprising that we urge you to look at IT governance from a holistic business perspective.

Effective service management requires constant vigilance and intricate choreography to ensure a balance among business priorities, customer expectations, available resources, and limitations on cost. IT is responsible for giving all internal and external customers and partners the resources they need, when they need them, without overstepping certain boundaries of resource and cost limitations. This focus has to be within the context of corporate governance requirements and an organization's key performance indicators (KPIs). A philosophy focused on continuous improvement in service management will help you optimize your IT infrastructure and business performance under the overarching umbrella of governance.

Measuring and Monitoring Performance

Measuring performance as a means to help improve performance is a concept that is well understood by competitive athletes. Imagine the countless hours spent during training measuring, recording, and monitoring changes in time and distance. But what if the runner were taking steroids? Was she in compliance? Clearly, even if all other measurements were positive, breaking the rules changes everything.

How does this example apply to IT governance? The principle really is the same.

Although measuring and monitoring may help you improve performance, that performance is irrelevant if you don't follow the company's governance rules.

Measurement methods

You can measure business performance by comparing production, sales, revenue, stock price, and customer satisfaction with your goals. You can measure IT performance by comparing server, application, and network uptime; service resolution time; budgets; and project completion dates with your goals. Businesses use all these measures to rate their performance compared with that of competitors and the expectations of customers, partners, and shareholders. But how can you measure the impact of IT performance on business results? It takes some fact-finding and true collaboration between IT and the business to settle on performance measures that support governance in service management.

A governance committee should answer the following types of questions to get started:

- ✔ How can IT performance measures support the business?
- ✔ What should management measure and monitor to ensure successful IT governance?

✔ Are customers able to get responses to requests in the expected amount of time?

✔ Is customer transaction data safe from unauthorized access?

✔ Can management get the right information at the right time?

✔ Can you demonstrate to business management that your organization can recover from anticipated outages without damaging customer loyalty?

✔ Are you able to monitor systems proactively so that you can make repairs before faulty services affect rules and regulations?

✔ Can you justify your IT investments to business management?

Proactive communication

Writing down key performance measurements is easy, but achieving them is complicated. Ironically, when IT manages services successfully from a business perspective, the business doesn't even notice. This outcome is like an old joke we like to tell:

Johnny was a quiet kid who never talked to his parents. One day he said, "This food is terrible!" His parents were shocked to hear his voice. "How come you never spoke before?" they asked. Johnny replied, "Up until now, everything was perfect."

What's Johnny trying to tell you? Maintain a clear dialogue with business management to understand what the business needs. When IT services are in perfect harmony with business objectives, you may never hear a word. But you certainly will hear many words loud and clear when a service failure leads to business disruptions. A much better policy is to take a proactive approach to demonstrate that IT management is paying attention. Good IT governance doesn't happen by accident.

Making Governance Work

Having a lot of oversight and collaboration with the business is important, but it won't be enough if you can't meet your goals. You need to measure results by monitoring IT goals based on business goals, such as whether customer complaints went down by 10 percent or the company increased sales by installing customer kiosks at all its stores.

In this book, we don't focus on how well your servers are performing in your data center. The reality is that management cares about the business results and making sure that the supporting characters, such as the data center, do their parts.

Don't get too comfortable, though: It isn't enough to monitor performance in isolation. In the corporate world, many organizations advance performance and achieve compliance by increasing automation, but automating every-thing makes it easy to lose sight of the human element in managing service the right way.

Standardization and automation help remove some risk and potential for error, but not all of it, because employees and other businesses stakeholders make decisions every day that put companies at risk. No amount of control in the health care industry, for example, ensures that patients will be given the correct medicines 100 percent of the time. The human element plays a big role in all governance issues.

Making governance work requires a combination of the following:

✔ Automation

✔ Optimization of processes

✔ Focus on KPIs

✔ Attention to the human element

This work sounds hard — and it is — but leveraging standards and best prac-tices can help, as we discuss in the following section.

People and groups have countless opportunities to make mistakes — deliberate or unintentional — that interfere with adherence to corporate, industry, and government rules and policies. No company can expect technol-ogy to correct for or protect against all instances of human error or fraud. Increasing use of IT service management in combination with increased stan-dardization and automation of workflows, however, can help organizations govern with confidence.

Developing Best Practices

Putting IT governance into action by following industry best practices helps you manage IT services with greater control and consistency. To put IT governance into action, your company should develop its own best practices, such as the following:

✔ **Define the process flows.** The process must do these two things:

- **Involve both business and IT professionals at three levels: corporate, departmental, and IT.**

- **Measure how effectively each service delivers business value.** This measurement helps you answer questions about meeting service-level agreements (SLAs), such as whether IT understands the business process well enough to set up SLAs that make sense and whether it can meet SLAs in such areas as mean time to repair.

✔ **Identify the roles and responsibilities of everyone involved.** Companies typically establish best practices by learning from mistakes. False starts in service management strategies are likely to be associated with inappropriate plans for change. You should know how you will implement a consistent change management process with tighter communication among all parties who need to know about the change. In addition, you should be proactive about change, such as requiring submission of notice about a service change early enough to decrease incidents associated with the change.

For more insight into the service management and IT governance strategies of real companies, we suggest that you read the case studies in Part V of this book.

The following sections discuss several important IT governance best practices.

Establishing a governance body

It's important for IT to understand two things: the objectives of the business and the effect of service disruptions or outages on these objectives.

Creating a governance board consisting of representatives of corporate, departmental, and IT management will help encourage communication — the kind necessary to link IT service management and the business.

This governing body should be an ongoing concern that has authority across the enterprise and that has a mechanism for communicating business-objectives changes to the IT folks who manage the services.

Monitoring and measuring IT service performance

Many companies implement a *service dashboard,* which holds the different services and shows how your performance measures up to your goals. In addition to leveraging the governance board (refer to the preceding section), your team can use the dashboard to answer the following types of questions:

✔ How are we performing according to our established KPIs?

✔ How does our performance now compare with last week's or last year's?

✔ What are the goals of our KPIs?

✔ What are we aiming for?

✔ Are rules and processes implemented correctly?

✔ Does each service meet technical standards?

Cataloging control and compliance data

Many organizations use a service catalog as a record of IT services. The catalog can include information like the following:

✔ Whom to contact about a service

✔ Who has authority to change the service

✔ Which critical applications are related to the service

✔ Outages or other incidents related to the service

✔ Information about the relationships among services

✔ Documentation of all agreements between IT and the customer or user of the service

A banking institution's service catalog, for example, may contain information about the company's online banking service, the KPIs for that service, and the SLAs between IT and the online banking business. If an outage occurs, the bank's IT service management team can read the service catalog to locate the root cause of problems with the service.

Governance resources

Check out these organizations for information on how IT can collaborate with the business to improve service management and governance:

✔ The Information Technology Infrastructure Library (ITIL) for certification programs (www.itil-officialsite.com)

✔ The International Organization for Standardization (ISO) for standards on governance (www.iso.org)

In addition to ITIL and ISO, many companies implement service management applications to automate and monitor IT controls. These applications can help companies ensure that the right IT controls are established to support the compliance requirements of regulations such as the Sarbanes-Oxley Act of 2002 and the Health Insurance Portability and Accountability Act (HIPAA).

For an introduction to service management standards and best practices, as well as more information on ISO, refer to Chapter 4. For more information on ITIL, see Chapter 5.

Part IV
Nitty-Gritty Service Management

The 5th Wave   By Rich Tennant

"It appears a server in Atlanta is about to go down, there's printer backup in Baltimore and an accountant in Chicago is about to make level 3 of the game 'Tomb Pirate.'"

In this part . . .

From a practical perspective, the nitty-gritty is every service management process that we haven't discussed yet. In this part, we take you on a journey from managing the data center to planning its evolution. In the course of this journey, you visit the desktop, mobile devices, data management, virtualization, the cloud, IT security, and business service management. It's quite a journey, with many interesting stops on the way.

Chapter 11

Managing the Data Center

*W*e have spent a lot of time talking about the fact that a business itself is a set of services focused on achieving the right customer experience. In the case of an automated teller machine (ATM), the customer wants to walk up to the machine and in quick order get a wad of cash. If the customer has the right card, the right security code, and enough money in the bank account, everything works like magic.

If only magic were possible! Reality is much more complicated. When we speak of managing the data center, what we really mean is managing the whole corporate IT resource — which, for the vast majority of organizations, has its heart in the data center.

In this chapter, we focus on the optimization of all the service management processes that constitute the operational activities of the data center. An inherent conflict exists between highly efficient use of assets and a guaranteed customer or user experience.

Understanding the Siloed Nature of the Data Center

A data center isn't a neatly packaged IT system; it's a messy combination of hardware, software, data storage, and infrastructure. The typical data center has myriad servers running different operating systems and a large variety of applications. In addition, many organizations have created multiple data centers over time to support specific departments or divisions in different geographic locations.

As long as hardware, energy, and physical space were relatively cheap, no one really bothered to think about the need to manage data center resources closely. If something broke, replacing it often was easier than figuring out where the problem was. If performance slowed, adding a couple more servers was a simple way to keep users from complaining. Over the past couple of years, however, three events changed everything:

✔ Data centers became expensive in terms of space and energy.

✔ The number of servers and other devices in use grew very large, making management of data and applications more complex and labor intensive.

✔ Compliance requirements, both external and internal, made oversight a business requirement.

Taken together, these events shifted organizations' approach from management of individual application silos (which could be added to the data center as new applications were requested) to overall management of data centers, based on the need to consolidate a broad set of services.

Organizations always had an incentive to optimize many aspects of data center activity, but the focus now is on managing a data center as a single coherent set of resources. This approach means managing a broad but poorly integrated IT ecosystem that spans the corporate supply chain from suppliers to customers while attempting to satisfy a series of competing demands, from the directives of corporate governance to energy efficiency.

Seeing the Data Center As a Factory

In many ways, you can think of a data center as being a factory. It resembles a factory in the sense that it has staff members who need to carry out regular, well-defined activities. It also has purpose-built machinery for processing a regular scheduled set of work. From an organizational perspective, the management goals include ensuring the quality of processes, having very few breakdowns, and holding down costs. The efficient and effective operation of the factory is critical to the success of the business.

Differences exist between a data center and a traditional factory, however. Specifically, in a data center the raw material being processed is information, and the mechanisms that process this raw material are business applications. All the activities of the data center involve catering to the needs of those business applications so that they perform as expected and are available when needed. The various types of management software are the tools that help data center staff keep the production line in good order.

Figure 11-1 illustrates this idea, with the data center running various workloads. Because this figure fundamentally depicts how a data center operates, it may make managing a data center appear to be relatively easy. A multitude of processes are involved, however.

Ultimately, what a data center does is run workloads. A *workload* is what it sounds like: a set of tasks required to meet customer or user demand (or possibly to complete tasks behind the scenes). As with everything else in the complex world of the data center, you find different types of workloads:

- ✔ **Continuous workloads** keep important business applications running all the time. An application that manages the transactions from hundreds of ATMs, for example, must run all the time.

- ✔ **Scheduled workloads** are put in place for tasks such as backups.

- ✔ **Unscheduled workloads** are intended to run only when a user requests service.

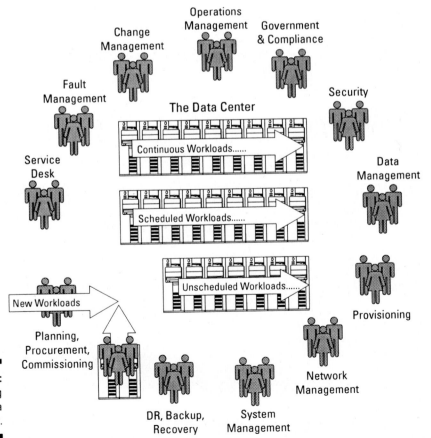

Figure 11-1:
Optimizing the data center.

Optimizing the Data Center

Optimization is a balancing act. If you want to provide a specific service level for an application, you must devote enough resources to ensure that the service level will be met. If you provide too many resources, however, you waste some of them. If you had no financial constraints, you could provide all the resources anyone could possibly need to cater to every possible level of application activity. In such a world, every server could have a duplicate server just in case of an outage. You could give every department twice the storage it needed just in case data volumes grew at dramatic rates.

That approach wasn't feasible even in the days of siloed computing, however, and it isn't at all desirable if you want to get the best possible value from the computer resources that are deployed.

Optimizing an entire data center is far more complex than optimizing for a specific application. Many things can be optimized in a way that provides adequate support for defined service levels yet keeps costs down.

Figure 11-2 represents the service management processes or activities that inevitably take place in management of the corporate IT resource. The processes shown in the figure are the ones that are relevant to optimization activity.

The figure separates these processes into groups, or layers, that can be considered together. We drew the figure as though it were a network connecting many applications, because it is quite likely that service management applications will relate to most of the processes depicted here and connect with one another via integration infrastructure.

Optimizing the data center as a whole is complicated because all the capabilities — facilities, workloads, hardware environments, data resources, software environments, and the infrastructure itself — have traditionally been handled as independent disciplines. The data center is rarely managed as a single unified environment, and the different areas typically don't orchestrate their activities.

The lack of integration generally is the result of explosive growth. IT management never expected that data centers would grow so large, and many of the problems that now exist were mild irritations or nonexistent when data centers were much smaller. The structure of the IT organization, combined with the service management software in use, reflects this lack of integration. Just as there are application silos, there are service management silos. This reality is compounded by the fact that many data centers are running out of space or seeing their costs escalate uncontrollably.

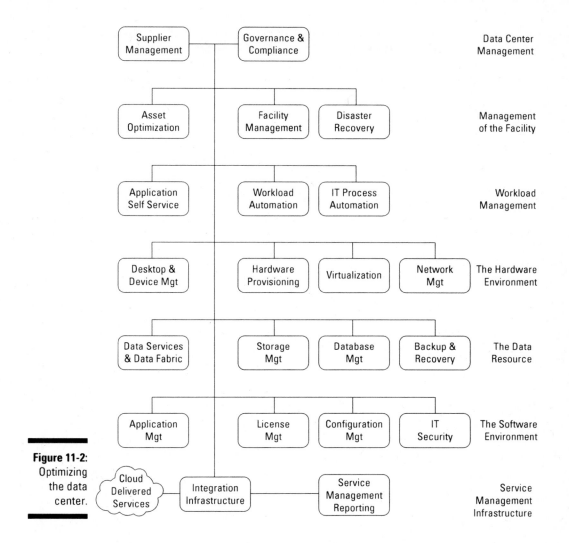

				Data Center Management
Supplier Management	Governance & Compliance			
Asset Optimization	Facility Management	Disaster Recovery		Management of the Facility
Application Self Service	Workload Automation	IT Process Automation		Workload Management
Desktop & Device Mgt	Hardware Provisioning	Virtualization	Network Mgt	The Hardware Environment
Data Services & Data Fabric	Storage Mgt	Database Mgt	Backup & Recovery	The Data Resource
Application Mgt	License Mgt	Configuration Mgt	IT Security	The Software Environment
Cloud Delivered Services	Integration Infrastructure	Service Management Reporting		Service Management Infrastructure

Figure 11-2: Optimizing the data center.

Several distinct factors mandate a holistic approach to data center management:

- ✔ Compliance, governance, and security requirements emanating from multiple sources

- ✔ Escalating power requirements and inefficient hardware use

- ✔ The advent of compelling virtualization technologies coupled with the need to implement them effectively to improve resource productivity

> ✔ Accelerated technology change (new technologies usually are difficult to integrate and tend to be disruptive)
>
> ✔ The automation of business processes across highly distributed environments encouraged by the introduction of a service oriented architecture (SOA)
>
> ✔ The need for service management to manage processes to support corporate goals directly

The need for this approach is even more urgent than you may think, because the needs of businesses change constantly. An organization often has a network of relationships with partners, suppliers, and customers that must be managed in a holistic manner. As companies become more and more dependent on these networks, it is imperative to manage the underlying technology that supports them in a predictable and dynamic manner.

What organizations now want most from their data centers are efficiency and predictability: predictable costs, staffing levels, and performance service levels for IT users and customers bound together in an efficient integrated operation.

In Figure 11-2, earlier in this section, we present a set of service management processes. In the following sections, we discuss these processes and explain how they may participate in the optimization of data center activities.

Managing the Data Center

At the highest level, organizations have to take a businesscentric view of optimizing the data center. You may have the best-looking data center in the world, but if it doesn't meet the performance needs of the organization or support the right customer experience, it will be a failure.

The top layer of Figure 11-2 (refer to "Optimizing the Data Center," earlier in this chapter) is data center management, containing two processes: supplier management, and governance and compliance. These two activities tend to strongly influence all the activities in the layers below to some degree.

Supplier management

Supplier management is about determining and maintaining relationships and contracts with key IT suppliers. Depending on how much money your company spends with these vendors, you can establish significant discounts for both purchases and support. Normally, any given business area works with more than one vendor, using a secondary supplier to provide a credible negotiating position with the primary supplier, for example. The conundrum in supplier management is that commitment to one supplier's strategic technology direction may make it impossible to implement alternative innovative technology in the data center when that technology comes from other sources.

Supplier management isn't a technology-supported activity (beyond the use of office software) and isn't likely ever to be well defined; generally, it's an art form. Who can know which vendors and what technology will dominate the market in five years' time? If the chief information officer (CIO) and his team are good at choosing technology winners and negotiating contracts, they will do well in this activity. The CIO might also work with vendors to establish a more predictable schedule for maintenance releases, patches, and back version support. Normally, however, they also need the confidence and assistance of the chief financial officer and chief executive officer to acquit themselves well. The decisions they make determine or constrain many technology choices at lower levels, and these constraints need to be known and understood when decisions are made.

The key performance indicators (KPIs) for supplier management are expressed in terms of the unit cost of specific units of technology, the discount the company achieves against list price, and the actual useful life cycle of the technology purchased.

Governance and compliance

Governance and compliance is the other key issue that has a big effect on data center strategy and many data center activities.

Compliance

Depending on your industry and even your subsection of your industry, you need to focus on different compliance initiatives.

Compliance can be awkward because it imposes rules and processes that may be expensive and rarely pay for themselves. You may incur criminal penalties for failing to abide by some regulations. Your CEO won't thank you when you tell her, as she walks away in handcuffs, that you saved thousands of dollars by ignoring regulations. For that reason, all compliance processes should be mandated by the board of directors, and all costs should be clear and visibly accounted for. The board will mandate specific costs and impose some constraints on how flexible some processes are, but these processes are mandatory.

Governance

IT governance is about implementing, maintaining, and improving IT management and support processes. In theory, it doesn't necessarily involve automation, although in practice, implementing IT governance effectively is difficult without a good deal of help from software. IT governance involves setting policy in all areas of IT activity. Especially in highly technical areas such as software security, not automating the implementation of policy is ineffective.

In many areas of IT, Information Technology Infrastructure Library (ITIL) standards can be implemented with little variance, and the implementation of the standard can be partly or wholly automated. (For more information on ITIL, see Chapter 5.)

It would be ideal if all IT policies and processes could be defined in a central repository and their implementation automated with little human intervention. Reality is far from that ideal, but in most data centers, much more could be done in this area. Typically, only a few elements of IT governance are automated. We discuss governance in greater depth in Chapter 10.

Managing the Facility

The second layer in Figure 11-2 (refer to "Optimizing the Data Center," earlier in this chapter) depicts service management processes that concern the data center facility as a whole. This layer contains three primary processes: asset optimization, facility management, and disaster recovery.

Asset optimization

This service management process is served by the asset management application that we discuss as part of the service management infrastructure in Chapter 9. There, we focus on the need to capture accurate information about the assets that are deployed in the corporate IT network or possibly used on a cloud basis, which is part of what the application is intended to do. (We discuss clouds in Chapter 15.)

The application's role is much bigger than just data gathering, however. Such an application also should be able to record and monitor the whole life cycle of any element of hardware or software, or combination of the two. In some organizations, this information is made freely available to at least some IT users so that they appreciate the costs and are able to calculate the return on investment associated with specific projects.

Ultimately, the IT asset management application (depending on what it does and how it's used) can contribute information to many important activities, including the creation and implementation of specific policies or service levels. It can also help with the assessment of risk and with meeting specific performance objectives of the business.

All these activities can be counted as asset optimization activities of a kind. Multiple dimensions are involved in the use of any given asset; hence, other KPIs may be associated with asset optimization.

Traditionally, optimizing physical assets, such as in manufacturing environments, has been viewed as being entirely separate from optimizing digital assets. That situation is changing under the umbrella of service management. As IT begins to align more closely with business processes, the management of IT assets and business assets is likely to merge into a single activity. Data centers are becoming part of a larger ecosystem of service management; therefore, they need to integrate with sensor-based systems and process automation systems.

Facility management

Facility management is the activity of caring for and feeding the physical data center. It embraces everything from disaster protection (such as sprinkler systems and fire-retardant materials) to environmental controls (such as air conditioning and power management) to physical security.

Speaking of physical security, an increasingly important innovation is for organizations to tie their physical security (such as doors with passcodes) to a systems-based security system. If an employee is fired, for example, automated systems typically are in place to remove that employee's passwords and prevent him from accessing systems. That same alert should trigger a change in the passcodes for the data center, as well as access to other physical environments that may need protection.

Significant economies of scale are involved in running a data center. When a data center runs out of space, the organization incurs a sudden, large, and unwelcome change in costs caused by the need to acquire a new, appropriately built facility to house more servers, which will need communications connections, power supply, air conditioning, security, and so on.

Data center space is the most expensive type of office space, so optimizing its use is important.

A good KPI for keeping an eye on facility costs and efficiency is average workload per square foot of floor space. There are many ways of defining workload in terms of hardware resources. Maintaining a KPI of this sort is useful for many purposes, particularly when you examine the cost of using a hosting provider or cloud computing (see Chapter 15).

Disaster recovery

The ability to recover from disasters is vitally important, and most organizations have rules of governance that dictate the provision of specific disaster-recovery capabilities. If a disaster befalls the corporate data center, which has no disaster-recovery capability, the company is unlikely to survive. Therefore, having business continuity procedures is a necessity. From a service management perspective, disaster recovery is a combination of the process, corporate policies, and readiness to act when the data center fails.

Disaster recovery can be expensive, especially in very large data centers with thousands of servers. Full disaster recovery mandates having an identical data center somewhere, ready to go into action immediately, complete with staff, operating procedures, preloaded applications, and up-to-data data. For most organizations, however, this plan is neither affordable nor feasible. Consequently, disaster-recovery plans normally provide for recovering only critical systems.

Disaster recovery can be complex, because as systems change and are upgraded, the disaster-recovery systems need to stay in step. The advent of SOA, for example, has posed some awkward problems for disaster-recovery systems. SOA-based systems typically are composed of services that are reused in different situations. Therefore, IT has to know the dependencies of these services across the organization. A related nuance is that disaster-recovery systems are rarely tested and sometimes not tested at all until a disaster occurs.

Luckily, technology developments make it increasingly easy to provide disaster recovery through the use of either cloud services or dual sites, with each data center providing disaster recovery for the other. (For details on clouds and virtualization, take a look at Chapter 15.)

Like any other IT activity, disaster recovery involves optimization issues. A company needs to link its service-level agreements and its asset optimization activities with the need for disaster recovery. As with everything in the service management world, compromises are likely to occur in terms of the disaster-recovery service-level targets and the necessary systems.

Useful facility-management KPIs

Other KPIs are likely to be useful. You can use the concept of a unit workload measurement, for example, based on calculating how an average application will behave with a typical or average level of service. For many years, Bill Gates thought of the power of a PC in terms of the Basic language compiler he once wrote as a measurement unit. We suggest that you do the same thing, using a typical business application.

Here are some KPIs that are likely to be worth tracking:

✔ Power costs (by unit workload)

✔ Average number of operational staff members (by unit workload)

✔ Average number of support staff members (by unit workload)

✔ Average software support costs (by unit workload)

✔ Average hardware support costs (by unit workload)

✔ Average data storage costs (by unit workload)

✔ Average server use (in terms of memory and CPU use)

✔ Average workload per square foot of floor space based on facility costs and efficiency

Keeping KPIs like these makes it possible to roughly allocate IT costs back to specific departments in the organization.

A disaster-recovery plan should cover issues such as e-commerce processes that touch suppliers and customers; e-mail, which is often the lifeblood of business operations; online customer service systems; customer and employee support systems; various systems that support the corporate infra-structure, such as sales, finance, and human resources; and research and development. Depending on the company's resources and income sources, management may need to consider other factors in a disaster-recovery plan.

Managing Workloads

The third layer in Figure 11-2 (refer to "Optimizing the Data Center," earlier in this chapter) groups those processes that relate to managing workloads: from an IT perspective, managing the corporate IT resource. Being simplistic, we could say that you have applications that you need to run and resources to run them, so all you're really doing is managing those workloads.

A few decades ago, in the age of the mainframe, workload management really was like that. It boiled down to scheduling jobs (often by writing complex job-control instructions) and monitoring the use of the computer resource. In those days few, if any, workloads ran around the clock; thus, workload management was a scheduling activity involving queuing up jobs to run and setting priorities between jobs. Some workloads had dependencies — a specific outcome from one program might alter what needed to be done next — but all dependencies usually could be automated via the job-control language.

In today's far more complex world, many more applications need to run, and many more computers exist to run them. Some workloads are permanent, running all the time. In most companies, e-mail is such an application. Quite a few companies also have Web-facing applications with resource requirements that can fluctuate dramatically. Virtualization capabilities make it possible (to some degree) to create virtual resource spaces. On its own, the World Wide Web increased the number of dependencies among applications, and when Web Services standards were created, the number of dependencies increased. SOA makes matters worse.

So workload management involves recording known dependencies among programs and applications — an activity that provides useful information to the configuration management database (CMDB), as noted in Chapter 9 — and scheduling those workloads to run within the available resources. This process has to be flexible so that an application's resources can be boosted when transaction rates escalate and reduced as those rates decline. In addition, a host of support functions have to run in conjunction with the business applications, including monitoring software and (where appropriate) backup jobs.

Application self-service

Increasingly, companies are giving users, customers, and partners direct access to applications that support everything from ordering to status inquiries. Customers and users really like to be able to access these resources directly, but this type of direct interaction with applications complicates workload management because it makes predicting future workloads harder. Behind self-service applications, you need the usual well-orchestrated set of service management capabilities.

Application self-service normally is automatic — that is, whenever the user requests a service, the process happens instantaneously, without any human intervention. To realize this level of sophistication, application self-service has to have three processes happening behind the scenes:

- Identity management capability (to make sure that the user has the authority to access the application)

✔ A portal interface (to make it easier for the user to access specific components or data elements)

✔ Resource provisioning capability to execute the user request (to bring the requested application resource to the right place at the right time)

If you're familiar with SOA, you may recognize the focus on components — and indeed, self-service applications are similar. Most SOA implementations work precisely this way. In such cases, services usually are recorded and made available in some sort of service catalog, perhaps called a service registry/ repository in SOA. This catalog may simply be a list of what applications a user can choose to run, and it may be automated to the point where the user simply selects a capability that is immediately made available through a portal. The service catalog could work in many ways, perhaps providing pointers to applications. If an application were sitting in a portal interface, the catalog could direct a user to that application.

If you want to know a lot more about SOA, we recommend that you take a look at *Service Oriented Architecture For Dummies,* 2nd Edition (Wiley). We think it's a great book, even if we did write it!

One risk in implementing self-service capabilities is creating an unexpected level of demand for resources, especially when Web-based applications are readily available to customers. If a major weather situation causes customers to reschedule flights online, for example, airline systems may experience a major unanticipated spike in access. As more and more customers rely on self-service applications, the workload management environment supporting application self-service needs to be highly automatic and sophisticated.

IT process automation

Implementing an efficient flow of work among people working on the same service management activity and teams working on related activities is one of the primary keys to optimizing the efficiency of the data center. We refer to the design and implementation of these workflows as *IT process automation.*

It's difficult to understate the contribution that the intelligent use of IT process automation can make. We can draw a clear parallel between this process and integration infrastructure, which we discuss in Chapter 9. The function of integration infrastructure is integrating all the service management software applications so that they can share data effectively and don't suffer the inherent inefficiencies of silo applications. Similarly, the function of IT process automation is integrating service management activities and processes so that they work in concert.

Workload automation

From the automation perspective, IT process automation implements workflows that schedule the progress of activities, passing work and information from one person to another, but it also involves integrating those workflows with the underlying service management applications that are used in some of the tasks.

To continue our analogy of the data center as a factory (refer to "Seeing the Data Center As a Factory," earlier in this chapter), IT process automation is about designing the flow of activities so that they happen in a timely manner and keep the production line rolling, whether those activities involve fixing problems that have occurred or commissioning new hardware and software to add to the data center. The ideal situation would be not only to have all important service management processes occurring as automated workflows, but also to have a dashboard-based reporting system that depicts all the activities in progress in the data center, providing alerts if bottlenecks arise.

Such a reporting system could also report on the data center's important KPIs, providing a real-time picture of the health of the whole data center.

Managing Hardware

Figure 11-2 (refer to "Optimizing the Data Center," earlier in this chapter) groups the following service management processes on the hardware-environment level:

- ✔ Desktop and device management
- ✔ Hardware provisioning
- ✔ Virtualization
- ✔ Network management

Most of these processes are discussed in other chapters, so except for the last two, we intend only to introduce them in the following sections.

Desktop and device management

The desktop traditionally has been managed as almost a separate domain by a separate team outside the data center, with the primary KPI being the annual cost of ownership (including support costs). This situation has changed recently, for two reasons:

1. Desktop virtualization is feasible now.
2. Increasing need exists to manage mobile devices — whether those devices are laptops, smartphones, or mobile phones — as extensions of the corporate network.

Hardware provisioning and virtualization

Traditionally, hardware provisioning was relatively simple. Hardware was bought, commissioned, and implemented with the knowledge that it would be designated for a specific application for most, if not all, of its useful life. Eventually, it would be replaced.

With the advent of virtualization, the provisioning of hardware became more complex but also more economical. Today, virtualization and hardware provisioning are inextricably bound together.

Network management

Network management constitutes the set of activities involved in maintaining, administering, and provisioning resources on the corporate network. The corporate network itself may embrace multiple sites and involve communications that span the globe.

The main focus of network management activity is simply monitoring traffic and keeping the network flowing, ideally identifying network resource problems before they affect the service levels of applications. In most cases, the primary KPI is based on network performance, because any traffic problems on the network will affect multiple applications.

An asset discovery application (which we mention in Chapter 9 in connection with the CMDB), if it exists, normally is under the control of the network management team because the application is likely to provide important data. The network management team is likely to work closely with the IT security team because members of IT security will be the first responders to any security attacks that the organization suffers.

Recent innovations in network technology are likely to change some network management processes. Previously, for example, the capacity of a network was controlled by the capacity of the physical network. Now, major network technology vendors such as Cisco and Brocade provide highly sophisticated network switches that can be configured as networks in a box. These switches make it possible to virtualize a network to reduce or increase bandwidth. Suppose that you have an exceptionally large data warehouse that needs to be backed up. If you virtualize the network, this typically complicated process is simplified dramatically and made more efficient. In such a case, bandwidth can be increased to speed the task and decreased when the task is finished.

In the longer term, bandwidth is likely to be provisioned automatically, just as virtual servers are provisioned automatically.

Network management is about to become more complicated with the addition of unified communications. In the vast majority of companies, voice communications, videoconferencing, and other forms of collaboration are separate from IT systems. This situation is slowly changing, inevitably making network management more complex.

Voice over IP (VoIP) is in the ascendancy, and companies are gradually adopting it, although not always in highly integrated ways. Nevertheless, adoption of VoIP is a move in the direction of unified communications, in which e-mail, Short Message Service (SMS) messages, chat, voice communications, and all forms of collaboration become computer applications.

Managing Data Resources

Managing highly distributed data has emerged as one of the most important issues for service management. This task has always been complex because of the vast volume of data that has to be managed in most corporations. The problem is exacerbated when data is managed as a service across departments and across partners and suppliers.

We devote Chapter 14 to data management, so in the following list, we simply define the processes included in it, as illustrated in Figure 11-2 (refer to "Optimizing the Data Center," earlier in this chapter). What has started to happen is that data itself has been packaged so that it can be transported with greater ease.

- **Data services and data fabric:** These processes move data around the network to make it available to the applications or services that need it (particularly business intelligence services).
- **Storage management:** This process manages data storage in all its forms.

✔ **Database management:** This process involves the specific tasks of managing database configuration and performance for critical applications and services.

✔ **Backup and recovery:** This process involves the management of backup and recovery, including the management of all dependencies among systems.

The primary KPI that an organization will want to measure is the cost per gigabyte of data stored in various strata of availability, from online to archived and stored.

Managing the Software Environment

The processes that we group on the software-environment level in Figure 11-2 (refer to "Optimizing the Data Center," earlier in this chapter) are covered elsewhere in this book, so we only introduce them here:

✔ **Application management:** This process normally involves specific software designed to monitor the performance of a specific application. The activity could also be described as performance monitoring at the application level.

✔ **License management:** The management of software licenses can be considered to be a separate activity or part of asset or supplier management. Either way, the primary KPI is expressed in terms of cost per user per application.

✔ **Configuration change management:** In its broadest definition, software configuration management covers the management of software releases and the management of changes in all configurations, complete with an audit trail (who did what, when, and how).

✔ **IT security:** IT security is a particularly complex activity, made more complex by the fact that currently, no security platform can be implemented to provide comprehensive IT security across a network.

With respect to optimization, the ultimate goal in the corporate environment is to use software efficiently in terms of resource consumption while delivering agreed-on service levels at both the business level and the application level.

Managing the Service Management Infrastructure

The final layer in Figure 11-2 (refer to "Optimizing the Data Center," earlier in this chapter) is service management infrastructure, which we discuss in Chapter 9. In the following sections, we discuss two additional elements: cloud computing and service management reporting.

Cloud computing

A *cloud* is a computing model that makes IT resources such as servers, middleware, and applications available as a service to business organizations in a self-service manner. We include cloud computing in Figure 11-2 simply to indicate that workloads (or perhaps parts of workloads) may be run in the cloud. In fact, all the layers we discuss in this chapter could be augmented from the cloud. We expect that this approach will become necessary over time, as organizations migrate some of their applications to the cloud or sign up to run new applications from the cloud. For more information on cloud computing, take a look at Chapter 15.

Service management reporting

The idea of a central console initially grew out of the fact that in the old days of the mainframe, a single screen reported the progress of all workloads to the computer operator. That setup was impossible in large networks. Instead, several consoles aggregated information from various parts of the network. In addition, purpose-specific consoles reported on activities such as network management or IT security.

Integration infrastructure

A central service management reporting capability depends on a functional CMDB and integration infrastructure that support the gathering of data from multiple sources and the passing of messages among service management applications. Such a capability can exist even if only some level of integration is available.

When this capability exists, it's a relatively simple matter to add reporting software to provide specific reporting capabilities that give insight into the behavior of any part of the IT network. Such reporting capabilities can easily be added to the service catalog and made available to anyone in the data center as self-service options.

Understanding Strategy and Maturity

The general strategic direction for service management, as we describe in Chapter 6, is evolution from system management through service management. This journey enables organizations to move from managing systems to managing the application services that run on those systems. The next stage of the journey is moving business service management (BSM) where it enables IT to be aligned with the goals of the business. As its name implies, BSM manages business services.

In this chapter, we look at the data center from an optimization perspective, highlighting various KPIs and specific areas of data center activity where optimization can be applied. Most of the optimization we discuss is already carried out within the data center in some way, in many cases informally. The nature of these optimizations will not change dramatically as an organization moves closer toward the goal of direct BSM, but the optimizations will have to be reconciled with the optimization of business services. When BSM is reality, it governs all other optimizations. We discuss BSM in more detail in Chapter 17.

In Figure 6-2 in Chapter 6, we define maturity in terms of this progression:

> Fragmented services⇨Standardized services⇨Integrated services⇨ Optimized services

As with strategy, the optimizations we discuss in this chapter are likely to be carried out in some way irrespective of the level of maturity. All such optimization activity becomes more effective as the industry moves to integrated services. The holistic optimization of the data center is possible only when the service management environment is fully integrated.

Chapter 12

Service Support and the Service Desk

*O*ne of the fundamental truths of service management is that when you do it well, the service management team is like the wizard behind the curtain in the Land of Oz. If your e-mail never goes down and your technical equipment never fails, you don't go looking behind the curtain to understand what went wrong.

The reality is that services do fail and errors do occur — and when they do, customers (or service users) need to have their questions answered and problems resolved. Whatever a problem is, it must be reported, diagnosed, evaluated, and fixed quickly.

This chapter defines the service desk, describes its parts, and explains its activity.

Watching the Service Desk in Action . . . or Inaction

For many businesses, the service desk is the first port of call in customer interactions. Imagine the lost productivity and revenue, and the all-around chaos, that would occur if companies didn't have effective systems to manage IT service delivery and deal with problems effectively when they arose.

Suppose that you manage a retail store for Poor Service Corp. You have 10 point-of-sale (POS) systems, 15 phones on voice over Internet Protocol (VoIP), 5 customer kiosks, and several back-office PCs and servers. That's a lot of technology that needs to be monitored and managed. Unfortunately, the service desk at Poor Service Corp. is inconsistent and disorganized. Users have a service desk number to call if the POS system or phone doesn't work, but when a kiosk fails, they must call a different number for service, and if any of the PCs fails, they have yet another number to call. Nobody is quite sure why, but that's how things work.

Everyone in your store avoids calling the service desk whenever possible; the desk workers often get things wrong on the first try and take a very long time to resolved problems. This type of service desk is inconsistent. In fact, one person who works at the service desk is very knowledgeable, but if he isn't around to answer questions, the rest of the team members are a little lost.

Frustrated employees sometimes just move to a different POS unit when one fails, and by the time someone calls the service desk, an urgent problem has developed (such as the failure of several devices). Also, recent equipment failures indicate a lack of compliance with Payment Card Industry (PCI) — data security standards required by the credit card companies you work with.

Can you see where this scenario is heading? The service support process takes too long, costs too much, and leaves you providing poor service to your customers.

A properly functioning service desk does the following things consistently and quickly to meet customers' service expectations:

1. Diagnoses a problem correctly.

2. Evaluates how to fix the problem.

3. Fixes the problem.

The ultimate goal of service management is to anticipate problems so that they never materialize and service desk calls are minimized.

Seeing How a Service Desk Works

A service desk provides a single point of contact for IT users and customers to report any issues they may have with the IT service (or, in some cases, with IT's customer service).

Lest you think that a service desk is a one-size-fits-all proposition, let us assure you that service desks come in many forms and styles:

- ✔ The local service desk (departmental)
- ✔ The consolidated service desk
- ✔ The Software as a Service (SaaS) service desk model

The service desk may be merged with the customer service desk, for example. The first responder to any call may be a call-center worker who isn't employed directly by the company but who can respond to several common problems before passing the call on to the "real" service desk.

Goals of the service desk

A service desk has several objectives:

- ✔ **Problem resolution:** First and foremost, the desk is there to help resolve issues and problems as quickly as possible. This task involves not only recognizing and resolving relatively simple issues, but also prioritizing problems that may have a greater impact. An outage at an insurance-company system that provides quotes to potential customers, for example, may take higher priority than a problem with the part of the company intranet that provides information about the employee discount program. The service desk has to know what's mission-critical and what isn't.

- ✔ **Service restoration:** The service desk works to restore service as quickly as possible to maintain service-level agreements (SLAs). These SLAs often take some time to put in place and require a lot of negotiation. Therefore, a key service desk role is ensuring that the agreements are enforced to the best of the company's ability, which means tracking and monitoring service levels.

- ✔ **System support:** The service desk provides system support, which includes dealing with any incidents and problems, and may also involve dealing with issues such as change and configuration management.

Handling service desk issues takes a lot of activity. These processes include recording requests, assessing issues, routing requests, diagnosing and resolving the problem, tracking notification, and reporting, to name a few.

Functions of the service desk

Many service desks deal with issues beyond incident and problem reporting. What actually happens inside the service desk can be fairly sophisticated.

A fairly comprehensive service desk may offer the following set of functions:

- **Communication via multiple channels:** The desk supports a wide variety of communication styles, including phone, e-mail, online forms, and even mobile communications. This communication is a two-way street: People can use the channels to report issues, and IT can use the channels to notify customers about the status and resolution of issues.

- **Incident and problem management:** The desk supports the assessment, prioritization, resolution, notification, and reporting of small incidents or major problems. An *incident* becomes a *problem* when it happens more than a few times. Management includes recording, routing, and resolving an issue; notifying interested parties of the status of the issue; and reporting on the issue.

- **Change management:** The desk supports the management of change requests, including information about how various parts of a system interact. Often, a system change actually causes an incident or a problem.

- **Configuration management:** The desk supports mapping of IT resources to the business processes that they support. Configuration management often entails the use of a configuration management database, which we describe in the sidebar "Providing visibility into your company's infrastructure," later in this chapter.

- **Knowledge base:** If service desk personnel don't have the right information to do their jobs, the jobs won't get done efficiently or effectively. Knowledge management ensures that people get the information that they need to do their jobs correctly. Service management systems often link to a database that stores information about past incidents and how they were resolved; this database speeds incident resolution.

Managing Events

The event management process involves three simple steps:

- Event reporting
- Problem diagnosis
- Problem remediation and verification

We cover all these steps in detail in the following sections.

Reporting on events

The service desk receives notifications of events (issues) via phone, fax, e-mail, Web, and mobile devices or directly from automated monitoring capabilities deployed within IT systems. Then it attempts to solve the underlying problems, normally by passing details of the event to the support staff.

Figure 12-1 illustrates the processes by which incidents are reported to the service desk:

1. An incident report comes from either of two sources:
   - Customers or employees
   - Monitoring software that raises automatic reports

2. The service desk immediately resolves any well-known issues, such as lost passwords or PC hardware failures.

   The vast majority of issues reported don't involve sophisticated diagnosis.

3. The service desk generates a trouble ticket summarizing everything that is known about the event

4. The problem moves into the diagnosis phase.

Diagnosing problems

Most service desks began as help desks that dealt reactively with incidents and problems, which remain important support issues. Two core service desk features are worth looking at, however.

Think of an incident as being an event that somehow interrupts or negatively affects the quality of a service. Front-line support staff can handle many relatively simple events, such as a printer failure or an employee's inability to reset his password, but they also have to determine when an event is a serious incident and deal with it effectively.

Figure 12-2 illustrates how a service desk typically manages and diagnoses incidents.

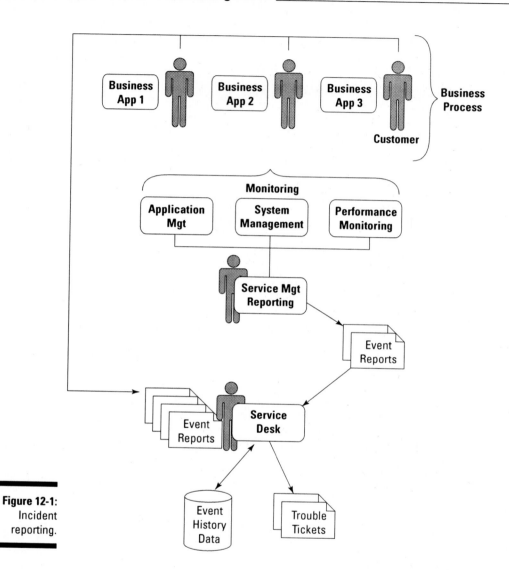

Figure 12-1:
Incident
reporting.

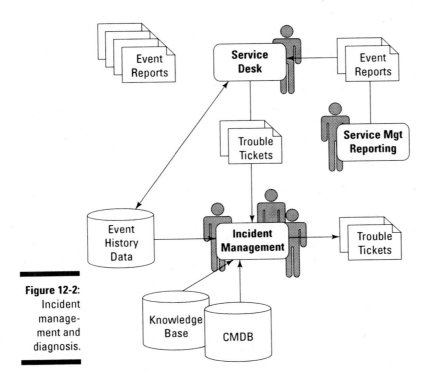

Figure 12-2:
Incident management and diagnosis.

Consider an example that shows how the process works. Janice works at the service desk of an electronics company. When she finishes her coffee and logs into her incident management system in the morning, she sees a helpful user interface tailored for her job. What does she see? Typically, this screen displays all the incidents she's dealing with, alerts about outages, some status reports, and a function that allows her to create a new incident report.

When the phone rings, Janice picks it up. Someone in the customer service department says that his printer isn't working. Janice must create a new incident trouble ticket. Because this kind of incident happens all the time, her service desk has templates for it. She asks the user his name, and she pulls up information about him and the printer to which he has access. The information about these particular assets is stored in the all-important configuration management database (CMDB) so that she can actually see the type of printer that isn't working. (See the nearby sidebar "Providing visibility into your company's infrastructure" for more information on CMDBs.)

Because the customer service department gets high priority at her company, Janice wants to deal with the problem right away. She asks the user what the error message is; then she pulls up her knowledge base and accesses possible solutions to this particular problem. Voilà — one of these solutions works, and she's done with that particular issue.

Next, she gets an e-mail from someone in sales who says that one of the company's product-ordering Web pages is degrading steadily. Janice creates a trouble ticket for this problem. The system automatically generates a severity code of 1 (meaning that the problem has to be dealt with immediately) and routes the ticket to Sarah, who's part of the Web site engineering team. Then Janice goes back to reading reports on other open incidents.

If multiple events of the same type occur, or if multiple events occur that appear to be related to the same underlying problem, in theory these events ought to fall into just one trouble ticket. In reality, however, the connection among events may be clear only to a subject-matter expert, so service desk staffers have to be aware of all open trouble tickets and their status.

Remediating and verifying problems

To continue the example from the preceding section, the trouble ticket goes to a specific support area where the problem is identified. After the problem has been fixed, its resolution is verified. Only at this point is the solution implemented.

Providing visibility into your company's infrastructure

A configuration management database (CMDB; see Chapter 9) contains information about all of a company's assets that make up the information system infrastructure. These assets are often referred to as *configuration items (CIs)*. These items may be servers, laptops, network elements, applications, and so on. In addition to this information, the CMDB may hold information about known errors, incidents, problems, changes, and release information. An important function of a CMDB is tracking changes in these items, because these changes can affect service.

The CMDB is an organization's information hub, holding all the relationships of system components. The idea of an information repository for information assets has been around for years, but with the growing importance of service management and the Information Technology Infrastructure Library (ITIL), it has gained more steam. (For details on ITIL, see Chapter 5.)

Remediation

Figure 12-3 illustrates various support areas that may get involved in the resolution of problems.

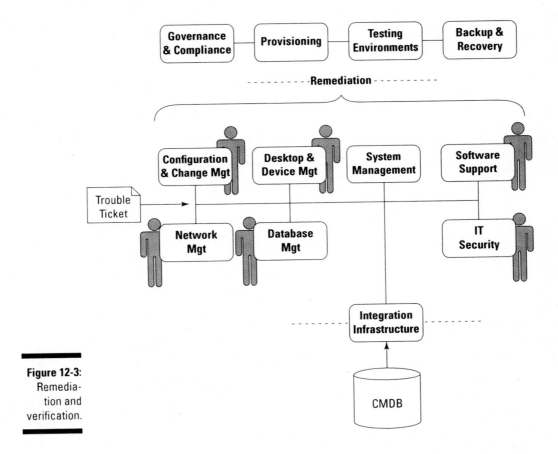

Figure 12-3:
Remedia-
tion and
verification.

Suppose that performance degradation has been reported in some application. The problem could stem from any of the following issues:

✔ **Configuration management:** Someone made an error while changing a configuration.

✔ **Change management:** An implemented software patch caused the problem.

✔ **Network:** The network gets overloaded when California wakes up.

- ✔ **Desktop or device:** Someone overloaded her PC, causing slow communications.
- ✔ **Database:** A database table needs to be optimized.
- ✔ **System management:** A server's processors failed.
- ✔ **IT security:** A denial-of-service attack is in progress.
- ✔ **Application:** A program has a bug.

The truth is that just about any area of service management can be involved in one way or another. Figure 12-3 indicates this possibility via the link from the CMDB to the integration infrastructure.

Suppose that Janice, on the service desk, passes a trouble ticket to Sarah, on the Web site engineering team. Sarah investigates the problem. She determines that the performance problem has to do with a server resource issue and that the server needs an upgrade (or that the Web site application needs a larger server). In the service management system, she notes the nature of the problem and the fact that this new server will be provisioned that day. She also updates the data on this problem and its solution in the knowledge base for future reference.

If someone in sales calls the service desk again, the desk will have a complete record of the whole event; it can report what the problem is and when it will be fixed.

TIP

Using the war-room technique

Occasionally, a problem comes up that stumps everyone. What's the cause? In this chapter's running example, the service desk employee knows who can best deal with the vast majority of problems, but she isn't sure exactly where a certain problem lies. Worse, the problem is a serious one that needs to be handled quickly because key service levels are being threatened.

Sometimes, performance problems are of that ilk. The problem may be in a database, in application software, in middleware, in the network, in server hardware — or in some combination of these elements. If the service desk simply passes the problem on to one of the teams that's responsible for one of these areas, that team may decide that the problem lies elsewhere and pass it back. The process can be repeated over and over, with the problem never being properly addressed.

The *war room* is designed to prevent such an outcome. It involves having members of all relevant support teams meet to form a short-lived group that resolves the problem collectively by analyzing it from every angle and determining a plan of action. Ideally, such a team can use the information-gathering capabilities of every team member.

Verification

The top of Figure 12-3 shows four processes involved in verification:

✔ Governance and compliance

✔ Provisioning

✔ Testing environments

✔ Backup and recovery

Sometimes, you know that a given action definitely solves a problem, as is often the case when hardware fails. The hardware is replaced, and the problem is solved immediately.

In the following circumstances, you must recover the application before implementing the solution:

✔ When the support engineer doesn't know for sure that a given solution will resolve the problem — and could make the problem worse

✔ When data has been corrupted

Suppose that you can't solve a problem the way you thought you could. First, make sure that the right people do the following things with any changes:

✔ Evaluate and authorize

✔ Record

✔ Test and validate

Standard processes are key in remediation and validation. If you don't have these processes in place, you'll never be able to keep track of anything. Also, the processes for remediation and verification are often defined as part of governance practice. (For more information on governance, refer to Chapter 10.) Make sure that you log everything you do to resolve a problem, including all attempts to solve it.

Tracking Service Key Performance Indicators

It's important that services, even relatively unimportant ones, have defined service levels. If you look at a service level another way, it's a key performance indicator (KPI).

Change and configuration management

Very often, application performance failures are caused by recent changes, either in programs or in software or hardware configurations. Changes affect service levels, sometimes positively and sometimes negatively, and a change in one part of a system can easily affect downstream parts of the system (or even other systems).

Statistics suggest that many performance problems and system failures stem from errors made when configurations are changed. Consequently, change and configuration management are moving under the purview of the service desk.

The change management process ensures that standard procedures are used to handle all changes to prevent negative effects on service quality. Configuration management provides a logical model of the infrastructure or a service by identifying, controlling, maintaining, and verifying the configuration items. The idea is to understand the relationships among all the services that are part of the enterprise. That way, if one service has a problem, you have a good idea of how the problem may affect another service.

A nurse may need access to patient records around the clock for example, so the system that supports records management and delivery needs to meet this criterion. On the other hand, a human resources system that lets employees see how much they've spent for out-of-pocket medical expenses may not be as critical, so a 24/7 service level would be unlikely.

Negotiating SLAs is often a dance between IT and the business. Some service levels are non-negotiable, such as the mission-critical one outlined in the preceding paragraph; others have more wiggle room. IT and the business must work together to establish these SLAs.

Typical SLAs include the following:

- Response times (possibly varying by transaction)
- Availability on any given day
- Overall uptime target
- Agreed-on response times and procedures in the event that a service goes down

Service-level metrics

When the agreements are in place, you must manage and track them. These service-level metrics or KPIs are stored in either of two places:

- ✔ The SLA management system
- ✔ The CMDB

Some service desk systems can link to the availability monitoring systems to confirm that mission-critical systems are identified and monitored as part of the SLA management process. This system helps IT prioritize issues and ensure that the right resources are allocated. Often, this monitoring can be done at the individual user level. The service-level management system can also link to the incident, problem, change, and configuration management systems to provide visibility into these functions. Typically, these systems also provide reports that outline certain SLA metrics for end users.

Service desk metrics

The KPIs for the service desk itself are expressed in terms of problem resolution. Ideally, incidents are classified according to type, and three specific times are recorded:

- ✔ **Time to identify problem:** In some circumstances, a problem may exist for a long time before it is reported, indicating that monitoring systems may need to be reviewed.
- ✔ **Time to diagnose:** This metric is the time between an event report and the identification of the cause of the problem.
- ✔ **Time to fix:** This metric is the time between diagnosis and system repair or resumption of service.

The analysis of the performance of the service desk and the support teams against these KPIs needs to be carried out intelligently. Culturally, it is important to encourage employees to report incidents and to continually improve the process of managing problems.

Also, comparing one month with another may not be comparing like with like. If everyone's using a new version of an operating system, for example, the number of incidents at the service desk may rise simply because of the operating-system change. Yet it may not be possible to revert to the older software (because it's no longer supported, for example).

Chapter 13

Desktop and Device Management

A long time ago, before laptop computers, personal digital assistants (PDAs), and cellphones, life on the desktop side was very peaceful. Customers all had terminals on their desktops that were more or less directly connected to a central computing resource. There was no user software to upgrade; there weren't many applications; user support wasn't too demanding. The only color that IT had to worry about was the pleasant green of the mainframe terminal.

But one day, a big, disruptive event occurred: The personal computer broke into the organization. Users were delighted with this sparkling new productivity tool, but they weren't particularly adept at taking care of it or even backing up the precious data that they created on it. Even when these wonderful devices were networked in local area networks, their management generally was the responsibility of each department and had little or nothing to do with IT.

The PC was enormously successful. Having delivered personal productivity applications, it displaced the mainframe's green screens and then became the platform for many client/server applications and networked applications such as e-mail and file sharing. At that point, the world of desktop management changed dramatically because it had to. The PC became the device through which most employees conducted business. The costs of local ad hoc support of PCs got out of hand, and companies had a clear financial reason to start managing desktops centrally.

With the passage of time, however, technology use grew, and companies had much more than just desktops to manage. Many users suddenly found a need for laptops so that they could work on the road. Workers began using handheld devices to measure and report on conditions on the factory floor. PDAs and cellphones soon had as much computer power as ancient mainframes. All these devices became part of the overall service management fabric.

In this chapter, we look at the importance of managing the desktop and the myriad devices that customers require to get their jobs done. We also look at management requirements and how desktop and device management fit into the overall service management environment.

Clients, Clients Everywhere . . .

Companies are at different stages of maturity when it comes to managing desktops and devices. At one end of the spectrum, client management is fragmented and reactive; organizations at the other end have automated client environment management to the point where PC applications are provisioned and patched automatically, and the PC environment is centrally controlled.

The flow in Figure 13-1 could apply to any company regardless of its current maturity; the chart shows the whole client management universe, including all processes that have to be carried out (whether they're automated or not). The processes discussed here are, in most cases, similar to the data center processes discussed in other chapters. The reality for most organizations is that the client environment is managed quite separately from the data center, with a separate support staff. For efficiency reasons and because the technology to enable it is improving fast, the management of the two domains will become more integrated in coming years.

Figure 13-1 shows client management consisting of a service's three fundamental elements:

- ✔ **People/organization:** The staff members in charge of the client management activities, including those implementing policy and troubleshooting. This group could include anyone from the person who stops by your desk to fix a PC when it goes wrong to employees in the data center monitoring the cost of computer assets.

- ✔ **Processes:** The organized activities involved in client management, including governance, assets, changes in security rules, and configuration changes.

- ✔ **Technology:** The supporting technology that helps manage client operations within the business. That technology could include patch management software, license management software, security software, and a host of other support applications.

Don't get suckered into thinking that you can improve client management simply by changing technology.

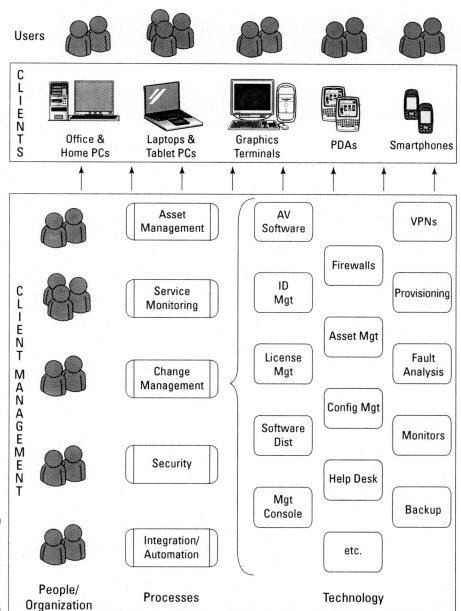

Figure 13-1:
Client management and the client domain.

Dividing Client Management into Five Process Areas

Look at the five process areas for successful client management illustrated in Figure 13-1 (in the preceding section):

- **Asset management:** No matter what the client environment is (cellphone, BlackBerry, laptop or desktop PC, Windows, or Mac), activities within that container need to be registered, monitored, and tracked based on both the hardware itself, the software that runs on the platform, and the use that is made of it by various groups of users.

- **Service monitoring:** Activities in this process area monitor what's happening at each client, as well as the tasks required to maintain the right level of service. The service desk provides coordination for monitoring.

- **Change management:** Activities in this process area involve managing and implementing all changes in applications and hardware. This area may include configuration management for applications that span the client and the data center, as well as license management.

- **Security:** Activities in this process area involve securing the whole client domain against external threats and authenticating which users can get into which facilities. Security may involve locking down administration capabilities and proactively managing the storage and backup of data files.

- **Integration/automation:** Activities in this process area aim to standardize all client management processes so that they work together to improve overall service, enhance overall governance, or reduce costs.

Each group of processes may be served by multiple software products and may be carried out by different groups in client management. All five process areas are carried out in some way in all organizations, with varying levels of sophistication. Most companies have some way to keep track of devices, for example; the tracking mechanism may be anything from a simple spreadsheet or an automated system that discovers all new devices as soon as they connect to the network.

As organizations mature, client management has to become business-driven rather than technology-driven. Consequently, a good way to begin improving client service management is to automate the technical management of the client so that it's largely invisible to users. Where you start depends on where you are, but taking all responsibility for PC administration, application provisioning, and IT security away from users is an intelligent goal.

The following sections cover the five process areas in detail.

Asset management

Desktop and device asset management helps you select, buy, use, and maintain desktop hardware and software. What must you do to manage desktops and mobile devices thoroughly? Here's a list of necessary activities:

✔ **Establish a detailed hardware asset register.** A *register* is a database that itemizes hardware assets and records all the details. It lets you analyze hardware assets (including peripherals) and provides a foundation for many user services, including provisioning and security. It also may be fed with information by asset discovery software.

✔ **Establish a software register.** A software register tracks all the software elements of devices. It complements the hardware register and offers a foundation for better automated provisioning of software.

✔ **Control software licenses.** Some users may be able to add new software to a desktop or mobile device, either because they have administrator capability or because some application self-service has been implemented. Controlling a glut of software is a difficult task. Watching software licenses reduces costs and efforts; it also eliminates the risk that the company will be running more versions of software than it has paid for.

✔ **Manage device costs.** By tracking device use, you can reduce redundancies, as well as maintain hardware more efficiently. Often, companies have devices that are no longer used but that still require time and effort to maintain.

Service monitoring

The client environment is one of the most vexing problems for IT management. Where client support is not well integrated with data center support, good reasons exist to establish an integrated support service. Then client monitoring goes beyond identifying a problem with a mobile or desktop device: The support service is driven by the data center's trouble-ticketing system, which tracks a problem to its resolution and quickly identifies situations in which the data center applications are the cause of the problem.

You can also support users by putting these components in place:

✔ **Automated client backup:** An automated backup system reduces the risk of data loss and speeds recovery times when failures occur. The sad truth is that most users simply don't have the discipline to manage their own backups, and a simple disk crash on a PC or laptop usually results in the loss of important data. (For more information about data loss and recovery time, see Chapter 14.)

- ✔ **Remote management and maintenance:** Because users may be spread around the country or the globe, service providers must be able to manage both client hardware and software remotely.

- ✔ **Client recovery:** Normally, this task involves restoring data from automated backups, but it also can involve reconfiguration or a software upgrade, depending on the problem diagnosis.

- ✔ **Root-cause analysis:** Many monitoring products place a software agent on the client device to capture the behavior of the hardware and software in real time. Simply knowing whether a failure is caused by hardware or software leads to faster recovery. The more information you can gather about CPU, memory, and application resource use, the easier it is to diagnose a problem.

- ✔ **Application monitoring:** Users are quick to blame IT when the performance of their applications is poor. Poor performance can have a multitude of causes, one of which is simply that the client device doesn't have enough power. Consequently, IT needs to be able to monitor client device performance based on actual application use. Application monitoring helps determine whether a performance problem can be resolved simply by a device upgrade.

- ✔ **Service-level maintenance:** Service levels should be applied both to hardware and applications running on client devices. Unless these service levels are defined accurately, they can't be monitored effectively. Because client management is an integral part of overall data center management, it can't be viewed in isolation. Service-level maintenance becomes even more important as organizations virtualize the client environments within the data center. (For more information on virtualization, see Chapter 15.)

Change management

Managing change means that you have to provide standardized processes for handling IT changes. Because the client device environment often lacks the centralized service management control that is typical in the data center, it can become the weak link in service management.

You should meet these key requirements for handling client-focused change management:

- ✔ **Hardware provisioning:** Rapid deployment of devices minimizes the time needed to support staff changes. New staff members have to be provisioned just as quickly as those leaving the organization.

- ✔ **Software distribution and upgrade:** Being able to distribute changed software to devices across the organization is mandatory in tight financial times. Many companies create a standard desktop client environment that facilitates distributing and changing software.

✔ **Patch management:** *Patches* are changes to software that are made to fix bugs rather than changes that upgrade software functionality. When well automated, patch management minimizes the impact of patch implementation while reducing the risk associated with the bugs that are being fixed. Many such fixes address IT security problems.

✔ **Configuration management:** This process lets your company automate the configuration settings in a desktop software environment, making it easier to manage the client environment. Specifically, it manages which applications are loaded and may include IT security settings that provide or deny administrative capabilities (see the following section).

Security

Ensuring the security of every user access device in a company can be tough. Even when IT sets up security, outside software can easily creep onto devices — particularly laptops and mobile devices, which are difficult to bolt down. Moreover, it's possible nowadays to run applications from a memory stick or thumb drive and to plug a variety of devices into USB ports.

Safeguard your access devices by using these approaches:

✔ **Secure access control:** This approach may involve just password control, or it may involve more sophisticated (token-based or biometric) authentication. Secure access control reduces security breaches.

✔ **Identity management:** Identity management defines the user in a global context for the whole corporate network. It makes it possible to link users directly to applications or even application functions. This approach delivers networkwide security, associating permissions with roles or with individual users.

✔ **Integrated threat management:** Normally, you have to counter a variety of security threats through several security products, both on the client and in the data center:

- Virtual private networks secure remote communications lines for using PCs from home or from remote offices.

- Intruder-detection systems monitor network traffic to identify intruders.

- White-listing products limit which programs are allowed to run.

✔ **Automated security policy:** Ultimately, with the right processes and technology, you can manage some aspects of IT security to some degree via policy. Some products manage logging activity so that the activities of all users throughout the network are logged, for example. Also, you can define policies within identity management software to designate who has the right to authorize access to particular services or applications.

Integration/automation

Integrating good client management into the overall service management framework can be complicated. Organizations are dealing with a variety of client environments, ranging from fully functional PCs to virtualized clients and wireless devices. To meet service levels, client management must be predicable and consistent.

Key ingredients in this approach include the following:

- **Standards:** Adopting client management standards precedes and prepares for all other integration work and enables greater flexibility over time. By *standards,* we mean standards in every layer of technology from hardware (standard PC models using standard components from the keyboard to networking cards) through communications and data access to client applications. The important point to understand is that when you deviate from any agreed-on standard, you risk increasing the number of points of failure and create potential integration problems. In recent years, most in-house software development has adopted Web Services standards, which has made it far easier to link applications both on clients and on servers.

- **Management by policy definition:** The ideal is to implement client management simply by defining policy directives in software and having them obeyed. Technically, reality is a long way from the ideal. It's possible, however, to enforce some rules directly in software (such as patch and configuration management software), and some software can be used to help automate compliance and governance. The better the implementation of service management capabilities becomes, the more feasible it is to move toward management by policy.

- **Governance and regulatory compliance:** Compliance often delivers side-effect benefits beyond simply being able to prove that IT operations are compliant when they're audited. One benefit may be that you can better meet internal audit requirements and, by analyzing some of the data gathered, gain deeper insight into the client domain. Specific benefits depend on your country and your industry.

   In many industry sectors nowadays, organizations have to abide by specific regulations, such as the Health Insurance Portability and Accountability Act (HIPAA) in the health care sector. Nearly all such regulations affect IT because they mandate a duty of care for customer data, and penalties are applied if these regulations are violated. Consequently, they're not optional. Luckily, however, many of these regulations are a boon because they mandate sensible IT practices, and companies rarely object to funding the necessary technology to meet compliance demands. (For more detailed information on compliance, see Chapter 10, which is devoted to this topic.)

Moving the Desktop into the Data Center

You can't do much to improve management of mobile devices (after you've integrated solid management processes, that is), but the same isn't true of managing desktop PCs. Most desktop expense lies in support: managing the PC population (software upgrades and the like) and fixing things when they go wrong.

In a typical enterprise situation, the annual support cost per PC is anywhere between three and five times the cost of the PC. Because PCs are outdated about every four years, the actual cost of ownership can be anywhere from 9 to 20 times the cost of the PC itself.

Although securing a good purchase price for PCs is important, keeping ownership costs under control is far more important. Keep costs low through effective automated desktop management processes. Bring the costs down even further by moving the desktop into the data center, so to speak.

Moving the desktop into the data center covers every possible means of replacing physical PCs with graphics terminals (also known as *thin clients;* see the nearby sidebar "Thin is in"). You can make these replacements in four ways, each of which is described in the following sections:

- ✔ Session-based computing
- ✔ Operating-system streaming
- ✔ True client virtualization
- ✔ PC blade

Thin is in

Thin client is another name for a graphics terminal. The name comes from the fact that such devices — although they're computers with CPUs, memory resources, keyboards, and mice — aren't PCs in the sense that they don't have disks or DVD drives. These devices also run an operating system, but the OS is used purely to emulate the user interface of a PC.

You could loosely describe every one of these techniques as being *client virtualization,* because in each technique, the PC is controlled from the data center (not from the desktop). In practice, however, only one of these techniques is based on true virtualization, which is the use of software to emulate a computing environment within another computer. Client virtualization involves emulating a whole PC in software on a data center server and displaying the user interface on a graphics terminal. Computers have become powerful enough to do this, and users are unlikely to be unable to detect the difference between client virtualization and a desktop PC.

All these arrangements simplify PC management considerably by making the following tasks easier:

- Enabling immediate setup of a new virtual PC if an actual PC fails
- Applying new patches
- Backing up data
- Dealing with viruses

It's a little early to put a figure on the benefits of moving the desktop into the data center, but anecdotal information suggests that this practice commonly reduces a PC's annual total cost of ownership by approximately 40 percent to 50 percent.

Session-based computing

In session-based computing, the user is really running a session on a server. The server is running a single instance of the Windows operating system with multiple sessions. Only the screen image is actually transmitted to the user, who may have a thin client or possibly an old PC. Products that provide this capability include Citrix MetaFrame and Microsoft Terminal Services.

Operating-system streaming

In this approach, the Windows OS software is passed to the client device — but only as much of the software that's needed at any point in time. Technically, this process is called *streaming.* Thus, the Windows OS and its applications are split between the client and the server. You can implement this approach by using PCs on the desktop (diskless PCs and laptops are options) or by using thin clients. Both Citrix and Hewlett-Packard provide this capability.

Real versus virtual desktops

It's easy to speak of PCs as though they're all the same, but they're not. In most organizations the 80–20 rule holds: At least 80 percent of PC users can get by with the current standard model, and the rest have specialized needs, such as dual screens or highly configured devices.

This approximate 80–20 split affects any initiative aimed at virtualizing the desktop, because you probably can't virtualize all PCs. Therefore, you end up with two client management processes: one for virtualized desktops and one for real desktops.

The truth is that some PC users (so-called *power users*) really do need a whole PC, even if that PC runs only one application (such as Adobe Photoshop) that requires as much processing power as you can provide. Such applications run unacceptably slowly in virtualized environments. Typically, IT developers also need high-end PCs to run their development environments.

True client virtualization

In true client virtualization, virtual PCs (complete emulations of a PC) are created on the server. The user has what appears on the server to be a complete PC, but in reality, the PC is virtual. Use the desktop with either a laptop or a thin client. VMware and Citrix both provide software that delivers this capability.

From a service management perspective, you should understand that desktop virtualization doesn't remove the need for management at the desktop. You still need to manage laptops and PCs that can't be virtualized, and that task may still place a heavy demand on support.

The PC blade

A *server blade* is a server computer contained entirely on a single computer board that can be slotted into a *blade cabinet* — a purpose-built computer cabinet with a built-in power supply.

In this arrangement, a whole PC is sitting on a server blade in the data center, which isn't shared in any way. Normally, the desktop is a thin client (refer to the sidebar "Thin is in," earlier in this chapter).

Meeting Service Expectations in Client Environments

Specific service levels are undoubtedly an investment choice. The relationship between extra investment and improved service levels is complex. It's far less expensive to raise desktop PC availability levels from 97 percent to 98 percent, for example, than to raise them from 98 to 99 percent. Sometimes, technology can make a difference for very little cost. A diskless PC, for example, provides far greater availability than one with a disk and may be suitable for some users. Such inexpensive service improvement possibilities are rare, however. Disks are mechanical devices that wear out and, hence, have a relatively high failure rate. You can reduce that failure rate by consolidating storage into arrays of disks that are designed so that the failure of any disk causes no problems.

You can't address end-to-end service-level issues in a simple manner; they're caused by factors such as technology incompatibilities, software patches, and user error. With the right attention to the client, however, you can improve the service level of the client device. To increase service levels across the board, you need to address each issue and problem area individually, and then monitor your success levels.

Desktops in the cloud

A desktop in the cloud has nothing to do with your local meterorologist. In effect, it refers to the approach in which you don't move the PCs into your data center; instead, you move them into the cloud. The process works this way:

1. You virtualize your desktops wherever they are, replacing them with thin clients.

2. The virtual PCs live *in the cloud,* which means that they live at one or more data centers run by service providers that house and support server hardware containing the virtual PCs.

All your software (administration/configuration and ownership) remains in your data center under your control, whether it's desktop or client/server applications. You deploy it into the cloud.

The business advantages are the same as in other forms of PC virtualization, reducing desktop ownership costs and support efforts in a big way. This approach also has some other advantages:

✔ The up-front investment is very low and transforms most client computing costs from fixed to variable (from capital to operating expense).

✔ It's quick to deploy and easy to scale incrementally.

✔ It's particularly attractive to companies that are running out of data center space.

User demand for improved service levels naturally increases over time because the amount of client-based (or usercentric) activity increases. Currently, voice over IP (VoIP) is fast becoming a desktop requirement, and video transmission may follow in its wake.

Following are two obvious key performance indicators for desktop management:

- ✔ **Annual support costs per device:** This metric is preferable to the total cost of ownership, which includes variable uncontrollable costs such as software licenses and device purchases.

- ✔ **Availability:** This metric, which measures uptime, gets close to 100 percent with virtualized desktops.

Chapter 14

Data Management in a Service Management World

*P*erhaps your company delivers an online service to small businesses. It helps businesses track and manage their consultant workload, managing contracts, project proposals, project management, expense reporting, and so on. This information comes from multiple customers in multiple locations. Your servers store all the data. You also provide your clients industry information that you pull from multiple sources and tailor to your clients. Service-level agreements (SLAs) make sure that your customers can access this service 24/7 and that if the system does goes down, you'll restore service in a certain amount of time.

One day, a customer reports that she can't access her account. Then more customers call your service desk with the same complaint. You realize that all the servers have shut down because of a flood. You can't restore the service and recover the data because you didn't back up the servers in the past month and didn't have a secondary storage facility. Heads roll. Lawsuits are filed. Your company goes out of business.

This extreme example shows the importance of data management in meeting customer expectations.

In this chapter, we look at the key issues that need to be part of your data management strategy: data delivery, storage, and retrieval; backup and restoration; disaster recovery; and archiving.

Creating a Data Management Strategy

Before you put together a data management strategy, you need to ask yourself these questions: "What is my valuable data? Is it finance, human resources, or sales data? What would the effect be if something happened to this data?" When you have a handle on how important various categories of data are, and on the risk associated with either not being able to access that data or losing that data, you can start to put together a data management strategy. The goal is to develop a strategy that minimizes the risk to your company. Ask yourself these basic questions when you're putting your strategy together:

- What categories should we put the data in?
- How quickly and how often do people need to access this data?
- What level of performance do we need to provide the people who use the data?
- Who needs to view, access, modify, and change the data?
- What continuity policies and procedures does the business have? In other words, what have we agreed to do in case of data loss or worse?
- What are the security requirements for accessing this data?
- How much capacity does the business need to store this data?
- What are the company's retention policies (that is, how long do we need to keep the data)? Do outside compliance and regulatory factors dictate those policies?
- How and where do we want to back up and restore data? Which data do we want to back up and restore?

All these questions need to be answered in the context of the value of the data and how much your company can afford to spend on the strategy, which can be a tricky balancing act. Having a clear idea of the importance of the data your company uses can help you set your priorities, however.

Reviewing the Elements of Data Management

Data management is a critical component of any service management strategy. It has five key elements:

- ✔ **Data delivery:** Companies are dealing with ever-increasing amounts of data of all types, from structured to unstructured (see the following section). You need a way to manage all this data. Your company, customers, and partners need this data, often in real time.

- ✔ **Data storage and retrieval:** Where are you going to store the data while customers are using it?

- ✔ **Data backup and restoration:** Along with storing the data, you have to make sure that you have a good backup and restoration plan. Then you have to make sure that the plan works!

- ✔ **Disaster recovery:** Disaster sometimes strikes. Make sure that you can get back any data you may have lost. Your company's survival may depend on it.

- ✔ **Data archiving:** Often, corporate compliance or other mandates require you to store data off-site for an extended period (such as years) before destroying it.

Before jumping into discussing these critical components, we want to make one thing clear: Data integrity and security are critical. Before you can safely do anything with your data, make sure that the data's integrity is beyond reproach and that data security measures are in place. Because the topic of security is so important, we devote Chapter 16 to it.

Typing your data for delivery

Data comes in many shapes and sizes, and a sound data management strategy needs to deal with any kind of data that a business collects and uses, which may include these types:

- ✔ **Structured data** generally has a defined length and format. Examples include numbers, dates, and groups of words and numbers called *strings* (for a customer's name, address, and so on). Structured data resides in a database or some other data store.

- ✔ **Unstructured data** doesn't follow a specified format. It includes anything from documents such as claims forms, expense reports, medical records, and presentations to Web content, images, and even streaming audio and video files.

- ✔ **Semistructured data**, such as an HTML document, has some structure but not enough to be called structured.

- ✔ **E-mail:** Don't forget about e-mail! Sometimes, companies have designated proprietary file systems just to store e-mail.

The reality is that a lot of data floats around your company and needs to flow to your customers, partners, and anyone else who needs it and has permission to use it. Way back when, in the dawn of computing, this wasn't the case. The monolithic mainframe typically contained data and software applications all in the same place. The software application called the data from the database. Data was often stored on a tape that was loaded onto the mainframe when needed.

As times changed, files began to be transported over computing networks — not much data at first, because moving a lot of data through a network wasn't affordable. Now companies can move massive amounts of data from one place to another over a network — in some companies, more than a terabyte of data a second!

In addition, some companies need to access data in real time, which might may be measured in milliseconds. A customer service representative who is speaking to a customer, for example, needs to get the customer's records to address an issue. Also, a large trading system may be handling massive amounts of information at lightning speed.

Getting at data: Storage and retrieval

Data access is critical to getting the job done. The examples in the preceding section illustrate just how critical it is to access the data that you've collected and created. But how are you going to store and get hold of this all-important information?

Here are some data storage systems that serve this purpose:

- ✔ **Database systems:** Databases usually store structured records. Various models are available; the most popular is the *relational database model (RDBM)*. In an RDBM, records are stored in tables (sometimes called *relations*). A customer table, for example, holds info such as customer ID, name, address, and age. Another table contains information about products purchased, as well as the customer ID. You can *query* (request information from) these two tables by using the customer ID as the common key.

✔ **In-memory databases:** Some companies need to deal with massive amounts of structured information, and they need to query that information on the fly. In-memory databases, which are becoming popular, usually store structured records in a cache (such as in the computer's CPU) for fast access.

✔ **Enterprise content management systems:** This type of system usually contains unstructured records: documents, faxes, call-center notes, claims, contracts, and other unstructured information that flows through the organization.

The system stores and provides online access to these documents, thereby preventing document loss and unauthorized content access, and making document retrieval much easier. Some content management systems classify documents according to type and provide a search capability for easier document retrieval.

A content management system can help an organization meet compliance guidelines. Certain content may be held in the system for a certain period — five years, for example — and then archived (or perhaps destroyed) in accordance with corporate compliance policies.

✔ **Web content-management systems:** This type of system stores all the elements of a Web page, including text and digital images. The role of this system is to simplify the publication of content to a Web site.

✔ **E-mail management systems:** Some companies keep their e-mails centrally stored in a proprietary e-mail management system.

✔ **File servers:** A *file server* is a networked computer that stores shared files.

Regardless of how you're storing the data, you must negotiate the following issues with the client:

✔ **Permission to access data:** In many companies, only people with specific job functions can access certain types of data. A marketing person probably wouldn't be able to access information related to manufacturing parts, for example.

✔ **Required performance levels:** You need to establish the service levels demanded of these systems with regard to returning data. A business may require 200-millisecond response time around the clock, for example.

✔ **Speed of data access and updating:** Data consumers may have certain expectations about how quickly they can access data and how timely the data is. All these considerations need to be negotiated between IT and the business. Sometimes, data subscribers can't get what they want because their requests are simply too expensive in terms of hardware costs.

✔ **Retention period:** A retention policy states how long the data should be held.

Securing data: Backup and recovery

Make sure that you have a backup copy of your data in case the data is lost, corrupted, or compromised.

Backup media

An enormous range of backup devices and media is available; each medium has pros and cons. For large-scale, enterprise backups, the following three types of media are most popular:

✔ **Tape:** Magnetic tape is one of the oldest backup media. Although it has a low cost per gigabyte of storage, the way that the data is written to the tape also means that retrieving data from the tape takes longer than with other media. If you need extremely fast response time from your backup, using tape would be difficult.

Also, magnetic tape isn't very durable. Think about your old VHS tapes, and you get the picture. We're not saying that you shouldn't use tape; many, many companies do because it's cheap and because buying more tape for more backups is easy. With tape, though, you need to take extra care that you have the right processes in place to protect the media from getting ripped.

Just so you don't think that magnetic tape is your only choice, you can try other options, such as WORM (Write Once, Read Many) tape, using a combination of hardware and software to make the data stored on the tape nonwritable and nonerasable.

✔ **Hard drive:** These drives are sometimes referred to as *fixed media.* Often, a hard drive is simply connected to the server or workstation for backup. Optionally, hard drives are put together in an array, sometimes referred to as a Redundant Array of Inexpensive Disks (RAID). You can configure a RAID setup in multiple ways that are beyond the scope of this book. Note, however, that retrieving data from a hard drive is easier than retrieving it from a tape.

✔ **Optical disc:** Some experts believe that optical discs are the most secure backup media because they're hardier than fixed media and tapes. (Think about DVDs and CDs.) You burn your data directly onto the disc. Accessing information stored on an optical disc takes longer than acessing data on a hard drive, however.

When deciding what kind of backup media to use, consider capacity (how much data can be stored per unit), cost per gigabyte of storage, durability, portability, and regulatory compliance.

Alternatively, you can back up data at a backup service (and store backup data on the network). Backup services have become increasingly popular. The services are convenient, and you don't have to buy or maintain any hardware or software yourself. But you need to do your homework to make sure that these services meet your needs in terms of scheduling backups, recovering information, ease of use, reliability, and so on.

Elements of a backup strategy

Not all data is created equal. Consider the following questions when devising a backup strategy:

✔ What is the company's critical data? How often do we need to back it up? Does the company have the right physical security in place to protect this media?

✔ Do we have the right priorities in terms of data backup? In other words, have we considered whether we need to have a different backup plan for more critical data or for data that falls under various compliance regulations?

✔ What should the backup data do?

✔ Do we need to send the backup off-site for secure storage?

✔ How often do we need to retrieve the data, and how quickly can we retrieve it?

✔ Does the staff need training to use this media?

✔ Can we get the data back to our applications in the amount of time specified in the SLA?

✔ Have we tested the backup plan to make sure that it works?

Backup can be expensive. You don't necessarily want to back up *every* piece of data every day and quickly fill your media. Sometimes, it makes sense to back up only what has changed. Determine what is optimal for your company based on service-level expectations.

Preparing for the worst: Disaster management

Bad things happen to good companies, so every company needs a disaster-recovery plan, which outlines what happens in case all (or part) of your system becomes unusable. The plan is a formal document that details the business-continuity effects of a disaster as well as the who, what, where, and when of addressing a disaster head-on, such as how long the company can afford for the system to be down and how the business will be affected.

Different companies have different strategies. Some have a complete facility ready to go if disaster strikes. Others prepare a *cold* facility, which has the equipment (such as computers) but isn't yet up and running. Still other companies simply back up their data and applications online — a method that takes more time.

Critical elements of a disaster-recovery plan include the following:

✔ **Application inventory:** Know what applications you're running and all the data you're using. If you don't have this information, how can you plan to restore what's necessary in priority order?

✔ **Risk analysis and business-impact analysis:** Any worthwhile plan includes a thorough analysis of how downtime will affect critical systems and data. Make sure that you also analyze any regulatory or compliance mandates, including which systems you must return first. This analysis involves determining both the effects and the magnitude of those effects. If your call-center customer information is destroyed, for example, you need to determine the effect of this loss and the potential magnitude of its effect on your business.

Risk analysis and business-impact analysis are disciplines in their own right. Standards bodies such the Information Technology Infrastructure Library (ITIL) reference various portals to help companies determine risk and impact and to develop business-continuity plans. For details on ITIL, see Chapter 5; for more information on ITIL and continuity management, check out www.itil-itsm-world.com/itil-8.htm.

✔ **Disaster-recovery teams:** The plan may involve people from across the organization, including employees from IT (hardware, software, communications, security, and facilities) and customer-facing staff members. Some team members are responsible for getting the hardware up and running when disaster strikes. Some are responsible for getting data back online. Some are responsible for communication — informing your customers, partners, and others about the situation and its status. Training may be an important part of the plan, so that everyone knows his or her role and exactly what to do in case of disaster.

✔ **Operating procedures:** You should establish what each person needs to do to get data up and running again.

✔ **Testing and maintenance:** Test the plan before you need it, and test it again on an ongoing basis to make sure that it still works.

Does your company already have well-articulated plans for data storage, retrieval, backup, and disaster management? If so, you probably feel that you're in good shape, and we hope that you are — but even well-thought-out backup and recovery plans are worth very little if you have low-quality data. Place a high priority on ensuring the accuracy and trustworthiness of data at the outset of any data management plan.

Storing data long-term: Archiving

Archiving is the process of loading data into long-term storage before you consider destroying it. We're talking about both digital data and paper documents here. Many companies still have to contend with archiving their paper-based documents.

You need to archive your data for several reasons:

✔ **Compliance:** Government bodies have various regulations about how long a company needs to store certain types of information. In the United States, for example, publicly traded companies must comply with the Sarbanes-Oxley Act of 2002, which stipulates that electronic data must be kept for three to seven years.

✔ **Offloading of records:** To lower the cost of storage, you may want to move your data from more expensive, highly reliable devices that can deliver data quickly to less expensive yet still reliable devices that allow you to get to the data if you need to.

✔ **E-discovery:** Sometimes, you need to locate specific information that you need in a court case or a legal dispute.

✔ **Peace of mind:** Although you may not think that you need all your data, you'll be glad that you can find it when you need it.

Keeping inactive data on your active servers or workstations usually isn't cost-effective. Many companies transition this data to another system that may be less expensive to maintain. If you do the same thing, make sure that you don't introduce errors into the process when you move the data. Also make sure that the new system can handle the load.

Some companies outsource archiving to a third party that specializes in storing data until the time comes to destroy it. Some of these organizations can index the data so that you can get to it if necessary.

Chapter 15

Virtualizing the Computing Environment

In This Chapter

▶ Seeing how virtualization evolved

▶ Knowing how virtualization works

▶ Dealing with management issues

▶ Moving virtualization to the cloud

*W*hy are we putting virtualization and cloud computing together in a discussion of service management?

Virtualization (using computer resources to imitate other computer resources or even whole computers) is one of the technical foundations of *cloud computing* (providing computing services via the Internet). We think that these two concepts are important to the data center and its destiny.

In this chapter, we present an overview of virtualization: what it means and how it is structured. We follow that discussion by explaining cloud computing. We also look at how the combination of virtualization and cloud computing is transforming the way services are managed.

Understanding Virtualization

Many companies have adopted virtualization as a way to gain efficiency and manageability in their data center environments. Virtualization has become a pragmatic way for organizations to shrink their server farms.

Essentially, virtualization decouples the software from the hardware. *Decoupling* means that software is put in a separate container so that it's isolated from operating systems.

Virtualization comes in many forms, because one resource is *emulating* (imitating) another resource. Here are some examples:

- **Virtual memory:** PCs have *virtual memory,* which is an area of the disk that's used as though it were memory. In essence, the computer more efficiently manages virtual memory; it simply puts information that won't be used for a while on disk, freeing memory space. Although disks are very slow in comparison with memory, the user may never notice the difference, especially if the system does a good job of managing virtual memory. The substitution works surprisingly well.

- **Software:** Companies have built software that can emulate a whole computer. That way, one computer can work as though it were actually 20 computers. If you have 1,000 computers and can reduce the number to 50, the gain is very significant. This reduction results in less money spent not only on computers, but also on power, air conditioning, maintenance, and floor space.

In a world in which almost everything is a service, virtualization is a fundamental mechanism for delivering services. Indeed, virtualization provides a platform for optimizing complex IT resources in a *scalable* manner (in a way that can grow efficiently), which is ideal for delivering services.

We can summarize the nature of virtualization with three terms:

- **Partitioning:** In virtualization, many applications and operating systems (OSes) are supported within a single physical system by *partitioning* (separating) the available resources.

- **Isolation:** Each virtual machine is isolated from its host physical system and other virtualized machines. One virtual-instance crash doesn't affect the other virtual machines. Data isn't shared between one virtual container and another.

- **Encapsulation:** A virtual machine can be represented (and even stored) as a single file, so you can identify it easily based on the service it provides. In essence, the encapsulation process could be a business service. This encapsulated virtual machine can be presented to an application as a complete entity. Therefore, encapsulation can protect each application so that it doesn't interfere with another application.

A short history of virtualization

IBM introduced virtualization in the early 1960s to enable users to run more than one operating system on a mainframe. Mainframe virtualization became less relevant to computing needs in the 1980s and 1990s. Indeed, in the 1990s, companies stopped worrying about the efficiency of the computer platform because computers were getting so powerful.

For more than a decade, IT organizations expanded the capabilities of their data centers by adding more and more servers. Servers had become so cheap that each time a new application was added, it was easier to buy a new server than to try to share resources with other applications. Eventually, organizations realized that the chore of maintaining, upgrading, and managing a large and growing number of servers was getting out of hand. The number of support-staff employees required to operate the data center was climbing swiftly, so the manpower cost of maintaining the data center (as a percentage of the total cost) was rising. At the same time, other costs were growing in an unpredicted manner, particularly the costs of electricity (to power the computers), air conditioning (to cool them), and floor space.

Scheduling a revolution

One of the main problems was that the servers that people had been happily adding to their networks were running horribly inefficiently. In the days of the mainframe, great efforts were made to use 100 percent of the computer's CPU and memory resources. Even under normal circumstances, it was possible to achieve better than 95 percent utilization. On the cheap servers that IT departments had been deploying, however, CPU efficiency was often 6 percent or less — sometimes as low as 2 percent. Memory and disk input/output (I/O) usage were similarly low.

This situation seems almost insane until you realize that applications simply don't require a great deal of resources, and with the servers that were being delivered by the time the year 2000 rolled around, you didn't put more than one application on a server. Why? Because the operating systems that everyone bought — Windows and Linux, mostly — didn't include any capability to schedule the use of resources effectively between competing applications. In a competitive hardware market, vendors began increasing the power of servers at an affordable price. Most of these servers had more power than typical applications needed. The same inefficiencies of Windows and Linux didn't address the efficiency problem, however. If an organization decided to stay with older but lower-powered hardware, it couldn't find people to maintain those aging platforms.

So if you had an application that only ever needed 5 percent of a current CPU, what were you going to do other than provide it with its own server? Some companies actually used old PCs for some applications of this kind, maintaining the PCs themselves, but there's a limit to the amount of old equipment that you can reuse.

The solution to this squandering of resources was adding scheduling capability to computers, which is precisely what one IT vendor, VMware, introduced. Adding scheduling began to change the dynamics of computer optimization and set the stage for the modern virtualization revolution. The mainframe is dead; long live the mainframe!

Using a hypervisor in virtualization

If you've read about virtualization, you've bumped into the term *hypervisor.* You may have found this word to be a little scary. (We did when we first read it.) The concept isn't technically complicated, however.

A *hypervisor* is an operating system, but more like the kind that runs on main-frames than like Windows, for example. You need one if you're going to create a virtual machine. One twist: *The hypervisor can load an OS as though that OS were simply an application.* In fact, the hypervisor can load many operating systems that way.

You should understand the nature of the hypervisor. It's designed like a mainframe OS because it schedules the amount of access that these guest OSes have to the CPU; to memory; to disk I/O; and, in fact, to any other I/O mechanisms. You can set up the hypervisor to split the physical computer's resources. Resources can be split 50–50 or 80–20 between two guest OSes, for example.

The beauty of this arrangement is that the hypervisor does all the heavy lift-ing. The guest OS doesn't have any idea that it's running in a virtual partition; it thinks that it has a computer all to itself.

Hypervisors come in several types:

✔ **Native hypervisors,** which sit directly on the hardware platform

✔ **Embedded hypervisors,** which are integrated into a processor on a separate chip

✔ **Hosted hypervisors,** which run as a distinct software layer above both the hardware and the OS

Abstracting hardware assets

One of the benefits of virtualization is the way that it abstracts hardware assets, in essence allowing a single piece of hardware to be used for multiple tasks.

The following list summarizes hardware abstraction and its management:

✔ **File system virtualization:** Virtual machines can access different file sys-tems and storage resources via a common interface.

✔ **Virtual symmetric multiprocessing:** A single virtual machine can use multiple physical processors simultaneously and thus pretend to be a server cluster. It also can emulate a fairly large grid of physical servers.

✔ **Virtual high availability support:** If a virtual machine fails, that virtual machine needs to restart on another server automatically.

✔ **Distributed resource scheduler:** You could think of the scheduler as being the super-hypervisor that manages all the other hypervisors. This mechanism assigns and balances computing capability dynamically across a collection of hardware resources that support the virtual machines. Therefore, a process can be moved to a different resource when it becomes available.

✔ **Virtual infrastructure client console:** This console provides an interface that allows administrators to connect remotely to virtual center management servers or to an individual hypervisor so that the server and the hypervisor can be managed manually.

Managing Virtualization

To manage virtualization, you must keep track of where everything is, what everything has to accomplish, and for what purpose. You must also do the following things:

✔ Know and understand the relationships among all elements of the network.

✔ Be able to change things dynamically when elements within this universe change.

✔ Keep the placement of virtual resources in step with all the other information held in the configuration management database (CMDB). Given that few organizations have anything approaching a comprehensive CMDB, that's asking for a lot. In fact, the CMDB needs to know how all service management capabilities are integrated. (For more information on the CMDB, see Chapter 9.)

Foundational issues

Managing a virtual environment involves some foundational issues that determine how well the components function as a system. These issues include how licenses are managed, how workloads are controlled, and how the network itself is managed. The reality is that IT sits between the network's static virtualization and the dream of full automation. We discuss some foundational issues in the following sections.

License management

Many license agreements tie license fees to physical servers rather than virtual servers. Resolve these licenses before using the associated software in a virtual environment. The constraints of such licenses may become an obstacle to efficiency.

Service levels

Measuring, managing, and maintaining service levels can become more complicated simply because the environment itself is more complex.

Network management

The real target of network management becomes the virtual network, which may be harder to manage than the physical network.

Workload administration

Set policies to determine how new resources can be provisioned, and under what circumstances. Before a new resource can be introduced, it needs to be approved by management. Also, the administrator has to be sure that the right security policies are included.

Capacity planning

Although it's convenient to think that all servers deliver roughly the same capacity, they don't. With virtualization, you have more control of hardware purchases and can plan network resources accordingly.

IT process workflow

In virtualization, the workflow among different support groups in the data center changes; adjust procedures gradually.

Abstraction layer

Managing virtualization requires an *abstraction layer* that hides and manages things between the physical storage subsystems. The virtualization software needs to be able to present the whole storage resource to the virtualized environment as a unified, sharable resource. That process can be more difficult than it sounds. All the administrative functions that you'd need in a physical data center have to be deployed in a virtualized environment, for example. Following are some of the most important considerations:

- You have to factor in backup, recovery, and disaster recovery. Virtualized storage can be used to reinforce or replace existing backup and recovery capabilities. It can also create *mirrored systems* (duplicates of all system components) and, thus, might participate in disaster-recovery plans.

- You can back up whole virtual machines or collections of virtual machines in any given state as disk files. This technique is particularly useful in a virtualized environment after you change applications or complete configurations. You must test — and, therefore, simulate — this configuration before putting it in a production environment.

- You must manage the service levels of the applications running in a virtualized environment. The actual information delay from disk varies for data held locally, data held on a storage area network (SAN), and data held on network access storage (NAS), and the delay differences may matter. Test different storage options against service levels.

  For more information on SANs, see *Storage Area Networks For Dummies,* 2nd Edition, by Christopher Poelker and Alex Nikitin (Wiley Publishing, Inc.).

- In the long run, establish capacity planning to support the likely growth of the resource requirement for any application (or virtual machine).

Provisioning software

Provisioning software enables the manual adjustment of the virtualized environment. Using provisioning software, you can create new virtual machines and modify existing ones to add or reduce resources. This type of provisioning is essential to managing workloads and to moving applications and services from one physical environment to another.

Provisioning software enables management to prioritize actions based on a company's key performance indicators. It enables the following:

- Migration of running virtual machines from one physical server to another

- Automatic restart of a failed virtual machine on a separate physical server

- Clustering of virtual machines across different physical servers

Managing data center resources is hard under any circumstance — and even harder when those resources are running in virtual partitions. These managed resources need to provide the right level of performance, accountability, and predictability to users, suppliers, and customers. Virtualization must be managed carefully.

Virtualizing storage

Increasingly, organizations also need to virtualize storage. This trend currently works in favor of NASes rather than SANs, because a NAS is less expensive and more flexible than a SAN.

Because the virtualized environment has at least the same requirements as the traditional data center in terms of the actual amount of data stored, managing virtualized storage becomes very important.

In addition to application data, virtual machine images need to be stored. When virtual machines aren't in use, they're stored as disk files that can be instantiated at a moment's notice. Consequently, you need a way to store virtual-machine images centrally.

Hardware provisioning

Before virtualization, hardware provisioning was simply a matter of commissioning new hardware and configuring it to run new applications or possibly repurposing hardware to run some new application.

Virtualization makes this process a little simpler in one way: You don't have to link the setup of new hardware to the instantiation of a new application. Now you can add a server to the pool and enable it to run virtual machines. Thereafter, those virtual machines are ready as they're needed. When you add a new application, you simply configure it to run on a virtual machine.

Provisioning is now the act of allocating a virtual machine to a specific server from a central console. Be aware of a catch, however: You can run into trouble if you go too far. You may decide to virtualize entire sets of applications and virtualize the servers that those applications are running on, for example. Although you may get some optimization, you also create too many silos that are too hard to manage. (For more information on silos, see the nearby sidebar "Static versus dynamic virtualization.") You may have optimized your environment so much that you have no room to accommodate peak loads.

Static versus dynamic virtualization

Virtualization actually is even more complicated. There are two types of virtualization: static and dynamic. Static virtualization is difficult, but the dynamic type is even more so.

In *static virtualization,* application silos become virtualized application silos. (A *silo* is an isolated piece of software and hardware that doesn't have the ability to interact with other components; it's a world unto itself.) You use virtualization to reduce the number of servers, but the virtualization is done via a fixed pattern that ensures that applications always have sufficient resources to manage peak workloads. This arrangement makes life relatively simple because that virtual machine will stay on the same server. Static virtualization is significantly more efficient than no virtualization, but it doesn't make optimal use of server resources.

If you want to optimize your environment, you need to be able to allocate server resources dynamically, based on changing needs within the business. *Dynamic virtualization* is complex, however. It's so complex that the market currently doesn't offer products that can implement it effectively. But those products will be available in time, because the virtualization cat is out of the bag.

Why is dynamic virtualization inevitable? The workloads in the data center are dynamic, especially considering that Internet applications change their transaction rates wildly over time. As the key performance requirements of the environment change, the virtual environment must change to meet those needs. In the long run, envision a world in which the whole network is treated as though it were a single resource space that can be shared dynamically based on changing workloads.

The hypervisor (refer to "Using a hypervisor in virtualization," earlier in this chapter) lets a physical server run many virtual machines at the same time. In a sense, one server does the work of maybe ten. That arrangement is a neat one, but you may not be able to shift those kinds of workloads without consequences. A server running 20 virtual machines, for example, may still have the same network connection with the same traffic limitation, which could act as a bottleneck. Alternatively, if all those applications use local disks, many of them may need to use a SAN or NAS — and that requirement may have performance implications.

Security issues

Using virtual machines complicates IT security in a big way. Virtualization changes the definition of what a server is, so security is no longer trying to protect a physical server or collection of servers that an application runs on. Instead, it's protecting virtual machines or collections of virtual machines. Because most data centers support only static virtualization, it isn't yet well understood what will happen during dynamic virtualization. Definite issues have been identified, however, and we address several of them in the following sections.

Network monitoring

Current network defenses are based on physical networks. In the virtualized environment, the network is no longer physical; its configuration can actually change dynamically, which makes network monitoring difficult. To fix this problem, you must have software products that can monitor virtual networks and, ultimately, dynamic virtual networks.

Hypervisors

Just as an OS attack is possible, a hacker can take control of a hypervisor. If the hacker gains control of the hypervisor, he gains control of everything that it controls; therefore, he could do a lot of damage. (For more details, see "Using a hypervisor in virtualization," earlier in this chapter.)

Configuration and change management

The simple act of changing configurations or patching the software on virtual machines becomes much more complex if the software involved is locked away in virtual images, because in the virtual world, you no longer have a fixed static address to update the configuration.

Perimeter security

Providing perimeter security such as firewalls in a virtual environment is a little more complicated than in a normal network, because some virtual servers are outside a firewall.

This problem may not be too hard to solve, because you can isolate the virtual resource spaces. This approach places a constraint on how provisioning is carried out, however.

Taking Virtualization into the Cloud

Virtualization, as a technique for achieving efficiency in the data center and on the desktop, is here to stay. As we indicate earlier in this chapter, virtualization is rapidly becoming a requirement for managing a data center from a service-delivery perspective. Despite the economies that virtualization provides, however, companies are seeking even better economies when they're available.

In particular, companies have increasing interest in cloud computing (see the following section), prompted by the assumption that cloud-computing providers may achieve more effective economies of scale than can be achieved in the data center. In some contexts, this assumption is correct.

If you like, you can think of cloud computing as being the next stage of development for virtualization. The problem for the data center is that workloads are very mixed; the data center needs to execute internal transactional systems, Web transactional systems, messaging systems such as e-mail and chat, business intelligence systems, document management systems, workflow systems, and so on. With cloud computing, you can pick your spot and focus on getting efficiency from a predictable workload.

From this somewhat manual approach, you can move to industrial virtualization by making it a repeatable platform. This move requires forethought, however. What would such a platform need?

For this use of resources to be effective, you must implement a full-service management platform so that resources are safe from all forms of risk. As in traditional systems, the virtualized environment must be protected:

- ✔ The virtualized services offered must be secure.

- ✔ The virtualized services must be backed up and recovered as though they're physical systems.

- ✔ These resources need to have workload management, workflow, provisioning, and load balancing at the foundation to support the required type of customer experience.

Without this level of oversight, virtualization won't deliver the cost savings that it promises.

Defining cloud computing

Based on this background, we define *cloud computing* as a computing model that makes IT resources such as servers, storage, middleware, and business applications available as a service to business organizations in a self-service manner. Although all these terms are important, the important one is *self-service*.

In a self-service model, organizations look at their IT infrastructure not as a collection of technologies needed for a specific project, but as a *single resource space*. The difference between the cloud and the traditional data center is that the cloud is inherently flexible. To work in the real world, the cloud needs three things:

✔ **Virtualization:** The resources that will be available in a self-service model no longer have the same kinds of constraints that they face in the corporate environment.

✔ **Automation:** Automation means that the service is supported by an underlying platform that allows resources to be changed, moved, and managed without human intervention.

✔ **Standardization:** Standardization is also key. Standardized processes and interfaces are required behind the scenes. Interoperability is an essential ingredient of the cloud environment.

When you bring these elements together, you have something very powerful.

What type of cloud services will customers subscribe to? All the services that we describe as the foundation of virtualization (refer to "Understanding Virtualization," earlier in this chapter) are the same ones that you'd make available as part of the cloud. You want to be able to access CPU cycles, storage, networks, and applications, for example, or you may want to augment the physical environment with additional CPU cycles during a peak load. Alternatively, you may want to replace an entire data center with a virtualized data center that's based on a virtualized environment managed by a third-party company.

Cloud computing is in its very early stages. In fact, in many situations customers aren't even aware that they're using a cloud. Anyone who uses Google's Gmail service, for example, is leveraging a cloud, because Google's own search environment runs within its own cloud. In other situations, large corporations are experimenting with cloud computing as a potential way to transfer data center operations to a more flexible model.

Another example is Amazon.com, which sells access to CPU cycles and storage as a service of its cloud infrastructure. A customer may decide to use Amazon's cloud to test a brand-new application before purchasing it, because renting is easier than owning.

In cloud environments, customers add CPU cycles or storage as their needs grow. They're protected from the details, but this protection doesn't happen by magic. The provider has to do a lot of work behind the scenes to manage this highly dynamic environment.

Using the cloud as utility computing

For decades, thinkers have talked about the day when we would move to utility computing as a normal model of managing computing resources.

Computing power would be no different from electricity. When you need some extra light in a room, for example, you turn on the light switch, and the electric utility allocates more power to your house. You don't have an electrical grid in your home, and you don't have to acquire tools to tune the way that power is allocated to different rooms of your home. Like electrical power, computing power would be a highly managed utility.

Obviously, we're far from that scenario right now. The typical enterprise is filled with truly heterogeneous data centers, assorted servers, desktops, mobile devices, storage, networks, applications, and vast arrays of management infrastructures and tools. In fact, you may have been told that about 85 percent of these computing resources are underused.

In addition, at least 70 percent of the budget spent on IT keeps the current systems operational rather than focusing on customer service. The advent of cloud computing is changing all that. Organizations need to reduce risk; reduce costs; and improve overall service to their customers, suppliers, and partners. Most of all, they need to focus on the service levels of the primary transactions that define the business.

IT organizations that decide to proceed with business as usual are putting their companies at risk. Also, because most IT budgets aren't growing, meeting customer expectations and performance goals without violating the budget is imperative. In truth, the biggest problem that IT organizations have isn't just running data centers and the associated software, but managing the environment so that it meets the required level of service.

Veiling virtualization technology from the end user

Any vendor that wants to provide cloud services to its customers has a lot to live up to. All the virtualization technology that supports these requirements is hidden from the customer. Although the customer may expect to run a wide variety of software services on the cloud, she may have little, if any, input into the underlying services.

Cloud customers see only the interface to the resources. In this self-service mode, they have the freedom to expand and contract their services at will. Vendors providing cloud services have to provide a sophisticated service-level agreement (SLA) layer between the business and the IT organization. The vendors have a responsibility to provide management services, including a service desk to handle problems and real-time visibility of usage metrics and expenditures. For two reasons, it's the vendor's responsibility to provide a completely reliable level of customer service:

- ✔ The customer has the freedom to move to another vendor's cloud if he isn't satisfied with the level of service.

- ✔ Customers are using the cloud as a substitute for a data center; therefore, the cloud provider has a responsibility to both internal and external customers.

Overseeing and managing a cloud environment are complicated jobs. The provider of the cloud service must have all the management capabilities that are used in any virtualized environment. In addition, the provider must be able to monitor current use and anticipate how it may change. Therefore, the cloud environment needs to be able to provide new resources to a customer in real time. Also, a high level of management must be built into the platform. Much of that management needs to be *autonomic* — self-managing and self-correcting.

Any sophisticated customer leveraging a cloud will want an SLA with the cloud provider. That customer also needs a mechanism to ensure that service levels are being met (via a full set of service management capabilities).

Chapter 16

IT Security and Service Management

Security is a fundamental requirement if you're implementing true service management. You may think that someone else in your organization is responsible for security. Think again. Don't leave security to an independent department somewhere in the bowels of IT. This chapter shows you how, overall, security has to be baked into service management.

Unless you're fresh out of college, you know that before 1995, IT security wasn't a significant problem, so very little money was spent on it. By 2004, organizations around the world were spending more than $20 billion on IT security, and that figure is expected to rise to $79 billion by the end of 2010. What happened?

Our guess is that you already know what happened. The Internet happened, letting computers connect remotely to hundreds of millions of other computers and giving lots of bad guys ample opportunity to launch a new career. The bad guys got better at breaking into IT networks, so the cost of stopping them escalated.

IT security is a very awkward area of service management for three reasons:

- ✔ Almost all applications are built without any consideration for security.
- ✔ IT security delivers very few benefits beyond reducing the risk of security breaches.
- ✔ Measuring the success of any IT security investment is very difficult.

Before describing any IT security products or processes, we expand on these points.

Understanding the Universe of Security Risks

When software developers design a system, they don't incorporate security features that might keep that system and its data more secure.

Historically, developers didn't need to add security features, because computer operating systems had a built-in security perimeter based on login identity and *permissions* (rules specifying what programs users could run and what data files users could access). With the advent of networks, however, an operating system could be artificially extended to work across a network.

PCs had no security at all initially, but a password-and-permissions system was added for networkwide security based on login. In IT security circles, this system is called *perimeter security* because it establishes a secure perimeter around the network, the applications it runs, and the data stored within. Many of the security products that organizations deploy, such as firewalls and *virtual private networks* (VPNs, which are encrypted communication lines), are also perimeter-security products. They improve the security of the perimeter, which is a bit like plugging holes in the castle walls.

Currently, the IT industry faces a problem: Security approaches (including perimeter security) are becoming less effective. To understand why, you must know how security threats arise.

Inside and outside threats

About 70 percent of security breaches are caused by insiders (or by people getting help from insiders). This statistic is based on surveys of organizations that suffer breaches, but the truth is that no one is sure exactly what the figure is. Insiders rarely get caught, and proving insider involvement usually is impossible when a security attack comes from a computer outside the organization.

Nevertheless, the possibility that insiders will open a door for hackers or mount an inside attack makes it clear that perimeter security on its own will never be enough.

The outside threat is best described this way:

- ✔ Hackers can be very talented engineers. They use specially designed, very sophisticated software tools to gain access and subvert systems.

- ✔ Hackers can have networks of thousands of compromised PCs under their control. Such networks, called *botnets,* are extremely powerful.

- ✔ Hackers may have channels through which they can sell an organization's data. A whole economic ecosystem has been built around the sale of stolen data.

- ✔ Some hackers have financial channels through which they can extort money with impunity.

- ✔ Hackers are guns for hire and may be hired by your competitors to perform industrial sabotage.

In summary, both inside and outside threats are real and may be formidable. How do you protect against them?

Types of attacks on IT assets

The type of protection you need depends on what you're trying to prevent. Here's a list of bad things that can happen:

- ✔ **Denial-of-service (DOS) attack:** Drowning some external connection service (such as a Web server) in an avalanche of traffic, thereby preventing the service from working. Normally, the aim is to extort money ("We'll stop when you pay us") or to damage the service out of sheer delinquency.

- ✔ **Resource theft:** Stealing computer equipment, particularly laptops.

- ✔ **Firewall breach:** Breaking through a firewall to access servers on the corporate network directly. Not all firewalls work perfectly, and those that do can be misconfigured.

✔ **Virus infection:** Implanting a virus on some computer in the network to open a back door into the network. Many such viruses can be planted in many ways.

✔ **Software mischief:** Using password-cracking software or known security weaknesses in some software (any kind accessed via the Internet) to gain access to the network.

✔ **Social engineering:** Persuading an inside user to reveal his password.

Hackers sometimes call users, pretending to be the service desk, and trick them into revealing their passwords.

✔ **Data theft:** Stealing any data that commands commercial value, such as financial details on customers, commercial secrets, or financial results.

✔ **Data destruction:** Destroying or corrupting data in an attack.

✔ **Resource hijacking:** Taking control of some of an organization's computers to run malevolent software, such as a program that sends out spam.

✔ **Fraud:** Interfering with legitimate business applications to perpetrate a fraud, such as causing money to be sent to fraudulent accounts or redirecting ordered goods to temporary pickup addresses.

You can't block all attacks — and when we say that, we mean it. If you analyze the last four items in the preceding list, you quickly see that no simple solution can address these threats. A hacker can mount a successful attack in many ways, and unless you have an unlimited security budget, you can't block all those efforts completely.

You *can* reduce the risk of a successful attack, however. Here are a few methods:

✔ **Anti-DOS technology:** Neutralize DOS attacks (which are purely external threats) by investing in appropriate technology. You can use different products — both software and hardware based — depending on the kind of attack you're trying to protect against.

✔ **Physical and personal security:** Guard against resource theft by adding physical security in the office and employing personal vigilance outside the office.

✔ **Firewall maintenance:** Apply the right level of diligence to maintaining firewalls.

✔ **White-listing:** Stop all viruses by *white-listing:* telling the system exactly what software is allowed to run on any server in the network and blocking all other software. (For more information, see "HIPS and NIPS," later in this chapter.)

✔ **Automatic login termination:** Reduce the risk of password cracking by automatically terminating login attempts after a certain number of tries.

Taking a Structured Approach to IT Security

Most people in IT security know that the best they can do for any computer network is significantly reduce the risk of a successful attack. Therefore, IT security is an exercise in risk management.

In general, follow these steps to reduce the risk of suffering security breaches:

1. **Authenticate all people accessing the network.**

2. **Frame all access permissions so that any given user has access only to the applications and data that she's been granted specific permission to access.**

3. **Authenticate all software running on any computer — and all changes to such software.**

   You need to automate and authenticate software patches and configuration changes, as well as manage security patches in a proactive way.

4. **Formalize the process of requesting permission to access data or applications.**

5. **Monitor all network activity, and log all unusual activity.**

   In most cases, you should deploy intruder-detection technology.

6. **Log all user activity and program activity, and analyze it for unexpected behavior.**

7. **Encrypt, up to the point of use, all valuable data that needs extra protection.**

8. **Regularly check the network for vulnerabilities in all software exposed to the Internet or external users in any way.**

If you read these steps and don't think that they'll be too hard to carry out, you don't know how complex it is to implement all these rules across a large network. Very few networks come close to this level of protection.

The reality of IT security is that *point solutions* usually are put in place to cover specific vulnerabilities. Thus, companies use firewalls to protect the internal network from the Internet, antivirus software to protect individual computers against known viruses, and VPNs to protect external connections coming into the network. Such security products reduce the risk of specific threats but don't constitute an integrated approach to IT security. Right now, that approach doesn't exist outside the realm of government organizations such as the National Security Agency, and it may not exist inside such organizations, either.

But some important products can make a significant contribution to building an integrated IT security platform. They come in three categories:

- ✔ Identity management
- ✔ Detection and forensics
- ✔ Data encryption

We discuss these products separately in the following sections.

Implementing Identity Management

We discuss identity management systems in conjunction with the configuration management database in Chapter 18, focusing on the way systems capture data for use by other service management applications. The role of an identity management system is much wider, of course.

Identity management's primary goal is managing personal identity information so that access to computer resources, applications, data, and services is controlled properly. Identity management is the one area of IT security that offers genuine benefits beyond reducing the risk of security breaches.

Benefits of identity management

The benefits of identity management come in three flavors:

- ✔ **Improved security:** Such security improvements clearly have some financial value by virtue of the security breaches they prevent, but attaching a meaningful figure to that value is difficult.

- ✔ **Directly reduced costs:** Direct cost reductions come from the following benefits:

  - • **Improved user productivity:** Productivity improvement results from simplification of the sign-on interface (see "Single sign-on," later in this chapter) and the ability to get access rights changed quickly. Productivity is likely to improve further where you provide user self-service.

- **Improved customer and partner service:** This benefit is the same as the simplified procedures described in the preceding paragraph, but delivered to partners and customers.

- **Reduced help desk costs:** Reductions in help desk costs usually contribute significantly to overall cost reduction, mostly because IT doesn't have to field so many calls about forgotten passwords.

- **Reduced IT costs:** Identity management enables automatic *provisioning* — providing or revoking users' access rights to systems and applications. Provisioning happens whether you automate it or not. When provisioning is manual, normally it's carried out by members of the IT operational staff or departmental staff. Considerable time and cost savings are possible when you automate the process (see "Provisioning," later in this chapter).

✔ **Compliance:** If your company must meet IT security compliance, identity management will inevitably help in that area.

Aspects of identity management

In this section, we cover the various aspects of an identity management program.

Data collation and management

Identity data generally is scattered around systems. Establish a common database or directory as a first step in gaining control of this information. This step involves inputting data and gathering data from various user directories.

Integration

An identity management system must integrate effectively with other applications to exchange identity information. In particular, it must have a direct interface to the human resources system — the place where new joiners and leavers are first recorded. It also must have a direct interface with supply-chain systems (if partners and suppliers are to use corporate systems) and customer databases (if customers require access to some systems), although customer identity management normally is handled by a separate component of an identity management system.

Stronger authentication

When you require authentication stronger than passwords, the identity management system must work with products that provide that authentication, such as biometric systems (fingerprints, handprints, iris verification, and the like) and identity token systems.

Provisioning

When you link all systems that use identity information, you can automate provisioning. If this process is automated, a single status change (of an employee or anyone else with access rights) can be defined in the identity management system and sent across all affected systems from that point.

Implementing a new application or changes in department business processes may affect the access requirements of individual users or user roles. Provisioning cuts across departments, possibly involving human resources, IT, and other departments.

When the process is automated, errors in providing users a broader level of access than necessary occur far less frequently or not at all. Providing broad levels of access happens frequently in manual provisioning, because it's easier to specify broad access than to specify a much more detailed granular level of access. Additionally, an automated process never fails to revoke former employees' access to the network.

When provisioning is complex, perhaps requiring approvals by several people in different departments, it requires a workflow arrangement. Ideally, you base the provisioning process on user self-service backed by a well-thought-out approval process.

Single sign-on

Single sign-on means providing all users an interface that validates identity as soon as a user signs on anywhere; this interface requires the user to enter a single password. Thereafter, all systems should know the user and her permissions.

Some single-sign-on products don't provide the full gamut of identity management capabilities, but all identity management products deliver single-sign-on capability.

Rather than being assigned to individuals, permissions are often assigned to roles (accounts clerk, sales assistant, programmer, and so on). Therefore, single sign-on also means capturing information about the administration hierarchy. Single sign-on naturally goes with portal technology, with the user having a Web-based initial interface that provides access to all applications that he's entitled to access. Thus, single sign-on may need to interface with a portal product.

Security administration

Another benefit that identity management confers is a reduction in security administration costs. Security administrators no longer have to make manual authorization grants in dozens of systems; the identity management system handles that workflow automatically. This arrangement is particularly useful for organizations that have distributed security administration over several locations, because it enables security administration to be centralized.

Data analysis

After you centralize all user data, you can generate useful reports on resource and application use or carry out security audits. If you're having problems with internal hacking, for example, you can check a log that lists every user's activity (see the following section). Also, if you have logging software for databases and files, you can monitor who did what to any item of data and when, including who looked at specific items of data. This audit capability is important for implementing data privacy and data protection compliance.

Employing Detection and Forensics

In this section, we discuss three specific groups of IT security products:

- ✔ Activity logs
- ✔ Host-based intrusion protection systems and network-based intrusion protection systems
- ✔ Data audit

No one — intruder or legitimate user — should be able to use those resources without leaving evidence. You want to detect any illegitimate activity as soon as it happens, but in many situations, you can separate the legitimate from the illegitimate. If you don't detect an attack while it's happening, at least you have a record of what took place.

Activity logs

Many logging capabilities are included in operating systems, applications, databases, and devices such as hardware firewalls and network monitors. A cost is associated with invoking logging capabilities: Turning on logging requires the system to write log records constantly, and it also involves creating a process to manage and archive such data until it's no longer needed.

Log files often provide some evidence of how fraud was perpetrated, however. Perpetrators of digital fraud often escape justice simply because the victim doesn't have sufficient evidence to prove what they did.

HIPS and NIPS

Host-based intrusion protection systems (HIPS) and *network-based intrusion protection systems (NIPS)* are the same thing: a collection of capabilities that make it difficult for intruders to penetrate a network. These systems can include the following elements:

- **System and log-file monitors:** This software looks for traces of hackers in log files. The monitors can watch login accounts, for example, and issue alerts when account permissions change — often an indication that something untoward is going on.

- **Network intrusion-detection systems (NIDS):** These security programs monitor the packets of information that travel through a computer network, looking for any telltale signs of hacker activity. The effectiveness of a NIDS depends on its capability to sort real dangers from harmless threats and legitimate activity. An ineffective NIDS raises too many false alarms and, thus, wastes time.

- **Digital deception software:** This software deliberately misleads anyone who's attempting to attack the IT network. It can range from the simple spoofing of various service names to setting up traps known as *honeypots* or *honeynets*. (For more information, see the nearby sidebar "Fooling attackers by spoofing.")

    Setting traps is unusual and can be expensive. It's normally done by government sites or by companies that suspect digital industrial espionage.

- **White-listing software:** This software inventories valid executable programs running on a computer and prevents any other executables from running. White-listing severely hampers hackers, because even if they get access to a computer, they can't upload their own software to run on it. White-listing software reports on any attempt to run unauthenticated software. It also stops virus software stone dead.

- **Unified threat management:** This central function takes information from all the preceding components and identifies threats by analyzing the combined information.

Fooling attackers by spoofing

As a technical IT term, *spoofing* means pretending to be something else. In a so-called *phishing* attack, a false Web site pretends to be a genuine one. A phishing Web site might pretend to be a bank's Web site, for example, and try to tempt users to reveal their financial details. It's possible to spoof e-mail addresses and, under some circumstances, Internet Protocol (IP) addresses, but mounting an attack this way is difficult because a computer responds directly to the real address rather than to the spoofed address.

When you use spoofing as a defense, your aim is to confuse attacking software. Hackers employ sniffing software to look for servers running specific versions of, say, Microsoft Windows. If you set the operating system to give out false information, which is easy enough to do, that false information confuses the attacking software into passing on by.

Honeypots work by spoofing, too. They pretend to be vulnerable servers and thereby trick attackers into revealing details on where they're attacking from.

Data audit

Although databases log who changed any data, they normally don't log who *read* any piece of data. But read data is easily stolen. Enthusiasm for filling this gap increased considerably after the Sarbanes-Oxley legislation was enacted in 2002, specifically demanding that financial data be secured from unauthorized eyes. Consequently, a series of software products that log who looks at what quickly came into existence. These products generally are referred to as *data audit* products.

Encrypting Data

The IT world has a whole set of encryption techniques that can be regarded as completely safe. Thus, you can easily encrypt data and ensure that only the intended recipient can decrypt it.

You *could* encrypt everything. You could encrypt data when you write it to disc, when you send it down a wire, when you send it through the air by radio, and so on. Encrypting everything in a comprehensive way considerably reduces your exposure to data theft. Hackers wouldn't be able to cover their tracks, because they'd never be able to decrypt the log files.

Encryption poses a performance penalty, however, so focus encryption on specific data that needs protection.

Think about how you use encryption. A fairly recent case of data theft included data that was encrypted until it was delivered to the application that needed to use it. At that point, the data was decrypted for use — and that's exactly where the hacker struck. The loss could have been prevented if the application itself had controlled the decryption on a record-by-record basis.

Because of the complexities it adds, encryption is used less frequently than perhaps it should be. The media have covered many cases of stolen laptops containing valuable data — including military secrets. Those thefts wouldn't have been problems if all the data on those laptops had been encrypted properly.

Creating an IT Security Strategy

This book isn't *IT Security For Dummies,* so we won't go into creating a comprehensive IT security strategy. We do want to provide some pointers, though:

- In most circumstances, IT security needs to be approached from a risk management perspective. If your organization has risk management specialists, involve them in IT security planning.

- IT security monitoring has no simple key performance indicators, but be aware of what similar organizations spend on IT security. That way, you have some awareness of the level of investment. Similarly, it makes sense to keep track of time lost due to any kind of attack — a useful measurement of cost that you may be able to reduce over time.

- You need identity management for many reasons, and identity management offers many benefits. Give priority to improving identity management if your current capability is poor.

- Try to create general awareness of IT security risks by educating and warning staff members about specific dangers (such as social engineering; refer to "Types of attacks on IT assets," earlier in this chapter).

- Regularly have external IT security consultants check your company's IT security policy and IT network.

- Determine specific IT security policies for change management and patch management, and make sure that policies are well understood by your service management staff.

> ✔ Stay abreast of news about IT security breaches in other companies and the causes of those breaches.

> ✔ Review backup and disaster-recovery systems in light of IT security. Apart from anything else, IT security breaches can require complete application recovery.

When a security breach occurs on a specific computer, the applications running on that computer will likely have to be stopped. Consequently, security breaches can be the direct causes of service interruptions and can contribute to lower service levels. Also, data theft resulting from a security breach could result in a real or perceived breach of customers' trust in your organization.

All you can do right now, however, is reduce the risk of such occurrences. Current IT security technology doesn't allow for integration and, hence, a higher level of maturity.

Chapter 17

Business Service Management

A lot of business, technological, and organizational issues have to come together in proper service management. How can service management goals provide important benefits to your company's business goals? The reality is that companies are at different stages of implementing a service management strategy. But no matter where your company is, the fundamental premise is that service management is an integral part of your business strategy.

Why did we wait until now to discuss business service management? You first have to understand the parts of service management and how they work together; otherwise, you don't know what tools are at your disposal. Here's a way to think about this issue: Imagine that you're in your car starting out on a trip. You don't have a map, and you haven't decided where you want to go. You stop at the nearest gas station and ask for directions. But how can you possibly figure out which path is best if you don't even know which town you're going to? As the old saying goes, if you don't know where you're headed, any road will do.

In this chapter, we explain what business service management is and how a business can benefit from it.

Defining Business Service Management

Business service management (BSM) is an approach to bringing together the following to provide management a holistic view of the business:

- ✔ Business process
- ✔ Business services
- ✔ IT service levels

BSM provides a way to measure and monitor the whole so that management can have comprehensive and meaningful oversight. How is this approach different from traditional approaches to managing IT? BSM is actually a superset. Yes, you have to manage your data center, the sensors in equipment on your factory floor, the desktops across your company . . . we could go on for quite a while. But would that be enough? Clearly, the answer is no. All these tasks focus on making sure that part of the infrastructure is operational. The reality is that BSM takes all these facets of managing the parts and brings them together based on the company's goals.

Based on this definition, it should be clear that BSM isn't a product.

Every corporation, no matter what its size, operates based on business goals and rules that dictate how the business functions. What is the company's mission? Who are the stakeholders? What do the shareholders expect? After an organization analyzes these factors, it measures progress toward these goals.

Using Key Performance Indicators in Risk Management

Key performance indicators (KPIs) are quantifiable measurements, agreed to by the business, that reflect the critical success factors of an organization. If a company wants to be the most profitable in its industry, its KPIs are based on measuring profit and the prices of good and services. Contrast this example with a company that sells a sophisticated product to a small set of demanding customers. Its KPIs are related to product quality and customer satisfaction.

The more technology a company uses to achieve its business goals, the more of its KPIs focus on its IT infrastructure. A company such as Google or Netflix, for example, has a lot of KPIs related to the effectiveness and efficiency of its data centers.

To be meaningful, KPIs have to be measurable. Suppose that your company has a KPI related to the response time for your online customer portal. The KPI states that a customer should expect a 1-second response time. Suddenly, response time has changed to 1.7 seconds. You must drill down to see how significant this problem may be. Is the response-time degradation related to an increase in business? What would the cost to the company be if this level of service continues? What would the cost to the company be if it wants to get back to the 1-second response time? Putting this situation in context with overall corporate goals, you may decide that 1.7 seconds is actually all right because the level of risk is minimal.

You always must understand KPIs in the context of risk to the business overall.

The 1.7-second response time may not affect the overall success of your business, but other factors may be much more important. If 1.7 percent of all customer data is lost or compromised, for example, would that be a problem for the business? After all, 1.7 percent is a small percentage of your overall customers. The company may not be willing to live with this level of risk, however.

KPIs are a balancing act between a company's goals and its ability to achieve business objectives while minimizing risk. When the corporate board sets the agenda for how the company will behave and achieve its goals, a framework exists for approaching BSM. These objectives can't be achieved in a vacuum.

Putting Service Levels in Context

When you have a good understanding of your company's goals (and the level of risk it's willing to take), start thinking about the service levels you need to manage.

This process is trickier than it may sound. Your boss may say, "I want the best service the industry can provide! Nothing is too good to support my customers!" Who wouldn't want the best? The level of business service that your company can provide its customers and stakeholders, however, is conditional. Unlike our scenario of perfection (see the sidebar "The best-case scenario: Perfection," at the end of the chapter), most companies are constrained by costs. Deciding on strategic goals and objectives puts a company in a position to understand what it needs to do to achieve the right service levels for the business.

Business service levels

A *business service level* is a line of defense that you must apply to the circumstances that make a difference in meeting the company's goals. How important is the quality of service to the way the business operates? What is the impact of good quality on the profitability of the company? A business service level can have these types of ramifications in delivering profitability to the company.

Consider whether you need 100 percent uptime from your e-mail system, for example. Employees want e-mail to work all the time, obviously, but if e-mail is down for 20 minutes a day, will it affect the bottom line, make the company less competitive in the market, or reduce customer satisfaction by 10 percent? Probably not. Why is this an issue? Promising 100 percent or even 99.999 percent uptime for the e-mail system requires a lot of technology: specialized software, redundant servers, and so on. In reality, though, occasional e-mail downtime won't necessarily bring the company to its knees.

When *will* something make a difference in the business? Consider security. Is it okay to have a data security breach for 20 minutes a day? No one would do business with a company that's likely to lose private information.

The bottom line is that a business service level is a business decision. IT shouldn't strive to achieve better service levels than it promised based on the goals of the company.

You may have noticed that we focus on the business service levels that relate to IT services — for good reason. Some business service levels relate to how personnel treat customers on the phone or to how a company ships supplies and the like. These tasks are people-related tasks that can affect the overall management of end-to-end processes. If a task that requires approval sits in a manager's inbox for a week, dire consequences may result, affecting the manager's overall ability to direct the business. In reality, however, little synergy exists between these types of business service levels and IT.

The real benefit to the business comes from business service levels in which IT and business meet. Companies that sell technology-based products are more likely to have more business service levels that are controlled and affected by technology. If you took a peek under the covers at companies like Google, Amazon.com, and Netflix, you'd see a great deal of attention paid to business service levels.

IT service levels

After the business decides what's important and how much service it needs to keep customers happy for the right price, IT takes control. Providing the right level of service is the responsibility of the IT department, along with data center management.

These service levels are codified in service-level agreements (SLAs) between the business and the IT organization. The content of this agreement is based on meeting a set of expectations between the provider of a service and the consumer of the service. If you promise to provide e-mail to employees, for example, a set of rules governs how this contract will be executed.

That contract might read something like this:

1. We promise that 99.999 percent of the time, e-mail will be operational. If it does fail, we promise to fix it within 20 minutes.

2. We will monitor the performance of the e-mail system on a continual basis and will report the results to the business on a monthly basis.

This agreement may look very simple and straightforward — and it is. The IT organization has the infrastructure to meet this requirement. It has the tools to monitor the system on an ongoing basis. The business has determined that if the e-mail system fails on occasion, people may be annoyed, but the company will not suffer financially.

Other service levels are more complicated and have more consequences for a business. Often, companies have relationships with third-party IT service providers. An insurance broker, for example, might use a third-party service provider to pay claims on policies. In this case, the parties would establish a much more detailed SLA than our example SLA for internal e-mail service. The SLA might require the service provider to promise 100 percent security of its customer data, and it might require the company to guarantee payment within 24 hours of receipt of an invoice.

What happens if IT is not able to meet the level of service required by the business? Clearly, it's the overall responsibility of the chief information officer to ensure that SLAs are met. Depending on the specific SLA, the CIO's job may be at risk if the SLAs are not achieved. In some situations, failure to achieve a specific SLA can cause the company to lose significant business.

The more demands the company places on the service provider, the higher the cost. The company purchasing the service needs to decide how much risk it's willing to accept. If the IT service provider doesn't meet the provisions of the SLA, it incurs penalties based on the severity of the problem. For this contract to work, both parties — the provider of the service and the consumer of the service — need to be able to monitor the results.

The best-case scenario: Perfection

What would your company look like if it achieved BSM perfection? Let us tell you the story of ABC Fashion Giant. ABC has been in business for more than 100 years, providing low-cost copies of high-fashion clothing to discount stores across North America and Europe. As soon as a celebrity wears an outfit, its designers copy, manufacture, and distribute the clothing to customers.

The company's KPIs (refer to "Using Key Performance Indicators in Risk Management," earlier in this chapter) are to provide its customers sufficient-quality garments that emulate the most popular designs. Speed and efficiency are the keys to the company's success. ABC has maximized its profits by producing the right fashions for the lowest cost. Because it also must get the products delivered to customers as quickly as possible, its distribution network must be highly optimized. The company needs to have excellent data about costs, quality, and results of past efforts. It depends on an efficient data center to collect information from its factories, its distributors of raw materials, its supply chain, and its customer management system. To support this effort, the company has a detailed business process design that's managed by a center of excellence made up of professionals from all areas of the business.

Our perfect company has its act together. It has established a well-designed business dashboard that includes all information about inventory levels, quality metrics, and customer satisfaction. These indicators are compared with those of previous years, as well as with competitors' results. The dashboard reflects the KPIs set by the board. It also keeps track of business rules, governance metrics, and data center functions.

ABC's data center was designed based on the strategy of the business. It has optimized performance based on the business. Therefore, systems that support product sales to distributors and large store chains have redundant servers and mirrored sites in other cities. Key data is updated in real time. The management software is sophisticated enough to anticipate when a problem is starting to affect performance and, therefore, can provide new services on demand. Nothing is left to chance.

The IT management team uses sophisticated project management, so all changes to the data center and business processes are handled through a project portfolio management system. In addition, all data about services that are managed within the data center is stored in a service catalog (see Chapter 10), which includes all the rules governing the use and maintenance of services, its security, and characteristics. The catalog maintains and updates the status of the relationship between the services and the KPIs agreed on by the business and IT.

The company also understands the importance of securing the data about its manufacturing processes as well as customer data. Security (see Chapter 16) is a companywide initiative. Therefore, ABC hired a chief security officer who implemented a well-integrated security platform that is monitored in real time.

ABC Fashion Giant is the envy of its industry. Even when a hurricane caused a three-day power outage, ABC kept its operations up and running.

Seeing Business Service Management As a Balancing Act

Successful BSM requires taking a holistic view of the business. You must measure and monitor everything as it relates to everything else. If you don't take this holistic approach, you'll be doing the business a disservice.

Everything in your organization is a service. A *service* is simply a way of delivering value to a customer or stakeholder by facilitating expected business results.

The nearby sidebar "The best-case scenario: Perfection" describes an ideal example of BSM. The truth of the matter, though, is that you won't find a perfect solution to the struggle between satisfying all the desires of the business for service and the financial constraints on the IT organization. Also, although you may recognize elements of your own company in the sidebar, you won't find any such thing as a perfect company. Most companies are at different stages in their journey.

For more information about what some companies are doing for real, check out Part V, which offers some great case studies.

Chapter 18

Planning the Evolution of the Data Center

*T*he data center is at the heart of the computing environment. Anyone working there knows that a data center is dynamic, changing and maturing as business requirements evolve and as technology emerges. This chapter helps you plan for changes in the data center.

Data center management has two aspects, both of which are critical for service management success:

- ✔ **Day-to-day management** includes operational and support issues such as configuration, release, and provisioning. (See Chapter 9 for more details.)

- ✔ **Long-term evolution** incorporates all the changes that companies need to support long-term strategic plans.

At the heart of these components is the requirement that *project portfolio management (PPM)* play a pivotal role in managing the evolution of the data center. PPM is a process intended to help your organization acquire and view information about its projects according to their importance. PPM focuses on important aspects of projects, including issues such as cost, value to company goals, and impact on resources. Management must understand the value of the *collection* of assets.

In the case of the data center, management must understand

- How the combined assets are managed
- How they benefit the business today
- How they must change to meet future requirements

In this chapter, we discuss the primary areas of data center planning. In doing so, we focus primarily on what can be thought of as evolutionary change. IT changes so rapidly that you have to plan not only for changes in business requirements, but also for future changes in the technology that you deploy.

Approaching Service Management the Google Way

Companies and IT departments are under a great deal of pressure to improve the efficiency of their data centers. The reason may well be related to the publicly acknowledged efficiency and effectiveness of Google. In a mere decade, Google has become a hugely profitable organization, running the largest computer network in the world with hundreds of thousands of servers. Its data centers (for it has quite a few) are the envy of many chief information officers. These centers are efficient in terms of hardware use, power use, software architecture, and even location.

Google serves as an excellent example of the IT side of service management because for Google, the whole customer experience *is* IT. Even with the company's vast resources, customer satisfaction comes down to a single overriding issue: speed. Therefore, response time is the driver of Google's success. We humans are so impatient that we won't tolerate even short delays; if response time stretches out beyond 140–200 milliseconds, we're likely to take our business elsewhere. That's how it is in the search business.

Over its short history, Google's search latency has gone down from a whole second (1,000 milliseconds) to 200 milliseconds. Also, the company put the complete search index to the whole Web in computer memory shared across 1,000 machines that divide the query work. Every time you send Google a query, 1,000 computers jump into action.

Corporate and IT Strategizing, and Data Center Planning

Before you decide that your data center strategy should mimic Google's, you need to understand the context of that company's strategy. Google's IT strategy is fairly simple, because about three quarters of the company's revenue comes from advertising associated with its search service. It isn't a stretch to state that dominance in search is the pillar of Google's corporate strategy. In fact, you could boil down its IT service management strategy to the ability to provide the fastest, most accurate search capability in the industry. In effect, Google IT service management focuses on a single Web page. Like any other company, Google also has to manage its own security, compliance, and people.

Many business leaders look at Google's efficiency and effectiveness and want their own data centers to be equally well managed. Most companies have many more aspects to their business, however — and, therefore, to their service management strategy. If your company is a bank, insurance company, hospital, manufacturing concern, or retailer, providing the best possible service can have many dimensions and can involve a wide variety of activities in a multitude of contexts. Therefore, your IT strategy can be very complex because it likely involves many different systems.

Figure 18-1 shows the activities involved in data center planning, with a focus on both the operational and the evolutionary. Chapters 8 and 9 discuss many operational issues; in this chapter, we focus on planning for the long term.

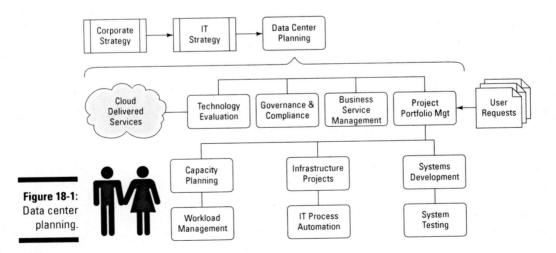

Figure 18-1: Data center planning.

The figure indicates the following:

- There is (or should be) a direct connection from corporate strategy through IT strategy to data center planning.
- The executive board determines corporate strategy and, ideally, explains it well enough so the whole company understands its goals.

As a consequence, IT strategy can be created with some sense, and the company's efforts and investments can be focused correctly. It's nice to imagine a world in which corporate strategy and IT strategy are defined in fine detail, well documented, and published, but we don't live in such a world. Nevertheless, efficiently run data centers exist because their goals have been set out and data center planning has been done in the light of those goals.

Change is the most important unifying theme of data center evolution. Because the data center is the manifestation of managing the services that define the business, you must make changes after a lot of thought. Therefore, planning is at the heart of data center evolution. When you look at the data center from a planning perspective, consider four areas of activities:

- Project portfolio management
- Technology evaluation
- Governance and compliance
- Business service management

We discuss these areas in detail in the following sections.

Project portfolio management

We devote most of this section to managing the data center by using a PPM approach. The biggest challenge facing IT is planning well and preparing for the unexpected.

When data center managers figure out how to finesse the planning, they can do two things: run an efficient operation and save money. But they don't have a wand that they can wave to achieve these goals, which require careful planning and the use of organizational skills.

We think that using a PPM approach goes a long way to meeting the goal of balancing IT with business needs (see Chapter 17). Good PPM helps you become proactive but isn't a project management system. Rather, it's a technique and set of best practices for planning and managing data center components.

Often, these best practices are built into PPM software. Examples of this software include CA Clarity PPM, Compuware Changepoint, Hewlett-Packard's HP PPM, Planview Enterprise PPM, and Serena Mariner.

Putting PPM in context

In some ways, PPM is the opposite of the old-fashioned fire-drill approach to IT. Rather than thinking of a software upgrade, a new application, or a new server as a *task,* you think of the combination as a *business project.* A project might be virtualizing the server population as a way of optimizing power in the data center, and checking overall identity management to secure current and future business initiatives.

In fact, enhancing any element of service management should automatically initiate a process of understanding the following:

- ✔ The current process
- ✔ The way data has been managed
- ✔ How other processes have been managed

This process isn't just an exercise. You simply can't make significant changes in your data center without managing the dependencies that will be affected.

Figure 18-1, earlier in this chapter, shows a set of user requests as inputs to PPM. We aren't talking about a plan for maintenance. Managing user requests in the context of PPM has a significant implication in planning for future capacity.

Managing change

Taking a PPM approach enables IT to consider the impact of data center changes on the business as a whole. New compliance requirements may lead to new software that manages those requirements, for example. The company may plan to add new online services, which will increase stress on existing servers and networks, and planned new partnerships will result in a different workload in the data center.

Typically, when large business initiatives occur, two types of IT projects occur: a software development project, and a data center delivery and implementation project. The data center portion can be a subproject of a larger effort, whereas initiatives to improve the data center may be projects in their own right.

Although anticipating future data center workload is never easy, a project orientation helps management plan better. Aside from efficiently managing data center evolution, PPM helps IT keep the data center from exceeding capacity or at least predicting accurately when capacity will be exceeded.

Planning isn't just for new applications and projects. Existing data center elements, such as the service desk, also are affected as the business changes. Also, you have limits on what you can achieve in any given data center. These limits may include floor space, power supply, personnel, development resources, or financing.

Coordinating downstream activities

Figure 18-2 depicts the activity that occurs downstream from PPM.

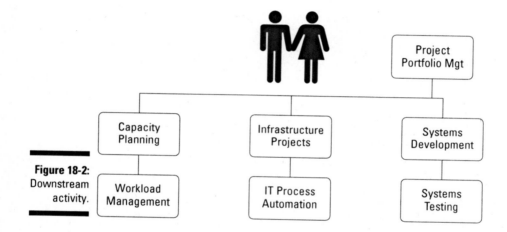

Figure 18-2: Downstream activity.

Three major activities occur downstream:

- **Capacity planning:** This activity used to be relatively simple; when adding a new application, the company added new hardware. Adding capacity is more complex with the introduction of virtualization (see Chapter 15) because then IT is managed as a resource pool. Capacity planning involves workload modeling, the activity of statistically modeling the load on the resources available for groups of applications. The goal is to predict the resource needs of the whole network over time, allowing for factors such as variations in application and network traffic.

- **Infrastructure projects:** As IT moves away toward a more integrated infrastructure, it also must move toward a more integrated set of service management processes and technology. Consequently, infrastructure projects such as establishing a federated configuration management database (CMDB; see Chapter 9) or virtualizing desktop computers are almost certain to involve changes in IT processes, which in turn may mean using processes that involve workflow and are based on

Information Technology Infrastructure Library (ITIL) definitions and models. (For more information on ITIL, see Chapter 5.)

✔ **Systems development:** Service oriented architecture (SOA) means both new applications and major changes to business processes. Because SOA makes application components available for use by other applications, it naturally creates new dependencies among applications or causes changes in existing dependencies. So when components are linked to build new applications or even to build end-to-end processes, existing software configurations are changed. This situation creates a testing issue, because now these components have to be tested to ensure that they work in all new contexts.

As a general rule, SOA increases the dependencies among applications and application components, and the effect needs to be modeled and tested. The same end-to-end modeling needs to be used in capacity planning for the resources needed to support the SOA services. (See Chapter 6 for more information on SOA.)

Technology evaluation

A data center can't handle change without a well-thought-out process. In most cases, data center management can't afford to adopt new technology until it's been proved. The alternative is to go through the expense of proving it yourself. But even if the new technology works well within its own context, you still have the problem of integrating it. After a technology is widely used, the integration problem diminishes and maybe even vanishes. Standards are established for its use that other technologies naturally adopt.

You may find it tempting to be the first on the block to purchase new, unproven technology — but doing so is risky. New technology is disruptive, and its success is uncertain, no matter how compelling the marketing story is.

Evaluating technology doesn't focus just on examining what new technologies can do; it also means considering when adopting those technologies makes sense. Unproven technology may be worth the risk if the pros (a major business advantage) dwarf the cons (usually, data center disruption and increased manual support costs). Such technology is rare for most data centers and businesses.

If you think about the data center as a type of factory, you see that change has to be well controlled. So if the company decides to adopt a new technology for, say, data storage, that technology must be tested exhaustively and then implemented gradually and in a strictly monitored fashion.

Governance and compliance

Governance and compliance rules impose a whole set of constraints on data center evolution. (Chapter 10 provides a lot of detail on governance.) Whether they're imposed by an industry or a government, rules dictate how personnel — support and operational staff — operate in the data center. Also, to some degree everything that's done in an organization is carried out according to governance and compliance.

Business service management

Business service management, which we discuss in detail in Chapter 17, makes sure that changes in the data center are in line with business goals.

Accurately defining service levels is an obvious requirement. When any significant change is made in data center processes, the rest of the business is likely to experience changes in service levels. In most cases, the changes are positive and improve business service levels. If a data center doesn't know the service levels it's supposed to achieve and is unable to measure them, however, IT may underinvest; consequently, data center operations may improve while business service levels are degraded. Alternatively, IT may overinvest, increasing data center costs and resources more than necessary.

Most organizations currently have undefined or vague service levels. Typically, service levels for the data center's mission-critical systems are known and, possibly, well defined. If a system fails, IT is in a difficult situation when responding to user complaints. A service level of 99.5 percent availability sounds impressive, for example, but it still means that users can expect system unavailability for a whole day over the course of a year. This result may be unacceptable for some systems, such as e-mail, but it may be fine if e-mail is never unavailable for more than 15 minutes at a time.

Some organizations also experience the phenomenon of *service-level creep*. Again, e-mail provides a good example. Employees depend on e-mail so much that even a 15-minute outage may affect the way that they do their jobs. If you don't review e-mail service levels regularly, IT doesn't find out that user expectations have changed until an outage occurs — which is the wrong time to discover a change in service demand.

If everyone agrees that the service level wasn't in the right spot and improving it will cost a significant amount of money, you can pretty much guarantee that the cost hasn't been budgeted. That situation is the opposite of planning; it's being caught unprepared. The data center planning cycle should naturally involve a review of service levels.

Drawing an Evolutionary Road Map for the Data Center

Focus on the following when you're planning data center evolution:

- ✔ **The service desk:** The service desk is the starting point for the resolution of service complaints. It constitutes the real-time response to service problems that software can't solve. If you audit a data center in terms of its capabilities, start by examining its fault-resolution process. (For more information about the service desk, we recommend reading Chapter 12.)

- ✔ **Configuration management database:** We don't believe that building a central CMDB (see Chapter 9) is worthwhile. We think that a federated data solution is inevitable. You _should_ focus on collecting the fundamental data that ought to reside in a CMDB, however, which means focusing early on the following:

  - Configuration management

  - Identity management

  - IT asset management and asset discovery

- ✔ **Project portfolio management:** If you skillfully carry out PPM, it becomes the driving mechanism for data center evolution. It lets you start planning the future so that the data center aligns itself to support business services directly.

A limited amount of change is possible in any given time frame. Every company starts from a different point, and to a great degree, its priorities are determined by the business.

Start Developing Your Service Strategy Now!

We hope that we've given you a taste of some of the important issues and approaches that make the service management journey so exciting. There's certainly a lot to think about.

We leave you with this thought: Service management is a businesscentric view. It starts with developing a service strategy based on internal and external market factors. The goal is to meet customer expectations. When you develop the services strategy, you're ready to develop your service management plan; the two go hand in hand. Good luck!

Part V
Real Life with Service Management

The 5th Wave   By Rich Tennant

Now maybe these folks got a decent disaster recovery plan and maybe they don't...

DANGER
WILD RHINOCEROS

In this part . . .

This part is where the rubber meets the road: real-life case studies that cover six industries. We'll go so far as to say that many of these case studies transcend industry boundaries. Don't look at just the case study for your own industry (although you may want to look at it first); also feast your eyes on what other people have discovered and accomplished in their service management journeys.

Chapter 19

Manufacturing

*I*n this chapter we look at the service management challenges of three companies — Elbit Systems of America, Cisco, and Varian Medical Systems — that manufacture highly complex and technologically advanced products and systems. These three very different companies have similar needs for servicing customers (internal and external) with the high level of attention that very technical products demand. All operate in industries such as health care and defense, which are highly regulated and secured.

What does this mean in terms of a service management strategy? All three companies invest substantial resources in research and development. Think of all the engineers and scientists working in technical environments that require the support of a complex technology infrastructure! In addition, globally based sales teams and technical consultants numbering in the thousands need consistent access to information about products, customers, and partners.

Securing facilities and data is a requirement for these manufacturing companies. They need to ensure compliance with the security demands of government and military customers and with industry regulations such as the Health Insurance and Portability and Accountability Act (HIPAA). Elbit Systems of America makes and supports many products used by the U.S. military to advance the security of the United States. Consultants do a lot of work at secure client sites, and Elbit Systems of America's own facilities, data, and applications need to meet similar security requirements. One of Elbit Systems of America's top service-management priorities was to more efficiently provide employees appropriate, secure access to facilities, applications, and data.

Cisco and Varian Medical Systems also have customers in the highly secure defense and security industries; however, their service-management efforts had a slightly different focus from Elbit Systems of America's. The goal of Cisco's service management program is to transform IT into a services business to enable Cisco's corporate strategy. Varian Medical Systems wanted to create a more efficient, timely response to service customers.

Elbit Systems of America

The five distinct business units of Elbit Systems of America — a wholly owned subsidiary of Elbit Systems, based in Israel — provide complex, high-performance technology to the defense, security, aviation, and medical instrumentation industries. Just to give you an idea, Elbit Systems of America's products and services include dismountable computer platforms for military vehicles, laser systems for military helicopters, and maintenance and logistics support of military electronic equipment.

Harry Butler, IT project manager for Elbit Systems of America, is responsible for making sure that all company employees get the IT services and support they need to get their jobs done. This mission may sound simple, but with thousands of employees involved, many of whom work at the high-security sites of client sites, it gets very complicated.

In 2001, Butler knew his team needed to take a new approach to service management to deliver consistently high-quality services to internal customers. IT needed a more holistic, proactive approach to managing services. As Butler put it, "It dawned on us that we could put out fires for the rest of our lives or actually go try to figure out what was causing the problems and why customers were upset." The company hired an outside consulting firm to assess the company's approach and make recommendations. The company established a service desk to deal with incident and problem management; then it implemented plans for a service catalog and a configuration management database (CMDB). Virtualization was a key part of the strategy. The IT team at Elbit Systems of America found out a lot along the way.

Implementing a service desk

The first order of business was deploying a service desk solution with a good incident-management system. IT initially targeted its internal customers — consultants and solution providers who need consistent access to secure information and IT services. What problems did the service desk need to handle? Generally, if an Elbit Systems of America employee can't access the applications he needs, he contacts the service desk with an urgent request. Suppose that a vice president of contracts needs to complete a proposal while he is onsite with a major client but can't access Elbit Systems of America's computers over the company's virtual private network (VPN). He must receive immediate assistance from the service desk if he wants to close the deal. At the same time, the service desk receives less-urgent calls. Before the service desk solution was implemented at Elbit Systems of America, however, IT gave all calls the same level of priority.

An important step in implementing the service desk was negotiating and agreeing on service levels with end users. Butler recognized that the old way — treating all calls as top priority — wasn't working. The company needed to balance available resources against the priorities of the business. The only way to do this effectively was for the business to articulate its needs and for IT to identify the cost tradeoffs. According to Butler, this negotiation process is ongoing, but IT has gotten good at it.

Streamlining business processes

After getting the service desk up to speed, Butler and his service management team had more time to devote to streamlining their approach to handling service requests. The intention was to automate some manual aspects of approving requests, such as authorizing file-share access.

With the help of senior executives, Butler's team reviewed the process for one of the most common service desk requests: permission to access secure facilities, files, or applications. This process involved many manual steps, ranging from users filling out paper forms to locating the person authorized to grant access rights. Sometimes a paper form was misplaced on its journey, and the company lost several days just trying to get employees access to facilities or applications. Other common requests, such as ordering a computer, also benefited from in-depth analysis.

Butler and his team found that too many paper forms needed to be routed through various steps for approval. All these common service requests were streamlined, and the new process was documented in a service catalog (see the following section).

Creating a service catalog

Sometimes the simplest ideas have the biggest impact. The IT services team had a 700-page catalog of IT services that included a lot of information, but the format wasn't very accessible and actionable. Elbit Systems of America took the very pragmatic approach of streamlining business processes for delivering IT services, implementing these processes, and documenting them by using service-catalog software.

How would you like to shorten a two-day process to two hours? That happened to employee requests for access after the service catalog implementation. Now employees can use the service catalog before a trip to request security clearance. If someone in Texas plans to travel to New Hampshire the following week, for example, she can use the service catalog to request physical security clearance so that when she arrives in New Hampshire, she can be ready to work. Previously, she had to e-mail someone requesting security clearance. If that person was on vacation and didn't get the notification e-mail, the consultant might not get clearance in time. He or she might waste several days this way that could have been used productively working. Now, if the person who is supposed to provide the service is gone, the system designates an alternate.

As the success of this small project permeated the organization, Butler's team was inundated with other requests. Human resources, for example, wanted the team to automate some of the time-consuming manual processes involved with new hires and employee exits. Finance requested that its check-approval process be automated, and the department included input in the service catalog. Now the team has a rather long list of services that need to get into the service catalog.

Implementing a CMDB

The configuration management database (CMDB) is at the heart of Elbit Systems of America's service-management strategy.

A CMDB stores all the information about all the assets across the company. In the case of e-mail, the company would store information about software such as Microsoft Outlook, the exchange servers, Internet access, routers, hubs, switches, firewalls, spam servers, e-mail–monitoring servers, and so on. It also has information about how exchange servers are connected to the Internet and to other servers. The IT team responsible for making sure everyone has e-mail must know what's included in the e-mail service. This makes it easier to fix a problem because, according to Butler, the reality is that you will never find one person in the organization that knows the entire hierarchy of how all servers are connected and interact with each other.

Now changes to the infrastructure are submitted 14 days in advance. They're discussed and visualized so that the team can see what pieces are going to be involved. In the case of e-mail, for example, team members see the upstream and downstream effects of changing the exchange server and can notify the people who are going to be affected by the changes. If a change order doesn't generate any potential problems, it's approved and becomes standard. The change-management process also helps identify rogue services. This process, then, helps reduce the number of problems in the infrastructure.

Employing virtualization

As the company's service management strategy expanded, so did the number of servers. As IT added new tools, each tool had its own server. The company ended up with a service desk server, a service catalog server, a local asset management server, and an enterprise asset manager server. Across the five business units, Elbit Systems of America had five separate servers at each of 13 locations, totaling 65 servers around the globe. This configuration was hard to manage.

After virtualizing five separate servers onto one at each of the 13 facilities, Elbit reduced the number of physical servers by 52. The company has cut down on the amount of hardware it has to maintain, and the solution is more flexible. For example, if it needs more disk space or more RAM, it can do it on the fly rather than ordering more RAM and waiting for maintenance to install it. Now IT just buys a healthy chunk of RAM for the server and allocates it. This process also saves space, as well as electricity and cooling costs.

Establishing best practices

Elbit Systems of America's service-management strategy has matured significantly since 2001. Butler offers the following thoughts on best practices based on the company's experiences:

- ✔ **Don't try to swallow the elephant all at once.** Butler cautions you to take service management one step at a time. Start by focusing on one IT service that will have a big impact on the business. Take the time to understand the processes so that you can streamline and create a more efficient approach. A learning curve is involved, so plan to allocate some extra time for the first few services you deploy.

- ✔ **Build credibility.** Initially, when IT negotiated with the business, the business didn't necessarily believe that a certain level of support would cost a certain amount of money. As the services rolled out and succeeded, the business started to understand how much it would cost to get a job done.

- ✔ **Build relationships.** Strong relationships go hand in hand with building credibility. It's essential that IT understand the business needs and that all stakeholders use a common language. Everyone must be open to new ideas and new approaches. As Butler puts it, "Just because we have always done it that way doesn't mean that's the way we always need to do it. It was important for both sides of the house to keep an open mind."

An important lesson from Elbit Systems of America's experience with service management is recognizing that everything is a service, from giving employees mobile online access to ensuring the security of facilities, providing access to those buildings, and providing a check-approval process. Elbit Systems of America evaluated the manual processes involved in delivering these services and moved to take a more comprehensive and automated approach.

Cisco

Customer experience matters to Cisco, one of the world's leading providers of hardware, software, and services for creating Internet solutions. Although the company is best known for its Internet Protocol (IP)-based network technologies, over time Cisco has dramatically expanded its business into new markets through strategic acquisitions. In adding companies such as WebEx and IronPort to the fold, Cisco has had to evolve its processes and systems to support multiple business models including traditional product, Software as a Service (SaaS), subscription, and IT as a service (ITaaS) offerings on a global scale. As one can imagine, such expansion over time has correspondingly led to a rather heterogeneous IT portfolio.

In order to evolve their operating model from support and delivery of individual technologies to a service provider model, Cisco has begun moving forward with the adoption of a comprehensive service management framework. The purpose of the framework is to facilitate the conversion of the many technical capabilities the IT organization provides into discreet customer-facing service offerings. One foundational building block in the execution of Cisco's service management framework is the construction of a multi-layer service catalog.

Using the multilayer service catalog

Sean Worthington, vice president of IT, Business Services, leads the team responsible for the construction of the services catalog. In addition to using the catalog to provide transparency into the portfolio of services across the enterprise, another goal is to clearly identify owners of those services. "That's a good barometer for me," says Worthington, "because if we have applications that we can't assign to a service, that begs the question 'What purpose are those applications servicing?' In this way, the catalog can be used as a guide to reduce the cost and complexity inherent in such a large enterprise IT environment. The company sees the catalog as a way to begin to streamline service delivery by getting rid of applications and technologies that aren't being used effectively.

"Conversely," says Worthington, "if it turns out there are a bunch of required services we've defined in our catalog where there's no application delivering them, that is an invalid outcome." In this way, Cisco can also use its service catalog to guide prudent investment in new capabilities. In building its catalog, Cisco has developed a taxonomy used to group IT capabilities into three categories of services: foundational, client, and business.

Foundational Services

Foundational services are consumed by internal groups, processes, or functions. This category includes such functions as database administration, hosting, storage, and network provisioning. The scope of these services is quite diverse. Worthington says, "That's why the creation of the catalog is very important but also not a terribly easy task."

Client Services

Client services are consumed by an individual and include the provisioning, management, and billing for services such as mobile devices, phones, PCs, and other items that get any employee up and running. The genesis of Cisco's service management efforts can be traced back to 1999 when they implemented an internally built application called Enterprise Management (EMAN) to automate client service delivery.

Business Services

The third category of services represents discreet business functions and is often exposed to the outside world. Under Guillermo Diaz Jr., vice president IT Customer Commerce, Services and Solutions, Cisco has executed a service oriented architecture (SOA) strategy as part of an ongoing commerce initiative. (Refer to Chapter 6 for additional information on SOA.) The commerce platform includes business services for product pricing, discounting, and configuration, services that will be offered to channel partners over time. Initially, these services will be used by multiple internal groups as they build business applications. Cisco envisions that over the next few years its channel partners will begin to use the same services — standard components from Cisco — and expose them as widgets or portlets to create their own online selling experiences. In addition to the commerce platform business services, IT also offers other services to internal groups, such as video conferencing and collaboration.

Enhancing the CMDB

At it continues to mature, the service catalog can further enhance the important process of configuration and change management, another pillar of Cisco's overarching service management framework. Worthington and Diaz believe that a solid CMDB is critical to the success of their overall plan to deliver services that meet customer requirements. Worthington refers to the CMDB as the "building list of materials for a service." The idea is to take the basic CMDB concept that's been with IT for quite a while and wrap value around it with the service catalog. Using the two together, the team can understand what each service offers and can list the components for a given service through the CMDB. Using the CMDB helps IT to understand how certain services work together to support the business.

Managing service-level agreements

These mechanisms in turn help manage the service-level agreements that go with individual services. Understanding the interdependencies between service components has been a key focus of Cisco's approach. For example, the business-level product pricing service might require 99.99 percent availability, but it depends upon other services from the catalog. This means that all the underlying services that support this service (such as database and network availability) also need to have the appropriate service levels in place to support the designated service level for pricing.

"As an IT client-facing person, I recognize that our clients and, ultimately, our end partners depend on IT services to always be available for their revenue generation," Diaz says. "We need to provide the right service-level agreements to our customers." Of course, tradeoffs can occur between meeting customer expectations and supplying the necessary resources. If you want to ensure a higher degree of availability for a particular service, you need to improve the resiliency of the underlying foundational components — which can add to the complexity of the architecture. Sometimes adding an incremental improvement to service availability requires an exponential increase in cost. How do you explain this to end users? According to Diaz, IT must be very clear about all the cost/benefit tradeoffs involved prior to establishing proper SLAs with customers. The service catalog and CMDB work in concert to clearly articulate these cost issues. Having an understanding for the interdependencies can, in some cases, enable more granular, tiered offerings for service consumers to choose from where service availability is properly balanced with associated cost.

Laying the groundwork for virtualization

Looking forward, as Cisco increasingly virtualizes its data-center environment; it must understand where a service is running and what its proper level of resiliency should be throughout the technology stack. In a virtualized world, you don't want a priority-1 service, running in a virtual machine, to be migrated to a priority-6 physical host for example; that arrangement certainly wouldn't meet service-level expectations. Both Diaz and Worthington agree that the service catalog will be increasingly important in the next generation of Cisco's data center.

Changing to a customer-experience mindset

According to Worthington, although moving IT to think of itself as an "internal service provider" is a big undertaking requiring detailed technical analysis, cultural change management is the "bigger challenge." The team believes that good change management depends on solid agreement and active steering-committee membership by all IT leaders. To address these challenges, Cisco has established an IT steering committee that brings together a broad team with diverse opinions and perspectives in order to facilitate this transformation. The goal of the group is to bring value to all layers of the organization as it manages change.

Worthington and Diaz believe that the impetus for transitioning to a service management philosophy should come from the top. The chief information officer (CIO) must be 100 percent committed and articulate this commitment clearly to all business stakeholders. Although the company is still early in the process, it expects that delivering on customer expectations with regard to services will be a big part of operational and performance reviews going forward.

Services need to be measured on criteria such as the number of capabilities delivered, the quality with which they're delivered, and the cost at which they're delivered. These criteria become measurements of the customer experience. Worthington says. "There is really only one set of metrics that matters; the rest are diagnostics. The ones that matter are the experience metrics."

By building a service management strategy based around this concept of customer experience, IT has increasingly delivered services in alignment with business requirements and priorities — further demonstrating its value as a strategic partner. The team responsible for service management has made sure as part of its analysis to tangibly demonstrate the financial benefits of its efforts. Diaz estimated that his Commerce IT team alone saved $1 million in the final quarter of 2008 through more efficient service management as supported by Worthington's group. Such results will likely further Cisco's program to transform IT into thinking of itself as a services business.

Varian Medical Systems

Varian Medical Systems provides equipment and solutions for cancer-treatment centers. In addition, the company provides industrial testing products and x-ray linear accelerators for cargo security. The company's more than 900 service representatives are responsible for the company's products, which are located in more than 5,000 locations worldwide. Varian implemented a service management strategy to add efficiency to equipment, device, and software service. The main goal was to evaluate the management process in terms of servicing the linear accelerators and software provided to oncology clinics.

Defining the challenges of the industry

When you understand how the equipment is used, recognizing the service challenge is easy. Radiation oncology treatment centers use linear accelerator machines to provide radiation treatment to cancer patients. The linear accelerator is a very large unit that must be located in a specially designed concrete room. Outside the concrete room, the medical oncology team uses computer software, medical imaging technology, and other equipment to plan, deliver, and monitor treatments. A lot of patient data must be recorded to determine optimum treatment and monitor the accuracy of ongoing treatment. Radiation oncology is a highly technical part of cancer treatment that requires precision in both the equipment and the health-care team.

Many problems can interrupt the continuous operation of the equipment. If the patient database goes down, for example, radiation treatment must stop because that database holds the information regarding patient equipment settings.

The main challenge for Varian was the time it took a technician to reach a site. Service calls generally involved several hours of travel time and then several hours to complete the repair. For customers in remote areas (such as in South America), the mean time to respond was much longer. Software questions could often be handled over the phone, but as Varian's products became more complex, it became increasingly difficult for customers to describe problems over the phone. Dan DuBeau, program manager, remote access and Mission Critical Application Protection (MICAP), says, "You can have a help desk representative on the phone with a customer, and they are talking two completely different languages." In 2000, the Varian team began looking at remote-access solutions with the expectation of improving the service level provided to customers.

Implementing a remote-access solution

Varian Medical Systems had two main goals for implementing a remote-access solution: decrease service call mean time to respond and decrease escalating travel costs. In addition, the company hoped to solve some of the communication problems that occurred when staff members tried to resolve customer problems over the phone.

Now when a customer uses Varian's software products, either managing patient information or setting up a treatment, IT support can access the customer's desktop remotely. A support representative can use the mouse and keyboard remotely, and the customer can see exactly what the Varian representative sees, watching the mouse move and viewing every keystroke. This solution is a great educational tool as well. Often, a customer needs to be trained. Also, if an on-site representative runs into something outside her area of expertise, she can have an expert from Varian access the application remotely and help the representative through the fix — a side benefit that Varian didn't expect.

Creating a rotating service desk

In addition to providing remote desktop support, Varian representatives work on the company service desk. Most service representatives work from home, and many of these representatives do it all, repairing a piece of equipment one day and working on a mainframe computer the next day. Varian also has two service forces out in the field.

The service representatives rotate their work responsibilities. A local representative in Seattle, for example, normally would drive or fly to a customer site to fix a problem with the equipment. One week of the year, however, he stays at home with a computer and instant-messaging software to take direct customer calls. If he gets a call that requires someone on-site, he redispatches that call; otherwise, he handles the call remotely.

After Varian implemented its remote desktop solutions, it took a while for all the representatives and customers to use the system. The reality is that nothing replaces face time with a customer, so initially, the representatives were hesitant to use the product. Now most customers — indeed the vast majority — insist on remote access.

The company also has become more proactive in its problem management. The idea is to track what the customer's doing now and send a dispatch to the customer before a problem occurs. Varian is currently looking at the lifetime of consumables — such as field lights on radiation therapy devices — to predict at what point a particular part of a machine will go out. Then Varian can send a service reminder and proactively change an important component before it fails.

Measuring the impact of service management

From a business standpoint, the company knew that it needed to determine the impact of the remote desktop solution. As DuBeau put it, "It is hard to measure what you are doing, but it is almost impossible to measure what you are *not* doing. And that's what we really want to measure." Varian is trying to measure how much has been saved by reducing travel time.

One metric that the company can track is remote-access usage hours, which totaled 17,000 in one month, including remote database upgrades and modifications. Varian used this metric and other data on service requests and responses to calculate cost savings and the new mean time to repair. The savings have been significant, amounting to a 20 percent overall reduction in expenses due to the following:

- ✔ Reduced numbers of overnight hotel stays and plane tickets
- ✔ Increase in productivity resulting from decreased travel time and better customer communication
- ✔ Reduced number of service representatives required due to the increase in productivity (one representative can do three jobs in the time it used to take to do one)

An additional benefit is that Varian has an accurate audit trail of what customers it has accessed, which helps customers meet compliance regulations such as HIPAA. The more the company automates its process, the easier it is to validate and verify that processes are sound. The true benefit of Varian's improved service management approach, of course, is one that can't be easily measured: delivering treatment to patients on time.

Chapter 20

Health Care

*T*he U.S. health care industry is facing a perfect storm of challenges. The Health Insurance Portability and Accountability Act (HIPAA) and other government regulations require providers to adhere to national standards for electronic records and transactions. Health care providers and payers must cope with many other pressures, including an aging population, a growing number of people without medical insurance, falling government reimbursement rates, and a growing shortage of qualified staff members.

In this difficult environment, health care insurance companies need to manage the relationships with health care providers and consumers. Pharmaceutical companies need to leverage data and best practices successfully across the entire health care system to ensure that they develop medicines to address emerging needs.

At the center of this storm, medical costs are skyrocketing. Controlling health care costs while ensuring quality of care has become a hot issue for this industry. Service management is emerging as an important strategy for meeting these challenges. Addressing problem and change management helps to decrease the down time of critical technology that clinicians and nurses use to treat patients and manage care, for example. The hospitals and insurance companies profiled in this chapter believe that service management helps reduce costs and ensure improved quality of care.

Innovation has become critical to success, so many companies are looking at ways to innovate. In this chapter, we profile four companies' service management efforts:

- ✔ The Medical Center of Central Georgia is using its service management system software to automate what were traditionally inefficient and/or paper-based business processes, and to manage customer service and change management.

- ✔ Independence Blue Cross deployed an operations control center to help monitor its systems and predict problems.

- ✔ Sisters of Mercy Health System transformed its clinical processes. IT supported this initiative by creating a more responsive technology infrastructure.

- ✔ Finally, Partners HealthCare deployed an innovative service oriented architecture strategy and is using a service catalog to help monitor the performance of its key services.

The Medical Center of Central Georgia

The Medical Center of Central Georgia, located in Macon, is a full-service acute-care hospital with more than 600 beds, serving about 750,000 residents. It's now the second-largest hospital in Georgia. The hospital system also includes a series of remote health care facilities; wellness centers; health clubs; and home care, home health, and hospice services throughout the city. The Medical Center of Central Georgia's core mission is to provide world-class care to its patients.

The IT department manages all servers, laptops, desktops, printers, scanners, and various applications. Five years ago, Information Services realized that it needed to improve service management and needed to automate many business processes. IT had previously deployed a homegrown system for managing problems, but the system was inadequate to meet the needs of Information Services and the organization. These inadequacies hindered process and workflow management, and eventually led to the need for a more robust system.

Ensuring high quality of care was a key concern. The IT team realized that it needed to change its approach. It began by implementing new service management software and processes and then expanded its vision to address change management. It also streamlined many of its business processes and reduced costs by using the service management software platform to automate and enforce business processes both within and outside IT.

Revamping the Technical Support Center

The Medical Center's Technical Support Center (TSC) supports IT as a whole and has been particularly successful with its client services. Client services technicians travel to different locations within the organization to deal with hardware and software issues. Before the service management system was implemented, each time a technician made a repair, he had to go back to the office or rely on a paging system to get the next service ticket. According to Patrice Briley, a lead analyst at the Medical Center, this service request could be in the same area the technician just left. The technician would have to go back to the area and then back to the office.

Now the organization is divided into zones. When a ticket is entered, the system makes logical decisions as to what zones and technician the ticket should be assigned; the routing is automatic. Rather than going back to a central area to get the next assignment or waiting for the TSC to make contact manually, the technician simply receives the next assignment by pager or e-mail. The actual work request is entered into the system, along with the necessary information to allow the system to process automatically. This new process also helps to improve quality of care by enabling the technicians to address problems faster and more efficiently. One big advantage of this approach, says systems analyst Isaac Ramsingh, is that the technicians "can be mobile rather than being tied to a physical computer or depending on an unreliable process to get the information they need. This has improved productivity tremendously."

The same system is used for change control management. Any request for changes to systems is entered into the application. An automatic approval process is then initiated, with the appropriate managers reviewing and approving or denying the request for change as appropriate. Reports from this system also drive committees responsible for managing changes, ensuring that each change is communicated effectively and any possible ill effects are identified. The intent is to thoroughly understand system interactions and proactively manage system changes.

Automating processes

The IT team is using the service management software platform to automate some of the manual, paper-intensive processes that encumbered IT productivity for years. One example is providing security access to systems for new employees. In the past, this task involved a paper-based process that may have involved as many as 10 or 11 system administrators. Now the new system takes the original request and splits it so that a subticket is sent to each system administrator involved, and manages the process of granting access to each of the systems required. New employees, or employees who have had their system access changed, can now sign into a centralized and secure Web page to retrieve all their system access information, like user IDs and passwords, along with documentation for each of their systems.

By leveraging the technology upon which the service management software was built the team has already developed nearly 20 independent applications to automate and manage various diverse processes. This kind of automation enables the company to cut costs, streamline business processes, and ensure adherence to policies and procedures.

Establishing best practices

Briley and Ramsingh mention several best practices that have emerged over the course of the Medical Center of Central Georgia's service management journey, including the following:

- ✔ **Bring the customer in up front.** When you are creating a system, it is important to get the users and business experts involved. This ensures the needs of the users are met and fosters a sense of ownership. This sense of ownership and buy-in results in greater acceptance and a better end product for everyone. According to Briley and Ramsingh, if you don't get the right folks involved at the onset of a project, it can result in a system that is poorly designed and not well accepted.

- ✔ **Communicate.** Communication is critical, especially when it comes to patient care. Being informed helps the staff take the necessary steps to ensure quality of care is not compromised. The TSC has become a single point of contact for dispersing information throughout the organization.

- ✔ **Build a knowledge base.** As a problem occurs, it is important to document the steps taken toward resolution. The next time the problem occurs, resolution can be reached more quickly. The end result is better customer service.

Independence Blue Cross

Independence Blue Cross (IBC) and its subsidiaries are the Philadelphia region's largest health insurers, with more than 3.4 million members. The company offers products and services such as managed care, traditional indemnity, pharmacy benefits management, Medicare, and Medicaid. IBC annually processes more than 32 million claims and responds to more than 6 million customer inquiries. IBC's information technology organization manages hundreds of applications that cover a wide area of business needs, from internal e-mail to external customer-facing systems. These include mission-critical solutions vital to the company's success, in which unscheduled down time is not an option. For example, an outage during the critical enrollment period could greatly hinder an individual's ability to choose an appropriate insurance product.

In 2002, IBC initiated a grass-roots movement to implement the Information Technology Infrastructure Library (ITIL) framework to improve the provisioning and control of IT services such as incident and problem management.

Although the objectives were on the right track, the effort failed to gain traction for several reasons. First, it didn't address key issues such as root cause analysis, notifications, and escalation. Also, although IBC had a change management process in place, it was weak in that it was loosely mandated and had no transparency or accountability structure, and its Web-based environment was unpredictable.

Fortunately, a more recent review and overhaul of the process has allowed IBC's Information Technology Team to institutionalize a vastly improved ITIL methodology, adding executive-level support and proactive capabilities. A crucial organizational change was the addition of an Operational Control Center (OCC), which monitors the systems and applications across the enterprise from the customer's point of view, thereby providing substantial business value.

Putting transparency back into the process

When Nick Robak, senior director of technology services, joined the team in 2005, he quickly saw a critical issue: the staff was handling incidents, but there was lack of accountability for any particular problem. This and other deficiencies in the service management process fueled the organization's effort to gain more control of resources as well as more credibility with the business.

With the assistance of systems integrator Liquid Hub, IBC pored through the hundreds of applications that it manages and assigned severity codes for problem classification. An example of a priority-one application is the one that all agents and brokers use when working with customers. This application provides customers comprehensive information about their policies and how those policies are set up. If that application becomes unavailable during the high-revenue or enrollment seasons, the company can be seriously affected.

After assigning the severity codes, IT identified the precise response mechanism that would be used to resolve each problem. Robak's team ensured that there was a well-defined and broadly communicated problem escalation, notification, and communication process. All details of the process were negotiated with the sponsors and stakeholders over a period of several months. This resulted in consensus by all parties, and allowed the incident and problem management process to be tightly governed by IT. The company quickly began reaping rewards. For example, the average time to repair has decreased by 50 percent.

Additionally, IT implemented a strict change-control process that, along with incident and problem management, has lowered the number of priority-one problems by 50 percent. "Before we focused the team on change management," Robak says, "certain areas of the organization utilized a change management process, while others didn't; we needed consistency." IT instituted a more orderly and enforceable change management policy that includes, for example, submitting change notices before changes can occur.

Getting proactive for the business: The OCC

After IBC implemented these improved incident, problem, and change management processes, it examined how to proactively identify issues before they became problems. As is typical at many large companies, when an incident occurs, everyone from the database person to the network and applications person might be asked to help solve the problem. Needless to say, this process is inefficient and unnecessarily drains resources. The goal was to move away from a purely reactive service desk that only addressed problems as they happened, and move toward the ability to show a holistic picture of service to the end user which includes proactive capabilities. To do this, the team looked at its services from the end-user perspective, gaining an end-to-end view of all the elements that make up a service, each of which could be monitored.

The idea to monitor services from an end-user perspective led to the creation of the OCC, which has a four-part mission:

- ✔ Proactively monitor the performance of critical business and technology services

- ✔ Routinely report ongoing operational metrics with a focus on improving them to match changing business priorities

- ✔ Coordinate performance improvements to resolve more incidents before they affect the consumer

- ✔ Deliver innovative solutions in process improvement, service quality, and increased systems performance to meet service-level agreements (SLAs)

The OCC is an organization that uses staff members from across Information Technology. Its members include service desk personnel, a Web environment administrator, enterprise monitoring personnel, SLA management and reporting experts, and those with executive dashboard expertise. The goal is that when the problem management staff is notified of an event or an anomaly, they can ask whether this issue is the start of a trend, and collaboration can begin among the members of the OCC to help predict and resolve larger issues.

If the OCC sounds a bit like a network operations center (NOC), which is used to monitor communications networks, that's because in some ways it is. Like a NOC, the OCC is housed in a separate room (with glass windows) where numerous large plasma screens provide a real-time view of activity across the company's systems. Unlike a NOC, however, the OCC monitors the business processes and services from the end-user perspective.

Monitoring and measuring are big parts of what the OCC does. According to Heath Durrans, director of managed infrastructure at LiquidHub, the primary purpose of the OCC is SLA management, which in this case is really business-level management. The goal is to meet customer expectations for service. If a system is failing to meet those service level objectives, the OCC needs to find out why. The OCC wants to know and report how the business is doing this month, and how that compares to its performance last month. It constantly monitors performance against expectations. The OCC might try, for example, to predict that a certain customer-facing application may go down on a certain day because of certain behavior and trends. It tracks both the application and how that application interacts with other applications and the infrastructure. The OCC supports both internal and external applications.

One internal service that the OCC monitors is how consumers get e-mail from the mail archive. How do you determine an acceptable performance level for retrieving e-mail? To answer this question, the team openly asked end users about their expectations for this service. It also mapped out all the hops — transfer between computers — that a message goes through across the entire infrastructure to retrieve an archived item. Then the OCC employed software agents and synthetic transactions to test availability, at the specified SLAs, to the end consumer. These test transactions are developed by IT to gauge how the system will respond under specific conditions.

The OCC has been a huge success. Robak says, "It's one of those projects that happens every couple of years where you see all the lights go on. Showing real evidence of what is going on with these applications and staving off problems before they happen has created a whole lot of support."

Identifying best practices

IBC has found that its internal and external customers are much happier now. Systems go down less often, and when they do, they're fixed more quickly. The team has identified certain best practices that have helped along the way:

- **Benchmarking:** Robak's team collected a three-month trend on service performance to use in negotiating SLAs. For example, it researched what a normal call response should be and then negotiated around that metric. However, a core OCC tenet is to not accept the norm but instead strive for service-performance excellence.

- **Negotiating:** IT must decide how to best support the business, but at the same time recognize the importance of balancing limited resources to ensure that critical systems remain stable.

✔ **Setting priorities:** IBC believes in the importance of both a unified ITIL practice that utilizes basic ITIL processes, and senior management endorsement and prioritization of these standards.

✔ **Measuring results:** IBC believes in gaining transparency in IT operations via clear reporting of operational metrics. These metrics also need to have built-in accountability. IBC knows who is responsible for fixing a particular problem and when that person needs to respond. All of the measurements and trends are provided to senior management on a regular basis.

Sisters of Mercy Health System

St. Louis-based Sisters of Mercy Health System (Mercy) operates 19 hospitals, physician practices, outpatient clinics, health plans, and related health and human services in Arkansas, Kansas, Louisiana, Mississippi, Missouri, Oklahoma, and Texas. Mercy is the ninth-largest Catholic health care system in the United States based on net patient service revenue.

Mercy began planning for a more integrated IT platform to serve the business and clinical needs of the health system in 2003. The initiative was motivated by Mercy's need to improve clinical service, quality, and safety while achieving operational efficiency and improving access to quality information. Mercy implemented applications to support enterprise resource planning (ERP) across its organization and to address clinical and revenue functions within its hospitals and physician clinics. Through this deployment, the health system aimed to update processes vital to quality clinical care, such as creating an electronic health record (EHR) for every Mercy patient. The EHR promised to reduce patient registration and scheduling hassles, manage and document all patient care, and aid in patient accounting. The technology infrastructure supporting these new applications demanded high levels of availability and service. Mercy had to establish a more comprehensive, integrated service management approach — and it didn't have a lot of time to complete this task when the applications went live.

Seeing the need for improved service management

Mercy's leaders, including those in the IT division, recognized the stark difference between its current state and the vision of the new deployment. A few clinical services and business processes were automated, and IT provided nearly 100 percent availability for these systems around the clock. Most clinical functions didn't heavily rely on IT infrastructure and service, however. If a doctor ordered something or created a prescription, she would write it out or dictate it.

Mercy's service desk operation needed to become more efficient to address the increased IT load from new clinicians and physicians utilizing the EHR. Additionally, in 2006, consultants examined Mercy's service management performance and found that poor processes and human error were leading to down time and other quality-of-service issues. Changes that weren't well planned or were rushed often resulted in problems. The trouble-ticketing system, which didn't distinguish among different types of problems and requests, was also causing problems: Nonurgent requests were sometimes resolved more quickly than urgent incidents.

Both senior IT and business executives agreed that they needed to strengthen the IT infrastructure and services quickly to support the project with the rock-solid availability it needed to succeed. IT leaders began talking about required uptime, planning for "3 nines" (99.99 percent availability of systems). Even at that high level, those that used Mercy's most important systems would still experience 8 hours and 46 minutes of down time per year. Additionally, it became clear that technology alone would not save the day. Equal focus on creating stronger processes was essential. Mercy needed to adopt service management and processes to ensure success. Mercy's deployment goal was very aggressive. Service desk, asset, incident, problem, change, and release management were all included in the initial six-month design period. The hospital system had many requirements for its service management solution, which had to be modular, flexible, and streamlined across different areas and processes.

Prescribing a service management solution

Mercy leaders decided on an integrated solution to meet high availability needs. With so much infrastructure and so many applications, the team needed information to flow seamlessly from one process to the next. If an end user created a service request that then became an incident, Mercy wanted data from the request to populate the incident record automatically. If the incident required a change, Mercy wanted the system to feed the incident and change action automatically through the approval and change-authorization process. In case the fix failed, Mercy's IT staff would have clear documentation to identify changes that could have caused the failure.

To meet its six-month deadline, Mercy "wanted to affect cultural change within our IT organization, so we did a big bang," said Will Showalter, chief information officer for Mercy. With strong executive sponsorship, he recruited business-process managers and owners to help evangelize the initiative and organized "synthesis sessions" to let everyone see design and provide input. All managers attended ITIL foundations courses, and the rest of the IT crew participated in a lighter version of ITIL training before they were trained on the new tools and processes.

Providing a service management makeover

Michael Zucker, director of process and quality for Mercy's IT division, led the service management effort. He would have liked extra time for testing, of course, but he didn't have that luxury. Mercy's IT staff not only had to be trained in the use a new tool, but also had to adopt a more disciplined approach. With the clock ticking, Zucker knew that the initial live deployment was bound to face some hitches. "We tried to be very proactive in our communication," he says. "Executive sponsors were saying, 'We are going to do it, so accept that — and once you accept that, here's a plan to handle it.'"

Setting expectations

Setting expectations became a top priority. Zucker's organization supplied end users and service desk staff information about potential problems and armed the service desk with guidance about how to address those problems.

This strategy helped the team navigate the inevitable bumps of the initial rollout in early 2008. Some IT staff members found the more rigorous service management process a bit cumbersome at first, but they got the message that it was important to "make sure they are thinking about it twice before taking action," Zucker remarks. Still, the time crunch took a toll; the January 2008 live deployment of the new application and processes was rough on many of Mercy's IT teams. But Mercy has been working steadily to smooth out those initial rough edges. "We might not be where we want to be yet, but we are heading in the right direction," says Showalter. "Continual process improvement and a focus on quality will always be with us."

The system now supports both infrastructure and clinical applications, serving as a single system recording work done by any of Mercy's 700 IT people. "Everything is recorded and managed here. It's our vehicle to communicate and make sure the work gets done," Showalter says. The integrated service management dashboard provides a much better reading on the health of systems and services, enabling IT to track more processes and metrics than before.

Refining the tracking system

Currently, Mercy is concentrating on refining the system through better discipline and additional metrics. Mercy already tracks availability at the network level and is working to measure availability at the individual application level. "All the support processes are interrelated, and we can look at them," Zucker says. "If something breaks down, it could be any number of things. Now if a user complains about slowness, we can more easily identify the root of the problem and direct it to the right service group to get it resolved faster."

Better discipline and visibility have helped Mercy improve accuracy, deliver higher availability, and respond more effectively when an issue does arise. Staff members can now distinguish between an incident (which requires immediate attention) and a request (which isn't urgent), and apply different metrics to each.

Mercy's IT division also introduced policies and metrics regarding standard and unplanned changes, and tracks these changes with specific key performance indicators. Improved metrics and tracking help identify processes that aren't compliant. If the metric mandates that all priority-one incidents need to be resolved within eight hours, the tools enable staff to spot any metrics that look suspicious and take remedial action.

Conducting customer and user surveys

Mercy conducts regular broad customer satisfaction surveys across the organization, uses a link from the system that provides feedback and ratings on service for individual incidents, and surveys users about specific incidents. User satisfaction and other key metrics improved in all categories from January 2008 to the same time the following year.

Achieving a healthy prognosis

In late 2008, Mercy installed an additional component that can move its asset-tracking functions to a configuration management database (CMDB). Currently, Mercy is adding new service-catalog functionality for different IT services to the CMDB, with 20 IT teams using the catalog management function to define individual service lines and the discrete services that they can provide to end users (and to one another). With this capability, IT staff members and users can view and order services as they would from an Internet-based retailer. Requests for infrastructure services (such as network or voice) and for clinical and business services are logged. The service catalog helps users throughout the organization find the services they need quickly and determine the right team for the job.

Going forward, Mercy's strong, consistent, and ongoing executive commitment will drive continuous improvements. The original implementation team, consisting of both business-process managers and IT personnel, now serves as a process board, discussing, prioritizing, and authorizing process changes. The application itself also helps enforce more discipline in processes and provides metrics that flag areas that are out of compliance.

Given that Mercy Health accomplished its service management transformation in record time, Mercy's IT leaders are often asked how the health system managed to get so much done in such a short time. They attribute its success to a few key factors:

- ✔ Strong executive sponsorship that established service management as a critical corporate priority

- ✔ Thorough evaluation and selection of comprehensive solutions that provided the necessary tools up front, as well as the ability to integrate additional components on Mercy's own schedule

- ✔ Set expectations up front, and established proactive, open, and collaborative processes to facilitate change

Partners HealthCare

Partners HealthCare, a not-for-profit organization, is the largest provider of medical services in Massachusetts. It was founded in 1994 by two of the top hospitals in the country, both in Boston: Brigham and Women's Hospital, and Massachusetts General Hospital. It includes large hospitals, community hospitals, primary care and specialty physicians, the two founding academic medical centers, specialty facilities, community health centers, and other health-related entities. Its goal is to provide "a continuum of coordinated high-quality care."

In 2000, Partners began to implement a service oriented architecture (SOA) strategy to share information in-network and among partners. In this way, patients can get the best possible care regardless of which facility they go to.

As Partners developed its portfolio of services, it realized that it needed a way to manage these services more effectively. Partners started a rudimentary process for vetting service requests, part of which involved arranging the services in a catalog that people could access. At first, the catalog was nothing more than a spreadsheet with information about the services; over time, it became a database that allowed users to request services.

As the services strategy evolved, IT had to provision these services and grant license to use them. This requirement set in motion a whole set of concerns related to use monitoring, performance monitoring, and security assurance. Partners needed to refine its approach to service management. This refinement included developing a monitoring and performance management strategy to ensure that services were meeting SLAs. In addition to monitoring service performance, the team made sure that it had a sound capacity management process in place so that unexpected spikes in service consumption didn't bring down the house.

Monitoring services

You can monitor a service at many levels. One of the first things that Partners needed to monitor was whether the consuming application was authorized to use a particular service. The IT team, under the direction of Steve Flammini, chief information officer of the information services group at Partners, implemented a security gateway to examine the credentials of the service call. That way, IT confirmed an authorized user and could attribute a level of use with that consumer.

The team also monitors the performance of the service at any given time and determines whether that performance meets its SLA requirements (if a SLA has been negotiated for the service). Flammini notes that in many cases, his team negotiates a SLA that is purely between the provider and the consumer. No blanket SLA applies to all consumers. IT works with different consumers to analyze their needs. If a specific performance level is required, a cost can be established, the consuming organization agrees, and the performance level can technically be met, the SLA is implemented.

A given application may need to do a medication lookup on a medication formula, for example; that service is a standard service. According to Flammini, you don't want several applications designing their own medication lookups. This service is a core piece of functionality that should be offered in the enterprise as a service. The SLA may be that when the consuming application (such as an electronic record in which prescriptions are written) issues a call to do a drug search, that result needs to be returned within 200 milliseconds. Before the implementation, the team does some load and performance testing, and performs simulations to ensure that the service can really turn this functionality around within that amount of time.

A lot of services used by a lot of applications can mean a lot of negotiation. The team delivers high-performance services that can scale, and in most cases those services are well within the performance window of any application's potential needs. The team can deliver this result because it has a sound underlying architecture and has done ample load testing.

Service performance may be affected by how often a service is consumed, so the team also tracks consumption patterns within the infrastructure. And, when a service doesn't meet its SLA, the team has to do some diagnostic investigation to see whether the service is being overly consumed. If someone applied to consume a service 10,000 times a day but actually calls it 100,000 times a day, that's overconsumption. The team looks at the consumption pattern and the infrastructure to find hot spots.

Planning capacity needs

In some cases, the team sees a much larger jump in usage on a particular service than it thought it would see. According to Flammini, the cause could be a bad design decision, an invocation bug, or explosive uptake in these services for various applications.

One example of a service that's experienced a large uptick in demand is the Enterprise Master Patient Index (EMPI), which was rolled out in 2005. In this identity-driven system, a patient's medical-record number is attached to all of his charts and paperwork. If a patient who's normally treated at one hospital in the network goes to another hospital or provider, that provider can request patient information by using these services. In effect, the EMPI is a unique customer identifier. Virtually all applications across the enterprise — whether they were developed in-house or purchased, and whether they are clinical, administrative, or data warehousing applications — depend on the EMPI as their source of patient information and identity. This service may be called upon tens of millions of times per day.

Partners on the back end must to be prepared to handle the growth. This requires capacity planning. According to Flammini, it sounds like "mother-hood and apple pie" to say that you have to sit down with IT and clinical systems leadership to understand how aggressively that organization wants to push out systems and understand their growth projections. However, the IT team needs to understand these plans so they don't get caught in a growth situation they may be unable to handle.

For example, in the case of the EMPI, IT sits down with the consumer to try to understand their consumption patterns. Are they going to have to call the EMPI service a dozen times each time they open a patient record — or just once? Or are they going to continually call upon a service for data, or will they store that data locally to avoid calling repeatedly?

Identifying team roles

What happens when a problem occurs? Where does the organization turn? Partners has multiple service-provider teams that are experts in certain clinical domains such as medications or the EMPI. Each team has designers, developers, and support people who really understand the inner workings of these services and can work with consumers to resolve issues.

In addition to the specialists, Partners has a group of generalists who support the infrastructure, look at the underlying technology platform, and monitor whether CPU use is out of bounds. This group also looks at various levels of the infrastructure.

Partners has had great success with its SOA strategy, and part of that success has come from learning to manage these services. Although the need for a service management strategy was an outgrowth of a technical requirement, the result is that the company is now using its services in applications that it hadn't even imagined, and the service management strategy is enabling IT to deliver real value to the organization.

Chapter 21

Retail

*T*he retail market is highly competitive. If consumers don't like what they see in your stores, they might simply take their business elsewhere. Retailers understand that today, more than ever, they must deliver a memorable and positive customer experience. For companies that focus on entertainment-related products, such as music and movies, the competition is even more intense.

Although mom-and-pop stores still exist, the trend has been toward larger chains and giant multinational corporations. To win the hearts and minds of customers, many large retail stores need to provide top-notch service as well as a memorable experience. They may provide some form of entertainment in the store itself (such as a light-and-sound show or memorabilia), or they may furnish kiosks where customers can listen to music or sample movies, which helps close the deal faster.

The key to customer satisfaction is the same whether you're in a small or large store: Exceed customer expectations.

In this chapter, we profile Virgin Entertainment Group and, in particular, its U.S. Virgin Megastores. The IT group servicing these stores realized that it needed to provide its customers an experience that was always on. This goal meant that the hardware and software used in the stores — especially the software that completed sales — had to be maintained properly, which led the company to deploy an aggressive service monitoring strategy.

Virgin Entertainment Group

Virgin Entertainment Group is a subsidiary of Richard Branson's Virgin Group conglomerate. The company has annual revenue of about $200 million. It sells everything from music, movies, books, and videogames to electronics and lifestyle fashion. It also has an e-commerce and social networking site. Although its stores in the United States are closing, the company owns and operates about 150 Virgin Megastores in France, Japan, Australia, and the Middle East, all owned by local companies with licensing agreements that lead back to Branson.

According to Robert Fort, chief information officer of Virgin Entertainment, the company had a critical need for real-time information about everything from sales to overall operational data. When Fort was walking through a store early in his tenure, he realized how important the customer experience was to the success of the brand. The company prides itself on providing a dynamic in-store environment, knowing that it has only a short time to make a positive impression on a customer. "Once we had established that customer experience, we realized it could be easily undermined by an inoperative kiosk or a register that was not working properly," he says. These kinds of problems could damage the company's bottom line.

(Store) room for improvement

Fort quickly determined that the company needed to monitor — proactively and persistently — all the services and features that it offered customers. By doing so, it could get right on top of any outages and, more important, "get out in front of those so that they don't even occur," he says.

Fort assessed his own organization and realized that he didn't have the resources to check every kiosk touchscreen. He wanted to monitor the uptime of all critical components, which included in-store technology and all the backbone components from IT, such as key servers, point-of-sale (POS) servers, and the registers right on down to the kiosks themselves.

A critical element of the monitoring strategy is its business focus. When a problem occurs, that problem is immediately tied to a business process. If a key network component fails, the IT department immediately becomes aware of which business processes are affected, such as credit processing or kiosks. Then it notifies the stores involved about the issue and takes corrective actions to prevent any effect on customers. A kiosk's failure at the same time as a credit failure is deemed to be less critical than the credit failure, so IT prioritizes its responses and resources appropriately.

The circle game

As the IT team embarked on its service monitoring effort, Fort realized that he needed to determine the most critical components of the Megastore infrastructure. He drew a series of concentric circles to help him organize his thoughts around these components. The innermost circle included core critical servers, network, and voice over IP (VoIP) components. The next circle contained the POS servers, which would bring all sales at a store to a screeching halt if they went down. This circle also contained credit services, which depend on the network to get customers' credit cards validated. (A store could continue to accept credit cards if the network was down, of course, but it would assume greater risk.) The next circle out included the registers, the circle beyond that one included the kiosks . . . you get the picture.

The failure of a single register or a single kiosk is less important than the failure of the whole system, but it still leaves a negative impression with customers. Typically, one register would fail and wouldn't be reported to the help desk. When the help desk finally got a call, the report was that multiple registers were down and associated monitors weren't functioning.

Overarching everything in the retail space is the Payment Card Industry (PCI) initiative, which includes mandates from card companies such as Visa MasterCard on how to protect customer data. Fort knew that he had to monitor the credit process very tightly, making sure that IT was aware of any outages or anomalies so that the company was PCI-compliant.

Monitor the infrastructure; think about the business

The team implemented a commercial monitoring application that could answer questions like these:

- ✔ Is the machine running?
- ✔ Does it have the appropriate amount of disk space?
- ✔ Does it have memory problems?
- ✔ Is it connected to the network?

The software also monitors application, database, and operating systems. In all, the team monitors more than 2,000 components. Any number of components make up a business process, and a failure in any physical component could affect one or more business processes. The team also can monitor individual business transactions such as credit card purchases, which helps Virgin remain compliant with PCI.

Fort is quick to point out that although the company is monitoring these components at a *technical level*, it receives information about the impact of events at a *business level*. At the technical level, you can imagine that the networks at each of the stores has a key router and switch to connect to the network cloud; behind those routers and switches are the POS servers and the individual registers, kiosks, media players, and digital signs.

At the technical level, someone may see the problem as being a router failure. At a business level, however, someone may see the problem as being an inability to process credit or sales. When a router goes down, the monitoring team not only sees red flags, but also knows which series of business processes is being affected, which helps the team determine the level of priority.

When IT knows the business impact, it can make the appropriate decision. A problem that might affect $100,000 worth of sales that day (if the registers go down, for example) gets top priority; it needs to be fixed no matter how much the repair costs. If, on the other hand, the issue might affect $20 worth of sales (a digital sign isn't working, for example), expediting a fix for it isn't worth a huge expense.

Don't light my fire

Automated monitoring meant a change for the network engineering team, which was used to a firefighting mentality. If something went wrong, team members got involved. It was a bit of a shift to look at a dashboard that lit up and a sent e-mail to report that something was amiss. The alert e-mail didn't necessarily say that the system had crashed — it might simply say that a database table increased by more than 10 percent in a single day — but it could predict a problem that needed investigation. The idea was to prevent the fire from coming.

This change affected many engineers' personal measures of success, because no one would necessarily know that he'd averted a potential disaster. In fact, several engineers left the organization to move to areas where they could start building new networks.

Fort attributes this situation to a maturity curve, saying that some personality types may find it unrewarding to monitor smoke instead of fighting raging fires. He imagines it this way: On the left side of a firefighting icon are the data-center-minded people, who are very process-oriented types who believe in governance and don't particularly care for fires. On the other side of the icon are the people who love fires, are always off to something new, and love to push boundaries. Fort believes that every organization going through service management will eventually move from one side of the icon to the other.

Chapter 22

Hospitality

*D*o you simply want a clean bed to sleep in when you travel, or do you opt for luxurious accommodations with a health club, infinity swimming pool, and Zen-style spa? Or do you insist on a green hotel with an environmental conscience? Whatever your preference, many of the largest hotel management companies operate multiple brands catering to a wide variety of market segments.

The competition in this industry is intense and has become even more challenging given the sharp decline in spending on leisure and business travel as both families and businesses tighten their budgets. Businesses in the hospitality industry use the diversity and quality of their services as a way to differentiate themselves from the competition. Although the quality of services such as housekeeping, restaurant meals, room service, and concierge assistance depends heavily on the performance of hotel staff, a lot of technical infrastructure is required in the background. The organization needs an agile and efficient infrastructure to focus on optimizing the customer experience. Guest profiles, housekeeping status, staffing reports, and other operations data must be available on demand to hotel management to ensure a positive experience for guests.

In addition, large hotel and resort companies employ many channels to serve customers, including the Web, call centers, travel partners, global distribution systems, travel agents, and other intermediaries. If you want your guests to keep coming back, they need on-demand access to room rates and availability from their preferred channels. Companies such as the one profiled in this chapter have implemented a service oriented architecture (SOA) to deploy these services more effectively. You can't deploy SOA, however, if you don't have the techniques in place to manage and govern these services. Managing the business services of an SOA environment is an integral part of a holistic approach to service management. (For more information on SOA, see Chapter 6.)

This chapter looks at the experience of one of the largest hotel groups in the world to show how it's leveraging a technology center of excellence to ensure effective governance of its many SOA-based business services.

InterContinental Hotels Group

InterContinental Hotels Group (IHG) includes a large, diverse group of well-known names in the hospitality industry: InterContinental Hotels & Resorts, Crowne Plaza Hotels & Resorts, Holiday Inn Hotels & Resorts, Holiday Inn Express, Staybridge Suites, Candlewood Suites, and Hotel Indigo. The organization also manages Priority Club Rewards, which is the world's largest hotel loyalty program, with more than 37 million members worldwide. The group manages more than 4,000 hotels in more than 100 countries.

Since 2002, IHG has deployed SOA to provide agility and efficiency. The following example illustrates how IHG leveraged SOA to improve its focus on customer service. Customer loyalty is very important to IHG, as evidenced by the success of its Priority Club reward system. The customer-loyalty division might access the SendGift service to send a thank-you gift to guests. On the other hand, the distribution division can reuse the same SendGift service to send coupons to other Priority Club members whom it feels might book a room at one of its hotels. As the company saw the number of services climbing — and the projected growth of the number of service consumers climbing even more rapidly — it recognized the need to ensure standards and governance. This situation happened when the company had deployed somewhere between 50 and 100 services.

Creating a center of excellence

IHG's chief information officer, Tom Conophy, who joined IHG in 2006, emphasized the need for governance as part of a disciplined service management process. He felt that the Global Technology organization needed to optimize its management of the growing number of business services. To do this, the company created what it called the Advanced Technology Platform (ATP). The vision and principles of service management and governance were embodied in the development of the ATP Center of Excellence (COE), instituted in 2008.

The ATP COE is a virtual body. Its members (all at director level or higher) are from departments across global technology at IHG that represent various service domains. A guest is one domain, for example. For a hotel company, the domain guest is very important. The person at the director level who owns the guest domain is the representative in the COE. Other domains include hotel, owner, product, revenue, and reservation.

Here's how the COE works: When the business generates a new initiative, a member of the IHG enterprise architecture team studies it, determines what domains it will affect, and contacts the domain owners. This research occurs in the early stages of a project, when funding has been approved but the service hasn't been designed, to give the governance team early involvement in the process. If a new service involves the guest domain, for example, the guest-domain owner is notified. Then the domain owner determines what kind of information will be requested, as well as any required changes. Because a change to one service may affect other services, a dialogue often begins among domain owners.

The COE provides a holistic view of all the managed business services and institutes a process for vetting decisions about services. The group has the power to mandate change. Its two top priorities are managing the life cycle of services and improving the process for managing provider–consumer relationships.

Managing the service life cycle

One of the COE's key goals is developing an ongoing process to manage services from a life-cycle perspective. Bill Peer, director of enterprise architecture in IHG Global Technology, says, "Once you have your services identified, they have a life cycle of their own. They have their own birth, generation, existence, and death. You need to accommodate all phases of life of these services." An enterprise the size of IHG has many domains staffed by people with varying levels of expertise. No one person can know everything about every service.

Unanticipated situations occur as services age. Many challenges occur in relationship to change management. A service may have operated just fine for several years under the direction of a particular business unit, but evolving business priorities shook things up a bit. A different business unit initiated a new business opportunity, which required an upgrade to the original service.

Before moving forward, the company had to answer the following types of questions:

- Who created this service?
- Who has the authority to make a change?
- Who do we need to contact to understand the full impact of making changes in the service?

✔ How many versions of this service should be maintained?

✔ Are different service versions compatible?

Before the development of the COE, questions such as these were hard to answer and possibly weren't considered at all.

Collaboration between domain owners

As services become more complex and more widely used, good communication among service providers and users became essential. At IHG, domain owners vary the types of communication about services depending on complexity. The logical approach for handling a trivial issue is using e-mail that gets captured, stored, and chronicled. When technical requirements demand greater interaction, the domain owners discuss the issues during a formal meeting. The enterprise architecture group facilitates meetings of this type. According to Peer, one of the key benefits of the COE is that the "collective knowledge of the group really makes this thing work."

Meeting service levels

Every service has a service-level minimum to adhere to. One application may have to respond in 100 milliseconds; another, in 150. Both applications use one or more services. IHG always develops its services to accommodate the shortest interval of time. That 100-millisecond response time becomes the service-level agreement (SLA) unless another request requires 75 milliseconds, in which case the response time can be adjusted. Therefore, different applications don't have unique response times. The team members understand that this approach involves trade-offs, but they chose it for its simplicity.

The group discusses hardware and operational cost implications before agreeing to change something, such as a response time. A business reason for lowering that response time may exist, yet the hardware costs may be prohibitive. The business always gets involved. The COE highlights the pros and cons of changing the SLA and then presents the details to the business to decide whether it can pay the price.

Sometimes, the process isn't as straightforward as getting one business unit to agree to a change. If an SLA has to be met for a broader project (such as a marketing or brand-driven project), the team turns to a businessperson in that guest domain. That person may or may not be in the reporting structure of the part of the business unit that's requesting the change, so getting the business units talking is important. The units can decide whether it's possible to share the cost and, if not, who will pay it.

Finding a balance

Peer is quick to point out the importance of finding a balance in the governance process. He believes that if governance is too formal, it stifles innovation. On the other hand, a governance process needs to be in place. His team's process appears to be working. Peer structured the process to make it part of the project-initiation request process, which has become an early indicator for the business coming down the pike. The COE has helped give multiple domain owners advance knowledge of changes in business services. Taking a life-cycle approach to service management helps IT be more responsive to business needs.

Chapter 23

Education

Computer technology is becoming ubiquitous in schools around the world. Students routinely use computers to research and write papers. Teachers use computer technology when planning lessons, enhancing classroom instruction, and posting assignments. Even some courses starting in middle school teach children how to use a computer for media design. As some of today's students begin using computers at home before they even learn to read, they feel very comfortable with the increasing use of technology. Finding the best way to integrate computer technology equitably across different schools in a community is often a hot topic of debate among educators, but for purposes of this chapter, put the debate aside.

Assuming that all things are equal, how do you maintain classroom technology? You can't have a technician waiting at every school. Besides, more and more computers are arriving while budgets are falling.

In this chapter, we consider the situation of Commission scolaire de la Région-de-Sherbrooke in Quebec, Canada. The school board's technology demands were increasing, and expanding the service team wasn't an option. The organization used a service management approach to help it manage and maintain its technology more effectively while still fulfilling its mission.

Commission scolaire de la Région-de-Sherbrooke

The Sherbrooke school board serves 20,000 students in Quebec. Its IT group is responsible for maintaining the computer technology in all the region's schools. The service technicians were well trained and good at their jobs, but the school board was facing a problem: The school's budget was falling because fewer students were enrolled, but the number of computers was increasing as technology became an integral part of the learning process. At one point, the IT department actually slowed computer purchases because of maintenance considerations.

Historically, different technicians had serviced different schools. Some of these technicians did everything — even replacing toner cartridges in the printers, planning computer purchases, and supporting software for teachers. Others were more focused on dealing with computer-related problems.

The IT department at the school board realized that it needed to provide quality, uniform service across the schools more effectively. Achieving this goal meant making some painful choices, such as deciding which services would have the best payback and support the school board's mission. Accordingly, IT reorganized the technical support team and implemented a service management strategy to help streamline maintenance.

Organizing to succeed

IT management's first step was tackling inconsistent service. To train the technicians to work together, IT sent them all to a program in which they simulated an airport and had to work together to schedule airplane departures. At first, as typically is the case, the process was chaotic; in other words, the team didn't come together well. The technicians soon realized the importance of organizing to meet a goal, however.

The next step was identifying a set of service management tools to help the team succeed. A service desk was at the top of the list. IT encountered a snag, though: In Quebec, most school-board technicians are part of a union. Implementing a service desk required talking to the union representatives to make sure that they understood the aim of the changes: not to change the job requirements, but to make technicians more efficient. The process took a bit of time, but eventually agreements were shored up, and the team was set to roll.

Deploying the strategy

The team began to deploy its service management strategy with a focus on three key areas:

- Asset management
- Desktop management
- Incident management

Asset management

A configuration management database (CMDB) stores all the asset information across the schools. Before the CMDB was implemented, the school board kept a semiautomated inventory of all computer-related hardware and software. As the number of computers exploded, keeping the list up to date was a difficult, time-consuming process. After implementing the asset management software, which did automatic discovery, the team had time to engage in more productive work. The tool also gave the management team the information it needed for use in budget planning, such as calculating the computers-to-students ratio for each school.

Desktop management

In addition to getting its hardware under control, IT was interested in managing its software installations more effectively. Instead of having technicians do the work at each site, the team used desktop management software that enabled IT to stream software installations to the school board's computers. This method also allowed IT to track what software was running on the school board's machines. Management refers to this system as "on-demand installation." If someone wants to install a Microsoft product on her machine, for example, she simply chooses it from a menu of supported programs, and the software is installed automatically.

Incident management

The school board is also trying to deal with incident management more productively. Before the service desk was launched, all the technicians spent a lot of time traveling. Now the team is transitioning to a remote management process, adding technicians to the process one at a time. First, the team asks one technician to do business as usual (such as traveling to different sites) while it monitors him; then the team asks him to do the same type of work remotely.

The school board will end up with a limited number of field workers; the rest of the technicians will work remotely, going to a school only for hardware problems (which must be repaired on-site). This system increases the time that technicians can spend solving requests.

Changing the way things are done

The new process takes some getting used to. For one thing, IT is specifying exactly what the technicians should do. Says Philippe Caron, adjoint director of IT, "People like a gray line because then they can ask a technician to do something that really isn't in his job description. Under the new process, school staff members have to do some things themselves." To help them along, IT is creating self-service documentation for tasks such as changing a printer cartridge.

Establishing best practices

Caron recommends that organizations begin with a framework to implement change successfully. "When the department of finance makes a decision, it bases its actions on laws. IT should also base its decisions on tangible policies and processes," he says.

After spending a lot of time researching frameworks, IT implemented the Information Technology Infrastructure Library (ITIL), which is a best-practices framework. (For more information about ITIL, see Chapter 5.) Caron's group suggests the following best practices, which Caron calls Think, Read, and Adapt:

- ✔ **Think:** This best practice involves considering questions such as how to implement the framework, whether successful applications and processes can be reused, how to identify the strengths and weaknesses of IT services, and how to identify and assess priorities.

- ✔ **Read:** Locate some documentation on the process you want to implement, and find examples of business-related experiences that relate to your company. Read as much as you can about the process you want to use.

- ✔ **Adapt:** Don't implement a framework directly; framework theories are created to meet many needs. Don't be afraid to implement only the parts of processes that fit your precise needs.

  Persuading people inside IT that a framework is needed is fairly easy; persuading others can take a bit longer.

Caron says that every day, people tell him that they're happy with the new service center. Although staff members miss seeing certain technicians at their schools, they like the on-demand service, which means that they don't have to wait for a preassigned service day. The most significant benefit has been enabling the school board to do a better job of achieving its mission: providing the best educational environment for its students so that all of them can learn, excel, and graduate.

Chapter 24

Service Provider

Service providers are in the business of managing other companies' IT operations. By providing technology-based services to multiple customers, they offer economies of scale and skill. Rather than bearing the costs of IT specialists and infrastructure on their own, customers can turn over part or all of their IT operations to service providers that offer a pool of highly specialized technical talent, resources, capabilities, and processes. By spreading these investments out over many customers, service providers can offer reduced IT costs and higher-quality services.

Before turning over any part of IT operations to a service provider, however, a customer must have confidence that the provider will satisfy the company's unique business, technological, and governance requirements. To do this cost-effectively for a broad range of customers, service providers need an accountable, responsive organization, as well as the tools and processes that enable them to deliver flexible, streamlined services.

In this chapter, we profile CIBER, Inc., an international system integration consultancy and outsourcing company. By definition, the company must provide service management capabilities to its clients to ensure that customer expectations are being met. An important part of this service is delivering on service-level agreement (SLA) commitments. The company is evolving its SLAs from technically focused to business focused as the trend becomes more prevalent.

CIBER

CIBER provides a wide variety of IT services, from physical data center services through different types of infrastructure software support to technical database administration, to customers throughout the United States, Europe, and Asia. Its IT Outsourcing Division (ITO) focuses on supplying operations and infrastructure outsourcing services to companies in a wide variety of industries.

In a typical scenario, an ITO transition project manager works with a new client to resolve architectural issues and optimize the IT environment before migrating to a hosted production environment. After a new customer's deployment is live, an ITO service manager takes over day-to-day management. As a primary component of the managed service, CIBER has implemented a robust monitoring and reporting capability to ensure that its SLAs are not being breached, as well as to prevent and remediate any incidents in the enterprise it is serving.

Service management solutions: Then and now

When ITO was formed, it used a basic service management solution. "This was good from a help desk perspective in terms of logging tickets but didn't give us a complete picture of the service," says Keenan Phelan, vice president of global managed services. As it grew, ITO needed a more robust, end-to-end solution that would give service managers the visibility to manage all aspects of daily service governance, satisfy SLA and key performance indicator obligations, and provide proactive guidance to clients.

In 2005, the organization chose an integrated service management solution to fulfill these requirements. Built on an information repository, the solution gives ITO ticketing and monitoring services that allow the team to react quickly to situations, as well as to govern and track information flow seamlessly to resolution. If a server goes down, for example, the system automatically alerts the Technical Operations Network Operating Center, which evaluates the alert. If something has failed, the center creates an incident ticket and routes it to designated ITO personnel, the customer, or a third party for resolution.

Troubleshooting

The integrated system also helps ITO troubleshoot and restore service as quickly as possible without affecting users. Recurring or major incidents are graduated to the problem management stage, at which staff members identify the root cause of the failure, whether it's a process, technology, or personnel. If a change is necessary, the problem rolls into the change management function, where staffers can make modifications and restore service. Along the way, Phelan says, "The system allows CIBER to react to the situation and govern communication to both end users and internal client IT contacts."

Reporting

ITO uses the reports that the system generates about SLA metrics, such as reaction times to calls, response times to resolve issues, and information on infrastructure health to take a more proactive approach to managing service. "Reviewing service-level agreements on a proactive basis with our customers helps to avoid problematic situations down the road . . . by addressing questions and issues that can become contentious *before* they become problems," Phelan says.

Service managers use these reports, along with knowledge of new IT trends, to advise clients in quarterly business reviews. As an example, they might provide insight on the cost and reliability benefits of relocating systems to a CIBER data center or about using virtualization solutions to reduce an organization's physical IT footprint. Says George Maroulakos, director of global service management, "Many times, the CIO of an organization will ask us to protect him from himself. . . . The strategic direction we provide improves the level and value of the service we offer and helps them protect themselves."

Service-level agreements: Business versus technical

ITO has always used technical SLAs — such as response times and availability levels — as measuring sticks for performance. CIBER, however, recently signed contracts with clients in the United Kingdom and United States to deliver jointly determined business SLAs. This type of SLA guarantees the outcome of a business process. A technical SLA might state that a system is up 99.9 percent of the time; the business SLA might state that the customer will get her report every day at 8 am. One SLA is technology-focused; the other is business-service-focused.

See Chapter 17 for a discussion of business service management.

ITO is finding that business SLAs can be double-edged swords. On the plus side, it can use the process of negotiating and fulfilling business SLA obligations to extend the client relationship beyond the IT organization and better understand client requirements. But business SLAs are more difficult for the service provider to craft and guarantee; they also carry more risk, because all the service levels that feed the business service must be met.

"Although business SLAs may appear simpler on paper, they don't simplify back-end requirements," Phelan says. For a client, the business SLA requirement for e-mail is simple: Users need to be able to send and receive e-mail and perform messaging activities around the clock. To provide this service level, ITO must meet the same technical SLAs for availability, reliability, and performance that it normally would.

Measuring business SLAs

Because measuring a business SLA is more *binary* — the provider either does or doesn't deliver on a single metric, rather than on a series of metrics — it's also more subjective. Notes Maroulakos, "You can look at a particular server or storage unit and say it was up or down; here's the data to prove it. But if, from a business perspective, a single user or a handful of users claim they can't *use* the service, how do you prove or disprove that?"

Furthermore, crafting penalties for a business SLA is much trickier. "In reality, no penalty can ever reimburse the client for a loss of service to a business-critical system, and for us, the potential damage to our reputation could be exponential," says Phelan.

Mitigating potential issues

ITO takes a proactive, collaborative approach to mitigate potential issues. It works with clients to develop precise SLAs that detail different levels of penalties and risk assignment. In the e-mail example from earlier in this chapter, for example, the client needs to give CIBER a wide range of authority; there is very little room for dependencies on internal IT or third parties. "If you're going to hold me responsible, you have to give me the authority to control the environment," Phelan says.

Even when the customer grants this authority, ITO still can't control everything. It can host the system in its data centers and control the network, server platforms, and software changes. It can hold dual contracts with carriers for redundancy, and it can control administration and management rights. But it can't control carrier failures or random acts of nature or man that could bring a system down.

Some customers also find it difficult to grasp the cost implications associated with guaranteeing higher levels of business service. "Sometimes a client starts off insisting on hyperavailability. But I can guarantee that they won't buy it, because when the CFO sees that if they accept three or four more hours of downtime, they can cut capital costs by up to 50 percent," Phelan says.

Although just a few customers have requested business SLAs to date, ITO sees increasing interest, particularly in industries such as retail, in which companies already use IT outsourcing extensively. In addition, Phelan says, "European countries have shown more interest — probably because they tend to be ahead of U.S. companies in ITIL [Information Technology Infrastructure Library; see Chapter 5] adoption and take a more disciplined approach." But, he adds, "If we were actively marketing it, a lot of U.S. clients would probably find it really interesting." Before it does this, however, ITO wants to make sure that it gets the details and processes right.

Lessons learned and best practices

Through years of managing IT infrastructure for its clients, ITO has developed many insights about implementing an effective service management strategy. Some of its top guidelines follow:

✔ **Service management systems aren't cure-alls.** Companies "can't take an environment that doesn't function well and put in a new systems management solution and suddenly make it function well," Phelan says. "You need to also resolve underlying architectural issues first."

✔ **Reality-check the cost of availability.** Each 9 after the decimal point in 99.999 percent availability costs exponentially more than the preceding one. Take a pragmatic approach, and determine the point of diminishing returns.

✔ **Internal issues don't solve themselves.** If you're planning to outsource infrastructure and service management, remember that internal operational issues won't automatically go away when you outsource. Work with the outsourcer up-front to identify architectural problems and address them before you hand off daily management.

✔ **Implement measurable technical SLAs before moving to business SLAs.** If you haven't yet established an SLA culture, it will be difficult to go directly to the more subjective business SLA right out the gate.

Part VI
The Part of Tens

The 5th Wave   By Rich Tennant

Oh come on —
how fatal
can it be?

FATAL
ERROR

In this part . . .

We know that you've already memorized this entire book. But in case you're interested, this part gives you some tips to consider as you make your way through service management. Because we're so nice, we also list some resources that you may find useful.

Chapter 25

Ten Service Management Dos and Don'ts

In This Chapter

▶ Balancing business objectives with service performance

▶ Understanding business processes

▶ Recognizing the importance of standards

▶ Choosing the right starting point

This chapter carves out a few dos and don'ts. We want you to benefit from the mistakes of other people — including us.

Do Remember Business Objectives

If you want to deliver high-quality service, you need to satisfy your customers' expectations. Sometimes, these expectations conflict with the policies and performance objectives of your business. Service management must find the right balance between optimizing performance/service delivery and meeting business objectives.

Service management needs to account for both customer satisfaction *and* business stakeholder requirements. You may spend too much money making customers very happy and lose money in the process, for example, so customer satisfaction needs to be balanced against costs to the company.

Don't Stop Optimizing after a Single Process

IT service management requires continuous process improvement. Although improving a single process may be satisfying, it won't be enough. You have to look at the overall processes that make the business operate efficiently.

Do Remember Business Processes

You have to understand the processes for all things IT, from application management, system management, and performance management to service desk, network management, and database management. When you know how to optimize service delivery, you can take a proactive approach to service management, such as analyzing and documenting workflows, optimizing performance, and conforming to regulatory requirements.

Do Plan for Cultural Change

What is your corporate culture? How well do employees adapt to changes in everything from new technology to new processes? It's common for employees to want to keep doing things the old-fashioned way. If you're going to change the way your IT organization works, however, you have to change the way people think about their jobs.

Cultural change is an important part of creating a businesscentric approach to service management. Your IT team needs to work together in a new way if you want to move from fighting the latest fire to donning fire-retardant pajamas. The responsibilities and roles for your IT service providers probably will change; clarify expectations at the beginning of your change process. You should be able to redefine your service-level agreements and get better at responding to business priorities. If the members of your IT team measure their performance by the number of crises they solve, they need to redefine the way they look at their jobs.

Don't Neglect Governance

IT governance is a combination of policy, process, controls, a stash of a consistent source of data about IT services, and the means to control those services — and it isn't easy to achieve. You must balance your focus on the key performance indicators of the business with performance of all IT components. IT governance is successful only if you align it with overall corporate governance requirements. Think about how you're going to get from where you are now to a well-coordinated approach that fits your corporate goals and objectives. This topic is an important one, so we refer you to Chapter 10 for more details on governance.

Do Keep Security in Mind

With all those services to manage, don't lose sight of who gets access to what. Concern yourself with the security of data, hardware, software, and physical assets. The convergence of physical security with the security of IT systems (fingerprint identity and electronic passcodes) is becoming an important part of comprehensive service management. We provide a lot more details on security in Chapter 16.

Don't Try to Manage Services without Standardization and Automation

You have a lot of smart people on your IT team. But if you have a lot of infrastructure components — and we expect that you do — no single person will know everything about all your servers or applications. The person who knows how to solve complicated service requests may leave the company someday. Improve standardization and automate processes to create a repeatable way to get the job done right.

Do Remember Industry Standards and Best Practices

Don't assume your requirements are so unique that you can't benefit from looking at established standards and best practices. Following best practices that other companies have successfully implemented will help you implement your service strategy faster.

Education is a good first step for your business. Send your team members to become certified in Information Technology Infrastructure Library (ITIL) practices, which we cover in Chapter 5. Study best-practices models that have been designed for your industry. Chapters 4 and 5 provide a lot more information on standards and best practices, and Chapter 26 tells you where to find some great resources on these standards.

Do Start with a Visible Project

Make sure that your initial service management project is well defined and well confined. Go for the biggest bang for the buck. Initially, try something visible, such as a service catalog that documents information about IT services. Many organizations begin by implementing a service desk that helps focus on solving immediate problems. Prove your success with a project that's achievable in a short time, with a significant effect on the business; then build incrementally.

Don't Postpone Service Management

Service management is a journey, and the sooner you begin, the sooner you'll get somewhere. Service management requires paying constant attention and balancing business priorities with available resources. A finely tuned and responsive IT service management approach drives business value.

Chapter 26

Ten Swell Service Management Resources

We've spoken with lots of people who have to manage the delivery of IT services at their companies, and we share some of their experiences with you in Part V. What's the number-one lesson? Don't reinvent the wheel! Take advantage of existing best practices by sending your team for certification programs and using others' experiences when planning.

This chapter lists resources that we hope you'll find useful as you plan and execute your service management strategy.

Hurwitz & Associates

www.hurwitz.com

We here at Hurwitz & Associates, the authors of *Service Management For Dummies* and *Service Oriented Architecture For Dummies,* 2nd Edition (along with other books, research reports, and commentary), are happy to help you with your service management questions. We can give a talk, do specialized research, and help you find the right technology partners. We invite you to subscribe to our monthly newsletter and visit our Web site.

ITIL

`www.itil-officialsite.com`

The Information Technology Infrastructure Library (ITIL) is a set of books on best practices for IT service management. ITIL was created in the United Kingdom in the 1980s and has become one of the most comprehensive sets of best practices on service management. The five core books in ITIL Version 3 — introduced in 2007 — focus on service strategy, service design, service transition, service operation, and continuous service improvement. ITIL emphasizes the importance of taking a life-cycle approach to service management. We have a lot more to say about implementing ITIL in Chapter 5.

ITIL Central

`http://itsm.fwtk.org`

Use the ITIL Central Web site to find helpful information about implementing ITIL best practices at your company and discover educational opportunities for yourself. The Web site offers an ITIL toolkit with materials to help you get started, including fact sheets on the major ITIL disciplines.

ISO

`www.iso.org`

The International Organization for Standardization (ISO) brings together representatives from all over the world to agree on international business standards. Many thousands of standards are related to all matters of doing business. The most relevant standards for technology are developed by the industry along with the International Electrotechnical Commission (IEC). Several of these standards — such as ISO 9001, ISO/IEC 20000, and ISO/IEC 38500 — are specific to the requirements for an effective service management system. We provide a short summary of the ISO service management standards in Chapter 4.

ISACA and COBIT

`www.isaca.org` and `www.isaca.org/cobit`

The Information Systems Audit and Control Association (ISACA) is a membership organization for information governance, control, security, and employee auditing. The organization has set many standards for IT auditing and control, and it offers a certification program in IT governance.

ISACA and its affiliate, the IT Governance Institute, first released the Control Objectives for Information and Related Technology (COBIT) in 1996. Many updates have been made since that time, including COBIT 4.1 in 2007.

COBIT is an IT governance framework and tool set designed to help businesses understand the relationship among technology, regulatory compliance, and controls, as well as the management of business risks. The COBIT publications are available free of charge on the Web site.

eSCM

www.itsqc.cmu.edu

The eSourcing Capability Model (eSCM) is a framework developed at Carnegie Mellon University that is intended to provide a best-practices model for improving relationships between customers and suppliers. eSCM has two distinct models:

- ✔ **eSCM-SP:** A best-practices model for service providers in IT-enabled sourcing. Use it as both an improvement road map and a certification standard.

- ✔ **eSCM-CL:** A best-practices model for client organizations and companies that outsource IT services to external service providers. The eSCM helps client organizations improve the results they get from their service providers.

CMMI

www.sei.cmu.edu/cmmi

Capability Maturity Model Integration (CMMI) is a process-improvement best-practices model used to improve processes in a project or organization. It was developed by the Software Engineering Institute of Carnegie Mellon University in connection with representatives of industry and government.

eTOM

www.tmforum.org/BusinessProcessFramework/1647/home.html

The enhanced Telecom Operations Map (eTOM) Business Process Framework helps build a common vocabulary for both business and functional processes in the communications industry. The framework helps businesses prioritize operational areas based on those that will have the greatest impact on the business. The framework covers life-cycle, operational, and corporate management.

TechTarget

`www.techtarget.com`

TechTarget.com is a comprehensive online resource for all sorts of IT-related information, providing links to IT communities that focus on different areas of interest. SearchCIO.com, for example, has lots of information about IT products and software vendors targeted to the needs of chief information officers and senior IT executives in large enterprises. Another site you may want to check out is SearchCompliance.com — which, as you may have guessed, focuses on information about creating a manageable compliance infrastructure.

Vendor Sites

All the major vendors that sell solutions for service management provide great resources online. We recommend that you check out vendors such as IBM, Computer Associates, Hewlett-Packard, BMC, Oracle, Progress Software, and Microsoft.

Glossary

access control: Determining who or what can go where, when, and how.

ACID: An acronym for *atomicity, consistency, isolation,* and *durability,* which are the main requirements for proper transaction processing.

API (application programming interface): A collection of subroutine calls that allow computer programs to use a software system.

architecture: In information processing, the design approach taken in developing a program or system.

archiving: The process by which database or file data that is seldom used or is outdated, but is required for historical or audit reasons, is copied to a cheaper form of storage. The storage medium may be online, tape, or optical disc.

asset management: Software that allows organizations to record all information about their hardware and software. Most such applications capture cost information, license information, and so on. Such information belongs in the configuration management database. *See also* CMDB.

audit: A check on the effectiveness of a task or set of tasks, and how the tasks are managed and documented.

audit trail: A trace of a sequence of events in a clerical or computer system. This audit usually identifies the creation or modification of any element in the system, who did it, and (possibly) why it was done.

authentication: The process by which the identity of a person or computer process is verified.

backup: A utility that copies databases, files, or subsets of databases and files to a storage medium. This copy can be used to restore the data in case of serious failure.

bandwidth: Technically, the range of frequencies over which a device can send or receive signals. The term is also used to denote the maximum data transfer rate, measured in bits per second, that a communications channel can handle.

Basel II: Known more formally as the International Convergence of Capital Measurement and Capital Standards — A Revised Framework. Basel II is an internationally recognized set of rules for evaluating a bank's finances in light of various risks. It's also one of the big compliance regulations making organizations do things that they wouldn't otherwise feel compelled to do. (Basel, by the way, is named after a very lovely city in Switzerland.)

batch: A noninteractive process that runs in a queue, usually when the system load is lowest, generally used for processing batches of information in a serial and usually efficient manner. Early computers were capable of only batch processing.

best practice: An effective way of doing something. It can relate to anything from writing program code to IT governance.

binding: Making the necessary connections among software components so that they can interact.

biometrics: Using a person's unique physical characteristics to prove his identity to a computer — by employing a fingerprint scanner or voice analyzer, for example.

black box: A component or device with an input and an output whose inner workings need not be understood by or accessible to the user.

BPEL (Business Process Execution Language): A computer language based on WSDL (Web Services Description Language, an XML format for describing Web Services) and designed for programming business services. *See also* XML.

BPM (business process management): A technology and methodology for controlling the activities — both automated and manual — needed to make a business function.

broker: In computer programming, a program that accepts requests from one software layer or component and translates them into a form that can be understood by another layer or component.

browser: A program that lets you access information on the Internet. Browsers used to run just on personal computers, but now they are on cellphones and personal digital assistants and soon will appear on refrigerators.

bus: A technology that connects multiple components so they can talk to one another. In essence, a bus is a connection capability. A bus can be software (such as an enterprise service bus) or hardware (such as a memory bus). *See also* ESB.

business process: The codification of rules and practices that constitute a business.

business process modeling: A technique for transforming how business operates into a codified source in code so that it can be translated into software.

business rules: Constraints or actions that refer to the actual commercial world but may need to be encapsulated in service management or business applications.

business service: An individual function or activity that is directly useful to the business.

center of excellence: A group of key people from all areas of the business and operations that focuses on best practices. A center of excellence provides a way for groups within the company to collaborate. This group also becomes a force for change, as it can leverage its growing knowledge to help business units benefit from experience.

change management: The management of change in operational processes and applications.

client/server: A model of computing in which the various processes are classified as either consumers of services (clients) or providers of services (servers). This classification was once used as the basis for dividing processes among the available processors.

cloud computing: A computing model that makes IT resources such as servers, middleware, and applications available as services to business organizations in a self-service manner.

CMDB (configuration management database): In general, a repository of service management data.

CMMI (Capability Maturity Model Integration): A process-improvement best practice used to improve processes in a project or overall. The Software Engineering Institute of Carnegie Mellon University developed CMMI along with representatives of industry and government.

COBIT (Control Objectives for Information and Related Technology): An IT framework with a focus on governance and managing technical and business risks.

component: A piece of computer software that can be used as a building block in larger systems. Components can be parts of business applications that have been made accessible through Web Service–related standards and technologies, such as WSDL, SOAP, and XML. *See* Web Services.

configuration: The complete description of the way in which the constituent elements of a software product or system interrelate, both in functional and physical terms.

configuration management: The management of configurations, normally involving holding configuration data in a database so that the data can be managed and changed where necessary.

container: In computer programming, a data structure or object used to manage collections of other objects in an organized way.

CRM (customer relationship management): Software intended to help you run your sales force and customer support operations.

data cleansing: Software used to identify potential data-quality problems. If a customer is listed multiple times in a customer database due to variations of the spelling of her name, the data-cleansing software makes corrections to help standardize the data.

data fabric: The part of the computer network devoted to transmissions.

data federation: Data access to a variety of data stores, using consistent rules and definitions that enable all the data stores to be treated as a single resource.

data profiling: A technique or process that helps you understand the content, structure, and relationships of your data. This process also helps you validate your data against technical and business rules.

data quality: Characteristics of data such as consistency, accuracy, reliability, completeness, timeliness, reasonableness, and validity. Data-quality software ensures that data elements are represented in a consistent way across different data stores or systems, making the data more trustworthy across the enterprise.

data transformation: A process by which the format of data is changed so it can be used by different applications.

data warehouse: A large data store containing the organization's historical data, which is used primarily for data analysis and data mining.

database: A computer system intended to store large amounts of information reliably and in an organized fashion. Most databases provide users convenient access to the data, along with helpful search capabilities.

distributed processing: Spreading the work of an information processing application among several computers.

early binding: Making necessary connections among software components when the software system is first put together or built.

ERP (Enterprise Resource Planning): A packaged set of business applications that combines business rules, process, and data management into a single integrated environment to support a business.

ESB (enterprise service bus): A distributed middleware software system that allows computer applications to communicate in a standardized way.

eSCM (eSourcing Capability Model): A framework developed at Carnegie Mellon University to provide a best-practices model for improving relationships between customers and suppliers in outsourcing agreements.

ETL (Extract – Transform – Load): Tools for locating and accessing data from a data store (data extraction), changing the structure or format of the data so it can be used by the business application (data transformation), and sending the data to the business application (data load).

eTOM (enhanced Telecom Operations Map): A framework that provides a business process model for the telecommunications industry.

fault tolerance: The ability of a system to provide uninterrupted service despite the failure of one or more of the system's components.

federation: The combination of disparate things so that they can act as one — as in federated states, data, or identity management — and making sure that all the right rules apply.

framework: A support structure for developing software products.

GPL (GNU General Public License): An open-source copyright license created by Richard Stallman that, in its strictest form, requires programs built on code licensed under GPL to adopt the same license.

granularity: An important software design concept, especially in relation to components, referring to the amount of detail or functionality — from fine to coarse — provided in a service component. One software component can do something quite simple, such as calculate a square root; another has a great deal of detail and functionality to represent a complex business rule or workflow. The first component is fine-grained, and the second is coarse-grained. Developers often aggregate fine-grained services into coarse-grained services to create a business service.

grid computing: A step beyond distributed processing, involving large numbers of networked computers (often geographically dispersed and possibly of different types and capabilities) that are harnessed to solve a common problem.

HIPAA (Health Insurance Portability and Accountability Act of 1996): A set of extensive regulations that health care organizations and providers in the United States must follow. One of the goals of this act is to place controls on the health care system to protect patients' right to privacy regarding information about their health. The policies and regulations place significant demands on technology systems that have anything to do with health care.

HTML (Hypertext Markup Language): A data-encoding scheme invented by Tim Berners-Lee in 1991 and the basic way that information is encoded over the World Wide Web.

HTTP (Hypertext Transport Protocol): The basic way that information is linked and transmitted over the World Wide Web. HTTPS is a version of HTTP with encryption for security.

identity management: Keeping track of a single user's (or asset's) identity throughout an engagement with a system or set of systems.

information integration: A process using software to link data sources in various departments or regions of the organization with an overall goal of creating more reliable, consistent, and trusted information.

infrastructure: The fundamental systems necessary for the ordinary operation of anything, be it a country or an IT department. The physical infrastructure that people rely on includes roads, electrical wiring, and water systems. In IT, infrastructure includes basic computer hardware, networks, operating systems, and other software that applications run on top of.

infrastructure services: Services provided by the infrastructure. In IT, these services include all the software needed to make devices talk to one another, for starters.

Internet: A huge computer network linking almost all the computers in the world and enabling them to communicate via standard protocols (TCP/IP) and data formats. *See also* SMTP, TCP/IP, and XML.

interoperability: The ability of a product to interface with many other products; usually used in the context of software.

IP (Internet Protocol): A codified technique for communicating data across a packet-switched network. IP can also mean intellectual property such as patents, trademarks, copyrights, and trade secrets. *See also* TCP/IP.

ISO (International Organization for Standardization): An organization that has developed more than 17,000 international standards, including standards for IT service management and corporate governance of information technology.

ITIL (Information Technology Infrastructure Library): A framework and set of standards for IT governance based on best practices.

JCA (J2EE Connector Architecture): A technology that enables Java programs to talk to other software, such as databases and legacy applications.

key performance indicator (KPI): An indicator used to measure the effectiveness of a process.

LAMP: An increasingly popular open-source approach to building Web applications. LAMP comprises the Linux operating system; the Apache Web server; a MySQL database; and a scripting language such as PHP, Perl, or Python.

late binding: Deferring the necessary connections among applications to when the connection is first needed. Late binding allows more flexibility for changes than early binding does, but it imposes some cost in processing time.

legacy application: Any application more than a few years old. When applications can't be disposed of and replaced easily, they become legacy applications. The good news is that they're still doing something useful when selected pieces of code can be turned into business services with new standardized interfaces.

loose coupling: An approach to distributed software applications in which components interact by passing data and requests to other components in a standardized way that minimizes dependencies among components. The emphasis is on simplicity and autonomy. Each component offers a small range of simple services to other components.

malware: The general term for computer software that intentionally does ill, such as viruses, Trojans, worms, and spyware.

markup language: A way of encoding information that uses plain text containing special tags often delimited by angle brackets (< and >). Specific markup languages are often created, based on XML, to standardize the interchange of information between different computer systems and services. *See also* XML.

mashup: A program (possibly installed on a Web page) that combines content from more than one source, such as Google Maps and a real-estate listing service.

290 Service Management For Dummies

master-slave: An arrangement in which one system or process is designated as a controller and other participating systems or processes respond to this controller. Should a master fail, the slaves are unable to continue.

metadata: The definitions, mappings, and other characteristics used to describe how to find, access, and use the company's data and software components.

metadata repository: A container of consistent definitions of business data and rules for mapping data to their actual physical locations in the system.

middleware: Multipurpose software that lives at a layer between the operating system and application in distributed computing environments.

mission critical: An application that a business cannot afford to be without at any time.

MOM (Message Oriented Middleware): A precursor to the enterprise service bus. *See* ESB.

MySQL: An open-source option to SQL.

.NET: Pronounced *dot-net;* the latest Microsoft programming framework, with heavy emphasis on Web Services. *See also* Web Services.

network: The connection of computer systems (nodes) by communications channels and appropriate software.

OASIS (Organization for the Advancement of Structured Information Standards): A consortium promoting e-business and Web Services standards.

open source: A movement in the software industry that makes programs available along with the source code used to create them so that others can inspect and modify how programs work.

P2P (peer to peer): A networking system in which nodes in a network exchange data directly instead of going through a central server.

Perl (Practical Extraction and Report Language): A powerful scripting language in widespread use in system administration, Web development, and other activities.

PHP (PHP Hypertext Processor): An open-source scripting language (originally designed in Perl) used especially for producing dynamic Web pages.

portal: In computing, a window that contains a means of access, often a menu, to all the applications throughout the whole network that the user is able to run. Often, the window is segmented into smaller windows, or _portlets,_ that provide direct access to applications such as stock-market price feeds or e-mail.

programming in the large: An approach to developing business software that focuses on the various tasks or business processes needed to make the business function — processing an order, for example, or checking product availability — as opposed to more low-level technical tasks such as opening a file.

protocol: A set of rules that computers use to establish and maintain communication among themselves.

provisioning: Making resources available to users and software. A provisioning system makes applications available to users and makes server resources available to applications.

real time: A form of processing in which a computer system accepts and updates data at the same time, feeding back immediate results that influence the data source.

real-time event processing: A class of applications that demand timely response to actions that take place out in the world. Typical examples include automated stock trading and RFID. _See also_ RFID.

registry: A single source for all the metadata needed to gain access to a Web service or software component.

repository: A database for software and components, with an emphasis on revision control and configuration management (where they keep the good stuff, in other words).

response time: The time from the moment at which a transaction is submitted by a user or an application to the moment at which the final result of that transaction is made known to the user or application.

RFID (radio frequency identification): A technology that uses small, inexpensive chips attached to products (or even animals) that then transmit a unique identification number over a short distance to a special radio transmitter/receiver.

RPC (remote procedure call): A way for a program running on one computer to run a subprogram on another computer.

SaaS (Software as a Service): The delivery of computer applications over the Internet.

SAML: A standard framework for exchanging authentication and authorization information (that is, credentials) in an XML format called *assertions*.

Sarbanes-Oxley: The Public Company Accounting Reform and Investor Protection Act of 2002, a U.S. law enhancing standards for all U.S. public companies' boards of directors, resulting in substantial new requirements for corporate IT.

scalability: As regards to hardware, the ability to go from small to large amounts of processing power with the same architecture. It also applies to software products such as databases, in which case it refers to the consistency of performance per unit of power as hardware resources increase.

scripting language: A computer programming language that is interpreted and has access to all or most operating-system facilities. Common examples include Perl, Python, Ruby, and JavaScript. It is often easier to program in a scripting language, but the resulting programs generally run more slowly than those created in compiled languages such as C and C++.

semantics: In computer programming, what the data means as opposed to formatting rules (syntax).

server farm: A room filled with computer servers, often needed to run large Internet sites.

service: A purposeful activity carried out for the benefit of a known target. Services are often made up of a group of component services, some of which may also have component services. Services always transform something, and they complete by delivering an output.

service catalog: A directory of IT services provided across the enterprise, including information such as service description, access rights, and ownership.

service desk: A single point of contact for IT users and customers to report any issues they may have with the IT service (or, in some cases, with IT's customer service).

service-level agreement (SLA): A document that captures the understanding between a service user and a service provider as to quality and timeliness.

service management: Monitoring and optimizing a service to ensure that it meets the critical outcomes that the customer values and the stakeholders want to provide.

servlet: A program that runs on a Web server in response to an action taken by the user via a browser.

silo: In IT, an application with a single narrow focus, such as human resources management or inventory control, with no intention or preparation for use by others.

silver bullet: A proposed solution that seems too good to be true and usually is.

Six Sigma: A statistical term meaning six standard deviations from the norm and the name of a quality-improvement program that aims at reducing errors to one in a million.

SMTP (Simple Mail Transfer Protocol): The basic method used to transmit electronic mail (e-mail) over the Internet.

SOA (service oriented architecture): An approach to building applications that implements business processes or services by using a set of loosely coupled black-box components orchestrated to deliver a well-defined level of service.

SQL (Structured Query Language): The most popular computer language for accessing and manipulating databases.

SSL (Secure Sockets Layer): A popular method for making secure connections over the Internet, first introduced by Netscape.

standards: A core set of common, repeatable best practices and protocols that have been agreed on by a business or industry group. Typically, vendors, industry user groups, and end users collaborate to develop standards based on the broad expertise of a large number of stakeholders. Organizations can leverage these standards as a common foundation and innovate on top of them.

subroutine: A piece of computer code that can easily be used (called) by many other programs, as long as they are on the same computer and (usually) are written in the same programming language.

TCP/IP (Transmission Control Protocol/Internet Protocol): The complex stack of communications protocols that underlies the Internet. All data is broken into small packets that are sent independently over the network and reassembled at the final destination.

thin client: Client hardware in the client/server environment that is dependent on the server for loading applications. Most hardware designed for this purpose is similar to a cut-down PC, with no floppy disk drive or hard drive.

throughput: The rate at which transactions are completed in a system.

TLS (Transport Layer Security): A newer name for SSL. *See also* SSL.

TQM (Total Quality Management): A popular quality-improvement program.

transaction: A computer action that represents a business event, such as debiting an account. When a transaction starts, it must either complete or not happen at all.

UDDI (Universal Description, Discovery, and Integration): A platform-independent, XML-based services registry sponsored by OASIS. *See also* OASIS and XML.

virtualization: Emulation. Virtual memory is the use of a disk to store active areas of memory to make the available memory appear larger. In a virtual environment, one computer runs software that allows it to emulate another machine. This kind of emulation is commonly known as virtualization.

W3C: A handy way of referring to the World Wide Web Consortium, an organization that coordinates standards for the World Wide Web.

Web Service: A software component created with an interface consisting of a WSDL definition, an XML schema definition, and a WS-Policy definition. Collectively, components could be called a service contract — or, alternatively, an API. *See also* API, WSDL, WS-Policy, and XML.

workflow: This is a sequence of steps needed to carry out a business process. Workflow technology automates the passage of information between the steps.

World Wide Web: A system built on top of the Internet that displays hyper-linked pages of information that can contain a wide variety of data formats, including multimedia.

WSCI (Web Services Choreography Interface): An XML-based interface description language that describes the flow of messages exchanged by a Web Service when it participates in choreographed interactions with other services.

WSDL (Web Services Definition Language): An XML format for describing Web services.

WS-Policy: The Web Services Policy Framework, which provides a means of expressing the capabilities, requirements, and characteristics of software components in a Web Services system.

WSRP (Web Services for Remote Portlets): A protocol that allows portlets to communicate by using standard Web Services interfaces.

XML (eXtensible Markup Language): A way of presenting data as plain-text files that has become the lingua franca of SOA. In XML, as in HTML, data is delimited in tags that are enclosed in angle brackets (< and >), although the tags in XML can have many more meanings. *See also* SOA.

XML Schema: A language for defining and describing the structure of XML documents.

XSD (XML Schema Definition): The description of what can be in an XML document.

XSLT (eXtensible Stylesheet Language Transformations): A computer language, based on XML, that specifies how to change one XML document into another. *See also* XML.

Index

• *Q* •

• *R* •

BUSINESS, CAREERS & PERSONAL FINANCE

Accounting For Dummies, 4th Edition*
978-0-470-24600-9

Bookkeeping Workbook For Dummies†
978-0-470-16983-4

Commodities For Dummies
978-0-470-04928-0

Doing Business in China For Dummies
978-0-470-04929-7

E-Mail Marketing For Dummies
978-0-470-19087-6

Job Interviews For Dummies, 3rd Edition*†
978-0-470-17748-8

Personal Finance Workbook For Dummies*†
978-0-470-09933-9

Real Estate License Exams For Dummies
978-0-7645-7623-2

Six Sigma For Dummies
978-0-7645-6798-8

Small Business Kit For Dummies, 2nd Edition*†
978-0-7645-5984-6

Telephone Sales For Dummies
978-0-470-16836-3

BUSINESS PRODUCTIVITY & MICROSOFT OFFICE

Access 2007 For Dummies
978-0-470-03649-5

Excel 2007 For Dummies
978-0-470-03737-9

Office 2007 For Dummies
978-0-470-00923-9

Outlook 2007 For Dummies
978-0-470-03830-7

PowerPoint 2007 For Dummies
978-0-470-04059-1

Project 2007 For Dummies
978-0-470-03651-8

QuickBooks 2008 For Dummies
978-0-470-18470-7

Quicken 2008 For Dummies
978-0-470-17473-9

Salesforce.com For Dummies, 2nd Edition
978-0-470-04893-1

Word 2007 For Dummies
978-0-470-03658-7

EDUCATION, HISTORY, REFERENCE & TEST PREPARATION

African American History For Dummies
978-0-7645-5469-8

Algebra For Dummies
978-0-7645-5325-7

Algebra Workbook For Dummies
978-0-7645-8467-1

Art History For Dummies
978-0-470-09910-0

ASVAB For Dummies, 2nd Edition
978-0-470-10671-6

British Military History For Dummies
978-0-470-03213-8

Calculus For Dummies
978-0-7645-2498-1

Canadian History For Dummies, 2nd Edition
978-0-470-83656-9

Geometry Workbook For Dummies
978-0-471-79940-5

The SAT I For Dummies, 6th Edition
978-0-7645-7193-0

Series 7 Exam For Dummies
978-0-470-09932-2

World History For Dummies
978-0-7645-5242-7

FOOD, GARDEN, HOBBIES & HOME

Bridge For Dummies, 2nd Edition
978-0-471-92426-5

Coin Collecting For Dummies, 2nd Edition
978-0-470-22275-1

Cooking Basics For Dummies, 3rd Edition
978-0-7645-7206-7

Drawing For Dummies
978-0-7645-5476-6

Etiquette For Dummies, 2nd Edition
978-0-470-10672-3

Gardening Basics For Dummies*†
978-0-470-03749-2

Knitting Patterns For Dummies
978-0-470-04556-5

Living Gluten-Free For Dummies†
978-0-471-77383-2

Painting Do-It-Yourself For Dummies
978-0-470-17533-0

HEALTH, SELF HELP, PARENTING & PETS

Anger Management For Dummies
978-0-470-03715-7

Anxiety & Depression Workbook For Dummies
978-0-7645-9793-0

Dieting For Dummies, 2nd Edition
978-0-7645-4149-0

Dog Training For Dummies, 2nd Edition
978-0-7645-8418-3

Horseback Riding For Dummies
978-0-470-09719-9

Infertility For Dummies†
978-0-470-11518-3

Meditation For Dummies with CD-ROM, 2nd Edition
978-0-471-77774-8

Post-Traumatic Stress Disorder For Dummies
978-0-470-04922-8

Puppies For Dummies, 2nd Edition
978-0-470-03717-1

Thyroid For Dummies, 2nd Edition†
978-0-471-78755-6

Type 1 Diabetes For Dummies*†
978-0-470-17811-9

* Separate Canadian edition also available
† Separate U.K. edition also available

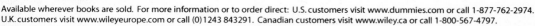

Available wherever books are sold. For more information or to order direct: U.S. customers visit www.dummies.com or call 1-877-762-2974.
U.K. customers visit www.wileyeurope.com or call (0)1243 843291. Canadian customers visit www.wiley.ca or call 1-800-567-4797.

INTERNET & DIGITAL MEDIA

AdWords For Dummies
978-0-470-15252-2

Blogging For Dummies, 2nd Edition
978-0-470-23017-6

**Digital Photography All-in-One
Desk Reference For Dummies, 3rd Edition**
978-0-470-03743-0

Digital Photography For Dummies, 5th Edition
978-0-7645-9802-9

**Digital SLR Cameras & Photography
For Dummies, 2nd Edition**
978-0-470-14927-0

**eBay Business All-in-One Desk Reference
For Dummies**
978-0-7645-8438-1

eBay For Dummies, 5th Edition*
978-0-470-04529-9

eBay Listings That Sell For Dummies
978-0-471-78912-3

Facebook For Dummies
978-0-470-26273-3

The Internet For Dummies, 11th Edition
978-0-470-12174-0

Investing Online For Dummies, 5th Edition
978-0-7645-8456-5

iPod & iTunes For Dummies, 5th Edition
978-0-470-17474-6

MySpace For Dummies
978-0-470-09529-4

Podcasting For Dummies
978-0-471-74898-4

**Search Engine Optimization
For Dummies, 2nd Edition**
978-0-471-97998-2

Second Life For Dummies
978-0-470-18025-9

**Starting an eBay Business For Dummies,
3rd Edition†**
978-0-470-14924-9

GRAPHICS, DESIGN & WEB DEVELOPMENT

**Adobe Creative Suite 3 Design Premium
All-in-One Desk Reference For Dummies**
978-0-470-11724-8

**Adobe Web Suite CS3 All-in-One Desk
Reference For Dummies**
978-0-470-12099-6

AutoCAD 2008 For Dummies
978-0-470-11650-0

**Building a Web Site For Dummies,
3rd Edition**
978-0-470-14928-7

**Creating Web Pages All-in-One Desk
Reference For Dummies, 3rd Edition**
978-0-470-09629-1

**Creating Web Pages For Dummies,
8th Edition**
978-0-470-08030-6

Dreamweaver CS3 For Dummies
978-0-470-11490-2

Flash CS3 For Dummies
978-0-470-12100-9

Google SketchUp For Dummies
978-0-470-13744-4

InDesign CS3 For Dummies
978-0-470-11865-8

**Photoshop CS3 All-in-One
Desk Reference For Dummies**
978-0-470-11195-6

Photoshop CS3 For Dummies
978-0-470-11193-2

Photoshop Elements 5 For Dummies
978-0-470-09810-3

SolidWorks For Dummies
978-0-7645-9555-4

Visio 2007 For Dummies
978-0-470-08983-5

Web Design For Dummies, 2nd Edition
978-0-471-78117-2

Web Sites Do-It-Yourself For Dummies
978-0-470-16903-2

Web Stores Do-It-Yourself For Dummies
978-0-470-17443-2

LANGUAGES, RELIGION & SPIRITUALITY

Arabic For Dummies
978-0-471-77270-5

Chinese For Dummies, Audio Set
978-0-470-12766-7

French For Dummies
978-0-7645-5193-2

German For Dummies
978-0-7645-5195-6

Hebrew For Dummies
978-0-7645-5489-6

Ingles Para Dummies
978-0-7645-5427-8

Italian For Dummies, Audio Set
978-0-470-09586-7

Italian Verbs For Dummies
978-0-471-77389-4

Japanese For Dummies
978-0-7645-5429-2

Latin For Dummies
978-0-7645-5431-5

Portuguese For Dummies
978-0-471-78738-9

Russian For Dummies
978-0-471-78001-4

Spanish Phrases For Dummies
978-0-7645-7204-3

Spanish For Dummies
978-0-7645-5194-9

Spanish For Dummies, Audio Set
978-0-470-09585-0

The Bible For Dummies
978-0-7645-5296-0

Catholicism For Dummies
978-0-7645-5391-2

The Historical Jesus For Dummies
978-0-470-16785-4

Islam For Dummies
978-0-7645-5503-9

**Spirituality For Dummies,
2nd Edition**
978-0-470-19142-2

NETWORKING AND PROGRAMMING

ASP.NET 3.5 For Dummies
978-0-470-19592-5

C# 2008 For Dummies
978-0-470-19109-5

Hacking For Dummies, 2nd Edition
978-0-470-05235-8

Home Networking For Dummies, 4th Edition
978-0-470-11806-1

Java For Dummies, 4th Edition
978-0-470-08716-9

**Microsoft® SQL Server™ 2008 All-in-One
Desk Reference For Dummies**
978-0-470-17954-3

**Networking All-in-One Desk Reference
For Dummies, 2nd Edition**
978-0-7645-9939-2

**Networking For Dummies,
8th Edition**
978-0-470-05620-2

SharePoint 2007 For Dummies
978-0-470-09941-4

**Wireless Home Networking
For Dummies, 2nd Edition**
978-0-471-74940-0

OPERATING SYSTEMS & COMPUTER BASICS

iMac For Dummies, 5th Edition
978-0-7645-8458-9

Laptops For Dummies, 2nd Edition
978-0-470-05432-1

Linux For Dummies, 8th Edition
978-0-470-11649-4

MacBook For Dummies
978-0-470-04859-7

**Mac OS X Leopard All-in-One
Desk Reference For Dummies**
978-0-470-05434-5

Mac OS X Leopard For Dummies
978-0-470-05433-8

Macs For Dummies, 9th Edition
978-0-470-04849-8

PCs For Dummies, 11th Edition
978-0-470-13728-4

Windows® Home Server For Dummies
978-0-470-18592-6

Windows Server 2008 For Dummies
978-0-470-18043-3

**Windows Vista All-in-One
Desk Reference For Dummies**
978-0-471-74941-7

Windows Vista For Dummies
978-0-471-75421-3

Windows Vista Security For Dummies
978-0-470-11805-4

SPORTS, FITNESS & MUSIC

Coaching Hockey For Dummies
978-0-470-83685-9

Coaching Soccer For Dummies
978-0-471-77381-8

Fitness For Dummies, 3rd Edition
978-0-7645-7851-9

Football For Dummies, 3rd Edition
978-0-470-12536-6

GarageBand For Dummies
978-0-7645-7323-1

Golf For Dummies, 3rd Edition
978-0-471-76871-5

Guitar For Dummies, 2nd Edition
978-0-7645-9904-0

**Home Recording For Musicians
For Dummies, 2nd Edition**
978-0-7645-8884-6

**iPod & iTunes For Dummies,
5th Edition**
978-0-470-17474-6

Music Theory For Dummies
978-0-7645-7838-0

Stretching For Dummies
978-0-470-06741-3

* Separate Canadian edition also available
† Separate U.K. edition also available

Available wherever books are sold. For more information or to order direct: U.S. customers visit www.dummies.com or call 1-877-762-2974.
U.K. customers visit www.wileyeurope.com or call (0) 1243 843291. Canadian customers visit www.wiley.ca or call 1-800-567-4797.

Printed in the United States of America
ED-02-22-13